The Jews of the United States, 1790-1840

The Jews of the United States
1790-1840
A Documentary History

Edited by
JOSEPH L. BLAU AND
SALO W. BARON

In Three Volumes

VOLUME ONE

Columbia University Press
New York and London 1963
The Jewish Publication Society of America
Philadelphia 5724

Joseph L. Blau is Professor of Religion, Columbia University.
Salo W. Baron is Professor Emeritus of Jewish History, Literature,
and Institutions on the Miller Foundation, Columbia University.

The edition of this work for The Jewish Publication Society of
America is Number 17-19 in the Jacob R. Schiff Series of Jewish
Contributions to American Democracy. A contribution from the
American Jewish Tercentenary Committee helped make publication
possible.

Preface

The volumes here presented were begun as part of a research project of the American Jewish Tercentenary Committee (Ralph E. Samuel, chairman; David Bernstein, executive director), in 1954, as one phase of the celebration of the three-hundredth anniversary of the permanent settlement of Jews on the North American continent. The original plan called for a series of ten chronological divisions, covering the entire course of American Jewish history since 1654. Salo Wittmayer Baron was designated to serve as editor-in-chief for the whole series; each division was to have had a special editor. What is presented here was envisaged as the second major division, to follow a collection of documents pertaining to the Colonial and Revolutionary periods. Joseph L. Blau was named as the editor for this division. A research staff was assembled, consisting of Drs. Saul Benison, Hyman Berman, Lloyd P. Gartner, Rudolph Glanz, and Moses Rischin. The editors and staff were, for a time, assisted by Mrs. Jeannette M. Baron and Professor Hyman B. Grinstein (who was to have served as editor of the fourth major division). Unfortunately, the funds available did not come up to expectations, so that the staff could not be maintained, work on the fourth time-division had to be halted, and the preparation of these volumes had to be interrupted frequently.

Despite these difficulties, the present division, covering the years 1790–1840, was virtually completed in 1957. Since that time, the editors have had the benefit of suggestions made to them particularly by Professor Richard B. Morris of Columbia University and Mr. Edwin Wolf, 2d, of the Library Company of Philadelphia. Both of these friends of the work kindly went over the entire manuscript painstakingly and called the editors' attention to many details. Mrs. Eleanor W. Blau has dedicated innumerable hours to assisting in the preparation of the final manuscript and to the reading of proof. In the latter task, Mrs. Jeannette M. Baron also shared. The staffs and directors of many libraries and the owners of many of the documents here printed have been gracious in extending aid and in granting permission to use their materials. These permissions are particularized elsewhere in these volumes. To all of these, and to all those others who have been involved in the ten-year course of this undertaking, we owe our sincere and heartfelt thanks.

No printed collection can completely represent the appearance of original manuscripts. We have, therefore, not tried to approximate such a complete representation but have, rather, arranged the materials for printing in the most convenient form. As far as has been feasible, the spelling of the originals has been preserved, without calling attention to unusual spellings or to inconsistencies except where, in the judgment of the editors, the reader might have attributed these to editorial failings rather than to the lapses of the original writers. In some instances, where the text would not have been clear without revision of the punctuation, the editors have introduced more modern styles of punctuation or have otherwise altered the punctuation of the original documents. Where the writers of the originals incorporated Hebrew words or phrases into their texts, the editors have replaced the Hebrew with a transliteration, in square brackets. Since many of the original manuscripts have suffered the ravages of time, there are places where the text is torn or blotted to the point of complete illegibility. Wherever possible, the editors have supplied, again in brackets, words or parts of words completed from the context. In some instances, it has been impossible to do even this with any adequacy; in such cases a bracketed space has been preferred to a wild guess. In general, the original texts have been modified or altered as little as possible.

The history of the Jews of the United States is part of the history of the United States as well as part of the history of the Jews. In the preparation of the introductory materials and notes for these volumes, the editors have made the effort consciously to demonstrate the interrelations of these two histories. For those readers whose primary interest is in the history of the Jews, they have tried to indicate how the experience of life in the United States, in the years of their concern, affected the traditional patterns of Jewish living. For those whose primary interest lies in the history of the United States, they have tried to show that, in every respect, the Jews of the United States have been a part in the making of that history. If this effort has been successful, then the labor and the heartbreak of the past ten years are justified.

J.L.B.
S.W.B.

Columbia University
October, 1963

Acknowledgments

The editors gratefully acknowledge permissions received for the inclusion of documents in these volumes from the following individuals and organizations: The Adams Manuscript Trust, Massachusetts Historical Society, Boston, Mass.; American Jewish Archives, Cincinnati, Ohio; American Jewish Historical Society, New York, N.Y.; American Philosophical Society, Philadelphia, Pa.; Congregation Ansche Chesed, New York, N.Y.; Congregation Mikveh Israel, Philadelphia, Pa.; Congregation Shearith Israel, New York, N.Y.; Department of Archives and History, State of Georgia, Atlanta, Ga.; The Historical Society of Pennsylvania, Philadelphia, Pa.; The Library Company of Philadelphia, Philadelphia, Pa.; The Library of Congress, Washington, D.C.; The Maryland Historical Society, Baltimore, Md.; Missouri Historical Society, St. Louis, Mo.; New York Historical Society, New York, N.Y.; The Rhode Island Historical Society, Providence, R.I.; The State Historical Society of Wisconsin, Madison, Wis.; Mr. J. Solis-Cohen, Jr., Philadelphia, Pa.; Mrs. Henry Taylor, Trevilians, Va.; The Trustees of Columbia University, New York, N.Y.; The University of North Carolina Library, Southern Historical Collection, Chapel Hill, N.C.; The Valentine Museum, Richmond, Va.; Mr. Edwin Wolf, 2d, Philadelphia, Pa.

Contents

Contents   xiii

xvi   *Contents*

General Introduction

From its inception, United States Jewish history had many extraordinary features. At a time when in Europe one hardly heard a whisper on Jewish Emancipation—the term itself was to be coined only after the Catholic Emancipation in England in 1828—Jews in the American colonies enjoyed a large measure of equality. This was rarely stated in formal laws. In fact, Jews, as such, were seldom mentioned in the colonial legal sources; their names appear in the records with reference to some business transactions or other activities unrelated to their Judaism. In many cases, we suspect the presence of Jews only through their Jewish-sounding names, a dubious method of identification at a time when the Protestant majority, particularly its Puritan wings, chose with preference Hebrew names borrowed from the Old Testament. Jews, for their part, frequently hastened to adopt English names or else retained Spanish or Portuguese family names which often make them indistinguishable from other colonials of Iberian descent. It has been suggested, for instance, that the earliest Jewish settler in the colony of Virginia, which was later to become the "mother of presidents," was Elias Legardo mentioned in 1621, merely because this combination of names sounds Jewish. More reliably, we may only consider one Moses Nehemiah of 1658 as the first known Jewish resident in that rather intolerant colony.

Only when the Jews appeared in large groups, as in New York (then New Amsterdam) in 1654, or in Georgia in 1733, was the question of Jewish status raised by the respective colonial administrations. An unfriendly governor in New Amsterdam, unfriendly not only to Jews but also to other religious dissenters from the then dominant Dutch Reformed Church, was overruled by the home directorate in Holland and ordered to allow the Jews the rights in question. In Georgia, on the contrary, the local administration favored the new Jewish arrivals much beyond the intention of the home offices in England. In any case, after short interludes of a struggle for individual rights, the Jews of New

Amsterdam attained most of their egalitarian objectives, and these were given an even broader scope under the British domination beginning in 1664. The Jewish question was so little present in the minds of the early English administrators that, after the first English governor, Richard Nicolls, had proclaimed, in 1665, the general principle that "no person shall be molested, fined or imprisoned for differing in judgment in matters of religion, who profess Christianity," his successor, Edmund Andros, omitted the latter reservation in his declaration of 1674 in which he promised to

permit all persons of what Religion soever quietly to inhabit within the precincts of our jurisdiction without giving them any disturbance or disquiet whatsoever for or by reason of their differing opinions in matters of religion provided they give no disturbance to the public peace nor do molest or disquiet others in the free exercise of their religion.

Probably, Andros never thought of the Jews when he issued that declaration, and, in 1683, the new governor, Thomas Dongan, and the Colonial Assembly, in promulgating another charter of liberties, could again glibly refer to the liberty of conscience to be enjoyed by all who "professed faith in God by Jesus Christ." Three years later, Dongan himself spoke again of all men "of what Religion soever" being allowed to live in the colony and freely to adhere to their beliefs.

From the point of view of the public, too, there hardly existed a Jewish question. On the few occasions when Jewish individuals appeared before courts, as did Jacob Lucena in Hartford in 1670 or Rowland Gideon in Boston in 1674, the courts leaned backward in favoring these Jewish parties *because* they were Jews. The only menace to Jewish rights, in fact to the very sojourn of Jews in the colony of Maryland, which arose in connection with the accusation of Jacob Lumbrozo in Baltimore in 1658 for alleged blasphemies against Jesus and the Trinitarian dogma, apparently ended without conviction and had no untoward consequences for the Jews.

No sharper contrast with the European conditions need be adduced than the status of Jews in public life. While in Europe, the attainment of political rights was considered the acme of emancipation and in many countries was not achieved until the mid-nineteenth century or later, in most colonies, it appears, Jews participated in elections with no one pointing an accusing finger. Jews were also entrusted with public offices without further ado. In New York in 1718, two Jews were sworn in as constables; they, in turn, appointed two non-Jews as their deputies. A year later another Jew, Moses Levy, preferred to pay the high fine of fifteen pounds rather than to accept that onerous assignment. Only once, when a defeated candidate in a New York election of 1737 complained to the Assembly that Jews had helped elect his opponent, did the Assembly take note of the disfranchisement of Jews in England and concluded that "they ought not to be admitted to vote for Representatives in this Colony." However, this decision neither annulled the earlier elections with Jewish participation nor did it prevent Jews from voting in subsequent elections such as that of 1761.

Most remarkably, on the eve of the American Revolution, Francis Salvador, who had come from England to South Carolina in December, 1773, little more than a year after his arrival, served in the First and Second Provincial Congresses of the colony, which soon turned into the first legislature of the newly founded state of South Carolina. Salvador was apparently destined to play a considerable role in the political development of that state, had he not fallen victim to an attack by Indians fighting on the English side at the beginning of the Revolution. There is no evidence that his Jewishness was in any way a handicap to his political career. Compared with such political equality the few obstacles to civil equality could easily be overcome. In many European countries, Jewish artisans were refused admission to the monopolistic Christian guilds, but American Jews seem never to have faced such handicaps. A famous silversmith, like Myer Myers in New York, was not only readily admitted to the Gold and Silversmiths Society in New York but was twice elected its president— once shortly before the Revolution and again in 1786.

More discrimination was practiced with respect to the Jewish faith. In early New Amsterdam, the small Jewish community had to pledge itself not to worship in public. There and elsewhere, Jews often encountered difficulties in securing permits for the establishment of cemeteries or the erection of synagogues. However, these difficulties were gradually overcome and in the seventeenth century there already were Jewish burial places in Newport, Rhode Island (1677), and in New York City (1682). By 1730, the Shearith Israel Congregation of New York was enabled to consecrate its first house of worship. In 1763, the Jewish community of Newport erected a beautiful synagogue which has since been declared a national shrine of the United States.

A most impressive step in the direction of Jewish equality was made by the English Parliament when it enacted, in 1740, its famous Naturalization Act for the British colonies in North America. Not only were Jews granted an opportunity to become naturalized citizens of all colonies on a par with the non-Jewish settlers but also, in two crucial articles, cognizance was taken of their religious scruples. The requirements that each petitioner submit a certificate that he had partaken of the Lord's Supper within the preceding three months and that he take an oath of abjuration "on the true faith of a Christian," were dropped in the case of Jews, so as to enable them to make full use of the new privilege. Curiously, more Jews of Jamaica than of those residing on the North American continent availed themselves of this new opportunity. In itself, this indifference is a clear indication that, in their ordinary pursuits, they found very few handicaps of a legal or political nature.

We hear of only one refusal to naturalize Jews. This happened to Aaron Lopez and Isaac Elizer of Newport, to whom the Assembly of Rhode Island and its Superior Court refused such burgher's rights in 1762 under the flimsy excuse that the colony was already overcrowded and that, hence, the purpose of the Naturalization Act to increase the colonial population had no bearing on it. This was one instance of the curious reversal of the tolerant policy of a colony which, a century earlier, had been founded by Roger Williams with the intent of providing complete religious liberty. However, Rhode Island itself had naturalized, without much ado, several other Jews, including Moses Lopez, Aaron's older brother. Aaron and Elizer, too, succeeded in circumventing the ill will of their colonial masters by securing naturalization in Taunton, Massachusetts, and New York, respectively; rights granted by one colony had automatic validity in all colonies.

Perhaps the most interesting effect of this incident was the following prediction entered by Ezra Stiles, then serving as pastor in Newport, in his *Literary Diary*, March 18, 1762:

I remark that Providence seems to make every Thing to work for Mortification to the Jews, and to prevent their incorporating into any Nation; that thus they may continue a distinct people. . . . [It] forbodes that the Jews will never become incorporated with the people of America, any more than in Europe, Asia and Africa.

Stiles was a poor prophet; this prediction came true only to the extent that the Jews retained their permanent identity as a religious group apart.

True, there were anti-Jewish individuals and groups in colonial America, as there were throughout the later history of the United States. But they were neither particularly vocal nor influential. They certainly did not affect the Jewish status before the outbreak of the American Revolution. At that time the five existing organized Jewish communities of New York, Newport, Philadelphia, Lancaster, and Charleston embraced a total of some 2,000 Jews living on very friendly terms with their neighbors and forming a small, but important, segment of their cities' population. Some individuals were also living in isolated settlements and retained more or less loose relations with the organized religious life of these major centers. Certainly from the standpoint of legal equality, the Swedish visitor, Peter Kalm, was quite right when, after reviewing the conditions in New York in 1748, he declared: "They [the Jews] enjoy all the privileges common to other inhabitants of this town and province."

In essence, therefore, the Revolution did not bring about a radical change in the Jewish position in American society. From the outset, Jews participated in the revolutionary movement on a par with their Christian fellow citizens. Like most other denominations, the Jewish community embraced a minority of Loyalists, a group of inactive sympathizers with either side of the struggle, but also a substantial majority of American patriots. Jewish youth volunteered for armed services on the revolutionary side, as it appears even beyond its ratio in the population. Most remarkable is the total acceptance of such Jewish fellow combatants by the non-Jewish revolutionary soldiers. Some Jews served as officers; for instance, Colonel Isaac Franks, one of George Washington's adjutants, or Major Benjamin Nonez, a relatively recent arrival from France in 1777, who fought at the side of both Lafayette and Washington. Another Jewish officer, David Franks, an assistant of Benedict Arnold, was suspected of having taken part in the latter's treason, but he was acquitted by the military tribunal. Most importantly, there never seems to have arisen any disciplinary problem between these Jewish officers and their Christian subordinates. They simply fought side by side for their common revolutionary ideals.

If the actual transformation in the Jewish status thus appeared to have been minor, the impact of the newly adopted Constitution of the United States on the psychology of the Jews in America and Europe was enormous. Here, the principle of separation of state and Church, that of general liberty of conscience, the nonapplication of religious tests in the appointment to any federal office, and the other nondiscriminatory freedoms included in the Bill of Rights were proclaimed for the first time as the fundamental law of the country. There still remained certain details to be ironed out. Particularly, the problem of states' rights versus federal rights remained to plague the public life of the United States for generations thereafter; indeed, until the present day. Not until the respective state constitutions incorporated such fully egalitarian provisions could the Jews of America claim to enjoy full equality of rights under the law. Moreover, the existing constitutional checks and balances, the old Anglo-Saxon tradition of not spelling out everything in systematic and logically consistent legal codes and the numerous opportunities left for a wide range of subsequent judicial interpretations, allowed for quite a few loopholes in the practical application of these laws to individual citizens and groups, including Jews. But as the story has unfolded itself during the one and three-quarter centuries since the adoption of the Constitution, American Jewry has had few reasons for complaint.

In 1789, Philadelphia, soon to be the capital city of the United States, was the scene of a splendid parade in honor of the new Constitution. Refreshment tables were placed at the end of the route for the enjoyment of all participants. One of the tables furnished only foods that conformed to Jewish dietary laws. There were, perhaps, no more than 3,000 Jews in the entire country at that time, only a handful of them in Philadelphia. Despite this lack of numerical strength, Jewish preferences were taken into consideration by the committee in charge of arrangements for this public celebration. Far more than any formal statements or legislative enactments, such a special provision suggests that the Jews living *in* the United States of America were truly *of* the United States of America. They were not merely, by a quirk of the law, citizens; they were also full participants in the life of the country, welcome as neighbors, as business associates, even as friends.

This is the story that stands out, above all specific details, in the many documents presented below. In the new American republic, the wandering Jew had at last found a second homeland, a place where he belonged, where he could put down roots, where he was not merely a more or less tolerated outsider. In respect to the position of the Jews, there was no striking change as a consequence of the adoption of the Constitution. Perhaps the most important difference was that what had been a matter of custom became the law of the land. With scattered exceptions, in states where older patterns of organic law survived in conflict with the new Constitutional frame, no paths were closed to Jews because of their adherence to the faith of their fathers. Every career was open to talent and ambition. During the first fifty years of national life under the Constitution, the Jews of the United States explored many of the avenues open to them, making the most of this heady freedom and of the opportunities offered to them.

Unfortunately, it is precisely this part of the history of the Jews of the United States to which least attention has been given. The Colonial Period and the Revolutionary War have been worked over time and again. The Civil War years and the decades immediately preceding them have been explored thoroughly and competently. The later years of mass immigration, chiefly from Eastern Europe, have been the subject of many studies. In all this, until recently, the half-century of the Early National Period has attracted very few students. Indeed, American-Jewish historians used to refer to this time as "the dead period." More recently, an apparent resurrection has taken place; it has become

clear in the process that it was the interest of earlier historians,
not the period itself, that was dead.

For during these fifty years, in the course of which the Jewish
population of the United States increased slowly, from 3,000 in
1790 to 6,000 in 1830, and then, more rapidly, to about 15,000 in
1840, it is possible to trace the lives of an unusually large proportion of the small Jewish group. The very minuteness of their numbers seems to increase the visibility of individuals. Similarly, Jewish
organizations and institutions were very few and scattered; once
again, the small number allows a great concentration on detail
without loss of the larger patterns of growth and decay. Furthermore, during these years, only a fragment of the life story of any
Jewish person was involved in the life of the Jewish group. There
had not yet developed any approximation to the all-embracing
Jewish communities of Europe. As a result, it is possible to see
with unusual clarity how the events of American life affected
Jewish participants. Even the culminating event of the period in
Jewish life, the coming to self-consciousness of the Jewish group
in the aftermath of the Damascus affair, in 1840, can be seen, in
the larger perspective of American technological history, as an
incidental by-product of the development of more rapid means
of communication, by steamship instead of sailing packet.

Here, then, are collected a number of documents illustrating all
phases of Jewish life in the United States between 1790 and 1840,
and demonstrating both what Jews of the time were like and what
the United States of America then was like. They have been
selected to reveal failures as well as successes, for not every peddler
became the owner of a department store nor every young scribbler
a distinguished writer. Here are the records of births, marriages
and deaths, schooling and friendship, commitment to private and
public business, religious duties and military service. Here, too, are
seen evidences of Jewish participation in the physical expansion
of the United States and of Jewish concern more fully to realize
its ideal possibilities.

Most of all, here are people. Except for a few official papers
and organizational plans, most of these documents—even most of
the business documents—readily yield insights into the lives of indi-

vidual Jews as they worked and played, struggled to gain a competence, established families, joined with their fellows to found synagogues and benevolent societies, faced characteristically the chances of life. Some of these people are already well-known; their careers hold enough general interest to have engaged the attention of biographers. This is especially the case of Mordecai Manuel Noah, publicist and politician, promoter and dramatist, certainly the most widely known American Jew of the age. Miss Rebecca Gratz is almost as celebrated, partly, no doubt because of the dubious legend that she was the original on whom Sir Walter Scott modeled the character of Rebecca in *Ivanhoe,* but partly, too, in her own right, by virtue of her lively letters to a large and diverse acquaintance.

Others, only slightly less interesting, emerge from anonymity in these documents. The Cohen brothers of Baltimore, orphaned early in life, became distinguished bankers in their adoptive city, American agents of the House of Rothschild, and contributors to the partially successful effort to remove pre-Revolutionary disabilities from the Jews of Maryland. Moses Myers founded a successful mercantile business in Norfolk, Virginia, and raised a family to succeed him; when France and England were at war, he was deputized by the French agent in America to refit and re-equip the French vessels that reached that port. Later, when Myers's business was hard hit by depression, a large number of his fellow-merchants supported him for the patronage position of Collector of the Port of Norfolk, in which he served with distinction. John Hays was a fur trader in the then remote sections of the middle west; he used his land-warrant for military service to purchase land and become a successful farmer. He held a number of public offices, of increasing responsibility, until he was named Receiver of Public Moneys at Jackson, Missouri. Young Moses Sheftall of Georgia studied medicine under Dr. Benjamin Rush of Philadelphia, the most distinguished medical man of the age; Dr. Moses Sheftall later returned to Philadelphia to conclude arrangements to marry the sister of the Revolutionary patriot, Dr. Solomon Bush, after some difficulties occasioned by the fact that Dr. Bush had abandoned Judaism. Later Dr. Sheftall wrote, out of his experience in medical practice, on the yellow fever.

There are dozens of such stories to be found in these documents. It is amazing how fully it is possible to explore and expose the lives of men and women who made but small ripples on the oceanic expanse of history. It is hard to realize how much of a human life is a matter of official record. Much of this is, of course, dry and factual detail; some part is, however, most personal. Consider, for example, the story of Solomon Lyon of Philadelphia, a relatively prosperous merchant and property owner. In 1780, his properties were assessed at the substantial sum of £6500; his tax in 1781 was £150; and in 1782, £275. In 1785, at a time when many of his fellow merchants went into bankruptcy, Lyon advertised in the *Independent Gazette* of Philadelphia that he was prepared to pay his creditors in full. Five years later, in 1790–91, he participated in the brokerage boom that accompanied the speculation in western land then going on; he advertised his brokerage service and he was privately criticized for his shrewd dealings by Benjamin Rush. He invested his profits in bank stocks and public securities: he was one of the Jewish stockholders in the Bank of North America; he invested in the Pennsylvania Population Company and in the company formed to provide a new water system for Philadelphia in 1800. It is possible that the extent of his capital investment by 1795 had entitled him to the social status of "gentleman," rather than "merchant" or "shopkeeper," even though he still kept a shop on Second Street between Vine and Callowhill.

Among Lyon's other commitments, he was a firm adherent of the local synagogue, Congregation Mikveh Israel. In 1790, he was one of the managers appointed by law to manage a lottery for the benefit of the Congregation, which badly needed £800. He was also a trustee of the first Jewish cemetery in Philadelphia. Among the bequests in his will (a great deal of valuable information can be gained from wills, which are instances of often highly personal documents that become part of the public and official record) was $200 left to Hyman Gratz as trustee; "as to One Hundred Dollars thereof to be appropriated for the repairs &c. of the Burial Ground of the Congregation to which I belong, and the remaining One Hundred Dollars to be appropriated for the repairs &c of the Burial Ground belonging to the new established Hebrew Congregation in the County of Philadelphia." The new congregation was Rodeph Shalom, the first synagogue in the United States to follow the customs and rituals of German (Ashkenazic) Jewry. Rodeph Shalom was first formed as a subordinate group (a *minyan*) within the older congregation, Mikveh Israel, in 1795 and not organized formally as a separate congregation until 1802. But in November, 1801, in anticipation of the separation, the new group had acquired a plot of land in Kensington as a cemetery.

On April 11, 1802, Solomon Lyon married a woman who had been converted to Judaism. He had lived with her for some time prior to their marriage; indeed, their first son had been circumcised by Jacob R. Cohen, Reader (*Hazzan*) of Congregation Mikveh Israel, on November 29, 1801. Lyon's will made ample provision for his "beloved Wife Sarah formerly called Rebecca," but he was apparently none too convinced of the thoroughness of her conversion, for he felt it necessary to specify that "it is my will and desire that my . . . children shall be brought up in the Religious Persuasion to which I belong and that my Son be placed under the tuition and instruction of Hassan Jacob Cohen or any other Teacher for the time being, officiating at the Hebrew Congregation to which I belong, until he attains the age of thirteen years." At least with respect to a daughter, Rachel, Lyon's caution in this regard was wasted; she married Wilson Jewell, a non-Jew, on April 26, 1824.

Prior to his association with the woman who later became his wife, Solomon Lyon had a housekeeper named Catherine Gordon who considered that she had claims against him. Lyon apparently agreed that these claims were valid, for, about the end of January, 1800, he consented to grant her an annuity of £100. Lyon further honored his commitment by making provision in his will for the continuation of the annuity to Catherine Gordon.

Needless to say, not every personal history can be as fully developed as that of Solomon Lyon. Yet the pages that follow are dotted with interesting and fascinating vignettes. Who would not wish to know more, for example, of twelve-year-old Edward Warren Moise, who applied for admission to West Point with the support of the Naval Officer of the Port of Charleston? Young Moise was never named to the United States Military Academy. Instead, he studied medicine in Charleston and moved early to

Woodville, Mississippi, where he carried on his medical practice. Later in life, he studied law and entered legal practice, achieving professional eminence in New Orleans, Louisiana, to which he removed in 1840. For many years, Moise was a member of the Louisiana House of Representatives and was, for several sessions, selected as Speaker of the House. In 1861, during the Civil War, when Louisiana was one of the states that seceded from the Federal Union, he served as a judge of the Confederate States Court in Louisiana. Still later, he was Attorney-General of the state. Surely his sponsor for the Military Academy was correct in judging that Moise "promises from Talents & general Conduct to be an usefull Member of Society," even though he was mistaken as to the sphere of that usefulness.

It is in such sketches that a documentary collection like this serves as a salutary reminder that history is about people. When a historian speaks of organizations, movements, trends and patterns, he is using a kind of shorthand; his subject is the day to day, year to year, lifetime to lifetime doings and sufferings of men and women of all stations in life, from the humblest to the greatest. Even behind the conscientiously impersonal language of the law there are persons who make laws and persons who interpret laws, persons who obey laws and persons who disobey laws, and, of course, persons who enforce laws. Because so many of these documents are letters exchanged by friends or other writings not intended for public view, the persons of the many dramas suggested below may appear without their public masks. The mild revelations thus occasioned will surely not detract from the reader's interest in these people.

Man is, however, a social being. His natural way is to organize to attain his goals. Any story of people is also, inevitably, a story of the various forms of social grouping that they invent or borrow the better to preserve or improve their lives. Over the centuries of European experience, the Jews developed a remarkably strong and useful form of community organization. There can be no doubt that the Jewish community of medieval and early modern Europe was one of the most important factors in the preservation of the Jewish people. Certainly, too, for those who migrated to the United

States, the community was the most familiar and traditional form of organization. Despite this, the Jews of the United States did not succeed in organizing communities on the European model. Instead, they developed an adapted form of the congregationalist polity—one of the forms of organization of the Protestant Christian groups, but by no means the only one.

The Jewish community in Europe had been, in effect, a government within a government. It had executive, legislative and judicial functions, exercised through appropriate agencies. The synagogue was one of these specialized agencies, for the expression of the religious life of the community. There were other agencies for educational, philanthropic, social, even fiscal expression. These various agencies were established by the community, supervised by the community, supported by the community, and responsible to the community. The officers of the community were, in effect, the supreme civil authorities in a tightly organized and controlled "welfare state." Rabbis, teachers, ritual slaughterers, performers of ritual circumcision, bakers of unleavened bread for Passover— all of these necessary functionaries of Jewish life were, so to say, the civil service of the community, employed by the community, and answerable to the communal officers. It was a most efficient and viable system.

Yet, the communal system never took root among the Jews of the United States. From the beginning, the congregation, the group of members of a synagogue, has been the only governing body of any force in American Jewish life. In the early days, the slaughterers, the bakers, the performers of circumcision, the teachers, and the readers who supplied the place of the rabbis were employed by the synagogues and supervised by the synagogal authorities. Later, but still within the years ending in 1840, there was a drift toward free enterprise in some of these religious functions. Ritual slaughter in conformity with the religious law, for example, became a free field for the independent entrepreneur. As a religious function, it was outside the sphere of the civil authorities, yet, in the absence of an organized community, it was too much for the synagogues to control. The result was chaos. Despite the difficulties of an inadequately controlled system, there was little strong support for the institution of a better form of policing.

Probably a major reason for the inability of the Jewish group to constitute itself a community was its variety. Among the earliest colonial arrivals, a majority came out of a Spanish or Portuguese Jewish background (Sephardim). They brought to their religious life in the New World a pattern of customs and traditions (*minhag*) developed in the Sephardic Jewries of Europe. By 1730, however, a majority of the Jews of America came from a Central European (Ashkenazic) background. Their customs and traditions, though based on the same law, had developed differently over the centuries of European experience. For a time, while the Jewish population was minute in any single city, one synagogue was all that could be maintained. Since synagogues of the Sephardic rite were already in existence, the first Ashkenazic arrivals had little choice. They had to join the existing synagogues and tolerate differences from the patterns in which they had been reared. Later, however, as the size of the Jewish group increased, Ashkenazic Jews first petitioned for the permission to hold services following their traditional rite in supplement to the Sephardic service. This compromise served only briefly. Soon after the beginning of the nineteenth century, Ashkenazic synagogues broke away from the older Sephardic synagogues in both Philadelphia and New York.

Once secession had been established as a possibility (and, we must remember, with a sharp increase of Jewish population after 1830), the fat was in the fire. For although Ashkenazic Jews may be considered as a unit in distinction to Sephardic Jews, they consist of many divergent national groups. Ashkenazim of English background and those of German background differed in many, perhaps minor, but still important details. Jews from Holland and those from Poland introduced still other variations. Even before 1840, in a major center of Jewish settlement like New York City (certainly the largest Jewish group after 1830 and possibly even a decade earlier), there were half-a-dozen synagogues, each one, after the first, owing its existence to the efforts of a small group of men to perpetuate the smallest of distinctions carried over from Europe. The sturdy independence of these small congregations precluded the development of community spirit or of communal institutions.

Reinforcing this internal basis for fragmentation was, of course, the example of American Christian denominationalism. Nowhere in Europe, not even in Holland, had the fragmentation of the Protestant denominations extended to anything like the number in America. Helped by the legal prohibition, in the Federal Constitution and most of the state constitutions, of an established church, spurred on by a democratic anti-intellectualism that encouraged the belief that the vaporizings of the unlettered were somehow closer to spiritual truth than the diligent studies of theological professionals, furthered by the well-established pattern of congregational autonomy, denominationalism became, in Sidney Mead's phrase, the "shape of American Protestantism." And, with the example of Protestantism in clear and open view, an equivalent fragmentation became "the shape" of American Judaism.

At the very end of the period with which we are here concerned, in the year 1840, the Damascus affair brought the Jews of America together in a wider unity of sentiment. Some of the leading spirits of the Jewish group in America, like Isaac Leeser in Philadelphia, had called, even before this, for a national organization of American Jews. In the aftermath of the Damascus affair, if ever, this call might have been heeded, but it was not. The pattern of American Jewish life was fixed. In response to a threat to its own integrity or to an anti-Semitic movement anywhere in the world, America's Jews would draw together for just long enough to meet the threat or contribute to the defeat of the movement. When the immediate purpose of the combination had been served, it broke apart again. The function of unity in American Jewish life was to be negative; unity was counteraction. Beyond this, it had no appeal to the average member of the Jewish group in the United States.

Though no formally organized community of American Jews was developed under the conditions of life in the United States, it would be unfair to suggest that communal feeling was lacking, too. Indeed, one aspect of synagogal history in this period that has great appeal is the frequency with which older or wealthier congregations gave help to newer groups. This was true even when the newer group was formed in a secession from the old. While it is improbable that there was no ill will on anyone's part to seceding members, it is worthy of remark that encouragement and financial assistance were so often available. Similarly, when an old congregation built a new synagogue, an appeal to other congregations for aid was usual and the response to such appeals was generous. In this respect, the congregations took a lively interest in the welfare of other Jewish groups, both in their own cities and elsewhere.

Another way in which the synagogue and their individual members took over what had been communal functions on the European Jewish scene was in respect to philanthropy. In the Jewish tradition, from Biblical times to the present day, philanthropy has never been regarded merely as an act of charity or almsgiving to the poor and the handicapped. It has, rather, been considered the fulfillment of a divine commandment, a religious obligation, and hence a source of spiritual vitality both for the donor and for the community. Philanthropic giving is an obligation, not an optional bounty. From the Colonial Period on, the records of Jewish synagogues in America show the attention that was paid to the carrying out of this religious imperative. In addition, outside of the organized congregations, many individuals formed and conscientiously supported benevolent societies. Some were for special purposes, such as the care of orphans or the proper burial of the indigent. Others were of a more general character, offering moral as well as financial assistance in all kinds of emergencies. On the whole, the Jews of the United States maintained the old tradition, both as a religious obligation and as a continuation of a prudential policy of not permitting other Jews to become a charge upon the general public welfare funds.

The documents below suggest still another form of the responsiveness of America's Jews to their coreligionists in other parts of the world. This was their desire somehow to help their brethren to share and enjoy the blessings of freedom and civil rights in the United States. In part, this was accomplished by direct means; an immigrant Jew, once he had succeeded in establishing an economic foothold in the New World, sent every penny he could spare to pay the way of relatives and friends following him to the more open society in America. There were also proposals—and even one formal attempt—to gain the same objective in a more systematic, large-scale fashion. The prevalence of a Jeffersonian agrarianism in the American public mind of the time led to these projects being formulated in terms of the formation of agricultural colonies. Mordecai Manuel Noah's "Ararat" scheme came nearest to actualization; perhaps both its near-realization and its ultimate failure can be attributed to Noah's own character traits. Soberer plans that might have proved viable lacked the dramatic flair that would have been needed to move them from paper to the land.

It has often been noted that such plans as these for Jewish resettlement are akin to the later developments of Zionism, in that they propose an essentially nonsupernatural, practical solution to the problem of the survival of Jewish masses in a hostile environment. There is no question that this similarity is present, but it is not the whole story. Noah, for instance, indicates an appreciation of the distinction between a miraculous and a natural solution by speaking at first of Ararat as a place of refuge where the Jews could await, without persecution, the Messianic era of return to the Holy Land. Nevertheless his own proclamations of this place of refuge assume a Messianic tone, as if the difference of which he was aware faded in his more expansive moments. It seems almost as if the closer "Ararat" approached foundation the more the distinction blurred in the mind of its projector. Perhaps, in the end, he had come to think of himself as a heaven-sent leader of world Jewry.

Amid these plans for agricultural settlement of large numbers of Jews in the United States, the land of Israel was not forgotten. Periodically messengers brought appeals to the American Jewish public from the mendicant Palestinian Jews. These messengers were well-received and given some financial aid. Furthermore, Noah certainly envisaged an ultimate restoration of all Jews to the Holy Land. Toward the end of the period dealt with in this collection, Isaac Leeser emerged as a prominent Jewish religious leader in Philadelphia. Early in his career, Leeser spoke of the belief in a miraculous restoration and held that there was no possible conflict between this hope for return to Zion and a patriotic loyalty to the United States. Some two decades after the sermon in which he took this position, Leeser's views on restoration took a more political turn; even at the later time, however, he continued to regard the return as a solution to the problems of Jews outside the United

States. Essentially, the pre-Zionism of such men as Noah and Leeser should, then, be considered as an extension of the religious and philanthropic concerns of American Jewry, not as a true anticipation of political Zionism.

We must not think of those Jews who came to the United States in these early days in the image of the East European immigrants of a later time. These were the enterprising, the bold, the venturesome, the daring, not those whose lives were "sicklied o'er with the pale cast of thought." They did not merely accept a life of danger when it was thrust upon them, but went out to live dangerously because to do so suited their temperament. Most of the Jews of the early national period, it is true, were occupied in commerce. Some few entered the professions of law and medicine. But a handful, too, voluntarily chose the military or naval life and some the life of the pioneer hunter or trapper. In the southern states, where the *code duello* still held sway, we hear of Jewish participants in duels of honor.

In general literary culture and, sad to say, particularly in knowledge of the religious literature of Judaism, the American Jews of the early nineteenth century were, with a few exceptions, notably deficient. Although they moved in the direction of an increased concern for both religious education and higher secular education, the results they achieved were scattered and inadequate. We may, perhaps, by an exercise of generosity, accept the few Jewish journalists of the age as literary men. There were, of course, no artists among the Jews. There were no men of science, unless the "chemists"—presumably manufacturers of pharmaceutical supplies and pharmacists—are regarded as scientists. Indeed, the only cultural activity in which the Jews of the United States made a significant contribution to American life was that of music. Even in music, however, in our period, Jews appear more prominently as impressarios than as performers.

This cultural deficiency excepted, and accounted for by the type of personality to be found in a pioneering role in a new country, there is scarcely an area or aspect of American life into which these documents fail to lead us. The history of the Jews in the United States between 1790 and 1840 is an integral part of the history of the United States. Here is not to be found an enclave (like, for example, the Amish or some more recent Jewish groups) whose internal development can be seen clearly in isolation from the life around it. In a sense, one can say that there was no Jewish life in the United States but only life in the United States as lived by Jews. It is this unique situation that has—thus far, at least— made the dialectic of Homeland and Exile a purely theoretical exercise among many Jews of the United States.

The Jews of the United States, 1790-1840

Part One
The Place of the Jews
in American Life

One of the distinctive features of American life has been that it
has served as the proving ground for ideas that had been discussed,
in Europe, as matters of theoretical interest, but had never been
tested in practice. It is not so much by virtue of originality of
thought as because of uniqueness of opportunity to test ideas
experimentally that the United States, in the early years of its
national existence, inaugurated policies that were watched with
interest—and, often, with skepticism—by leaders of thought and
by the informed public in Europe. To illustrate this by a major
example, it had long been said, in the writings of European masters
of political theory from the Stoics on down, that the people were
the ultimate source of the authority of government. In practice,
however, this theoretical nod in the direction of popular sovereignty
was entirely neglected, and where there was any concession at
all to the idea of representation of the interest of the "sovereign"
people, it was in a doctrine—theoretical once more—of "virtual
representation." In the United States, on the contrary, the idea of the
sovereignty of the people was taken as a basic premise of political
life, and, as a result, an attempt was made to develop a form of
representation that would be actual rather than virtual.

This, in turn, led to a necessity for deciding what was meant, in
a political sense, by the "people." Was it everyone who lived in
the United States? Or was it some fragmentary part, whether large
or small? Once again, the decision that the "people" meant all the
inhabitants of the land was not based on a new theory; the idea
had often been thought of by Europeans. It was the attempt to
realize practically the equation of the "people" with the whole
white population that was the novel contribution of life in the
United States. Now one aspect of religious freedom is implied in

the decision that the "people" means the whole people, namely, that religious differences cannot be allowed as grounds for political disfranchisement. The government must be and must remain religiously uncommitted, for if it should be religiously committed, civil preference would be given to one part of the people. Thus the "wall of separation between church and state" was not merely a shibboleth; nor was it entirely the result of the multiplicity of religious sects in the country, each afraid that some other sect might be established. It was rather, an inevitable consequence of the decision to base the political structure of the United States on the *actual* sovereignty and *actual* representation of *all* the people.

The relevance of this discussion to our concern for describing the place of the Jews in American life is direct and clear. For the first time in many centuries of Jewish experience, the Jews in America found themselves citizens, regarded as part of the "people of the United States," rather than as resident and more or less tolerated aliens. As citizens, the Jews had a right to vote, to run for office, to express their views and expect their expression to be listened to by their representatives. They were faced with no overt discrimination against entering into any profession or trade. Their legal and political status, as far as the federal government was concerned, was precisely the same as that of any other citizens of the United States. They were religiously of the Jewish people, but politically of the American people.

Certainly no one should think that the status of the Jews in America changed overnight from that of pariahs to that of welcome brothers. Much of the change had taken place in fact before it was enshrined in law; for law usually follows public attitudes. Legislation is, for the most part, the consequence of changes in patterns of living, not their cause. Much of the change did not take full effect until many years after the federal Constitution had been adopted; for the relation between the federal government and that of the states was different in the early years of the United States from what it has become. Today, we think of the United States as the fundamental political unit, and of state and local governments as traditional, if sometimes inconvenient, supplementary political units. A man today might describe himself as

an American citizen living in Virginia; in 1789, he would have
called himself a citizen of the Old Dominion of Virginia. The state
held his primary allegiance, and the federal government was an
often inconvenient agent of the states for conducting certain types
of business. The states were born before they were united; in
many cases, they operated until well on into the nineteenth century
under constitutions that were considerably older than the federal
Constitution and that preserved even older traditions surviving
from their colonial charters. In these circumstances, it was possible,
in some states, for a Jew to be merely a resident, without political
rights, even though a full citizen, and even an official, of the United
States.

The pattern was still further complicated by the degree of independence and self-determination that could be maintained by a
local governmental unit, like a county or a township. The seriousness
of this will be apparent when it is realized that it is on the local
level that the administration of the laws takes place in the first
instance. The federal Congress was, by the First Amendment to
the Constitution, inhibited from the making of laws "respecting
an establishment of religion." Certain state legislatures were instructed (as in Massachusetts) by their constitutions to make precisely the sort of law that was forbidden to Congress. Finally,
local governments, by statute, might, and in certain cases did,
extend the idea of "establishment" to a point at which it worked
a hardship on Jews to live in those communities.

By and large, however, the official situation of the Jews in
American life was more favorable than it had been in any other
country in the world prior to the French Revolution. In time, too,
even during the half-century of our concern, some of the anomalies
caused by the co-presence of three sets of partially overlapping
and partially incongruous laws were wiped out. At no time between 1789 and 1840 was there any *numerus clausus*, or restriction
against the Jews in any trade or profession, including officer rank
in the army and navy, on a national level. True, there was a period,
until 1826, when a Jew was excluded from the legal profession
in Maryland; but if he wished to practice law, he had only to
move to Pennsylvania, Virginia, South Carolina, or New York to
find ample scope for his professional ambitions. And from the

very beginning of national existence, Jews were to be found in government service, both civilian and military.

To this rapid survey indicating the official place of the Jews in American life, it should be added that, for the most part, the unofficial, personal, and business attitude of non-Jews was one of welcome. The story is told of Joseph Jonas, the first Jew to reach Cincinnati, that an old lady, who had never before seen a Jew, asked him to stand still while she examined him closely. Then she said, "Thee looks no different from anyone else." This is representative of much of the popular American acceptance of the Jews. In the early national period, when America's Jews came chiefly from western Europe, they looked no different from anyone else, and they could be readily absorbed into an already mixed population. There was certainly no trade, business, or profession that was overcrowded, so there was no need for an economic scapegoat. It is questionable whether anyone thought twice about the fact that the wife of President Andrew Jackson bought her dress fabrics from a Jewish firm in Philadelphia. No one would have thought to say that Rachel Jackson should have given her business to a Christian merchant; there was enough business for all, and businessmen really believed in free and open competition. Nor would it have occurred to anyone to suggest—as it might be suggested today—that by dealing with a Jewish firm, Mrs. Jackson was guaranteeing that her husband would get the "Jewish vote." The Jewish merchant, in his economic life, was regarded as a merchant, not as a Jew. He took part in organizations that aimed to increase the trade of his community, and where he had much to contribute, he was elected to office in these organizations. Only the itinerant Jewish peddler sometimes met difficulties, and it is perhaps most accurate to say that they were the difficulties that faced all peddlers, aggravated by the fact of his Jewishness. It is inaccurate and incorrect to read European anti-Semitism, or the later American anti-Semitism of the end of the nineteenth and first half of the twentieth century into the early national period of American Jewish history.

Finally, the important psychological question must be answered: Granting that the official place of the Jews in American life was relatively secure, and that their fellow-citizens were, on the whole, welcoming, did the Jews themselves feel comfortable in their place in American life? The record shows that they did, after a brief period when they were somewhat hesitant about accepting what seemed to be held out to them. They were aware of their good fortune and were ardent propagandists for further Jewish immigration to the United States. At this time, they did not feel that the coming of more Jews might disturb a balance; this is the clearest proof that they felt secure and at home. As soon as the sense of security was lost (say in the 1870s), American Jews began to discourage further Jewish immigration, to save themselves at the expense of their fellow-Jews. In the period of our concern, the United States of America was both a physical and a spiritual homeland for the Jews. Here, the Jew was not in an alien world, a world he never made and was only with reluctance allowed to live in; he was in a land of which he was one of the builders, and he took pride in what he had helped to build.

I

Official Papers, Foreign and Domestic, 1789-1820

From the time of the adoption of the Constitution of the United States of America, there has been no question of the *official* attitude of the federal government towards minority religious groups, including the Jews. Individual Jews have been eligible for posts of trust and responsibility under the government by virtue of the explicit provision of the Constitution prohibiting religious tests.[1] Although no Jew has ever been elected to the presidency, there is no technical reason why a Jew should not be selected; even the oath of office specified for the inauguration of the President contains no words to which a Jew might object.[2] Furthermore, the freedom of religion that was implicit in these provisions was defined with greater precision in the Bill of Rights, which several of the States insisted upon as a condition of their ratification of the Constitution.[3] From its very inception, the Constitution defined the official attitude of the nation as neutral in religious matters. If, as a practical matter, the acceptance of this definition can be traced in large part to the multiplicity of Protestant Christian denominations, none of which could afford to allow another an advantage, the principles that lay behind its formulation were those that had been expressed by Thomas Jefferson and James Madison at an earlier time and can be traced to the views of the English philosopher, John Locke.

There are a number of official statements and public papers that bear out the contention that the federal government maintained a neutral attitude toward the religious views of its citizens, as required by the Constitution. In the early foreign relations of the United States of America, the point was spelled out in the

1796 Treaty with Tripoli, a Muslim nation. Of the domestic reassertions of the principle of religious freedom, the most important was the Northwest Ordinance (1787),[4] the organic law under which the federal government administered the large territory that was later to be formed into the states of Ohio, Indiana, Illinois, Michigan, and Wisconsin. The importance of the Northwest Ordinance lies in the fact that the religious rights it specifies were taken over into the constitutions of all the states that were carved out of the Northwest Territory. When we turn our attention to public papers, we find that George Washington, in replying to congratulatory letters sent to him by the various Jewish congregations of the country on his election to the presidency, took the opportunity to affirm his belief in religious freedom. Washington's letter to the Jewish Congregation of Newport, Rhode Island, gave currency to the now-classic phrase, "to bigotry no sanction," which he quoted from the letter from the congregation. Thomas Jefferson, too, although on some occasions he had expressed an unfavorable private view of Judaism, in his historic letter in reply to an address of the Danbury, Connecticut, Baptist Association, in 1802, interpreted the religious freedom provision of the First Amendment to the Federal Constitution as setting up "a wall of separation between church and state." In personal letters, John Adams, Thomas Jefferson, and James Madison all affirmed their delight that in the United States of America Jewish civic disabilities had been removed.

1. TREATY WITH TRIPOLI, 1796 [5]

As the government of the United States of America is not in any sense founded on the Christian religion—as it has in itself no character of enmity against the laws, religion or tranquility of Musselmen . . . it is declared by the parties that no pretext arising from religious opinions shall ever produce an interruption of the harmony existing between the two countries.[6]

2. ADDRESS OF THE NEWPORT CONGREGATION [7]
TO THE PRESIDENT OF THE UNITED STATES [8]

[*August 17, 1790*]

Sir: Permit the children of the stock of Abraham to approach you with the most cordial affection and esteem for your person and merit, and to join with our fellow-citizens in welcoming you to Newport.[9]

With pleasure we reflect on those days of difficulty and danger when the God of Israel, who delivered David from the peril of the sword, shielded your head in the day of battle; and we rejoice to think that the same spirit which rested in the bosom of the greatly beloved Daniel, enabling him to preside over the provinces of the Babylonian Empire, rests and ever will rest upon you, enabling you to discharge the arduous duties of the Chief Magistrate of these States.

Deprived as we hitherto have been of the invaluable rights of free citizens, we now—with a deep sense of gratitude to the Almighty Disposer of all events—behold a government erected by the majesty of the people—a government which to bigotry gives no sanction, to persecution no assistance, but generously affording to all liberty of conscience and immunities of citizenship, deeming every one of whatever nation, tongue, or language, equal parts of the great governmental machine.

This so ample and extensive Federal Union, whose base is philanthropy, mutual confidence and public virtue, we cannot but acknowledge to be the work of the great God, who rules in the armies of the heavens and among the inhabitants of the earth, doing whatever seemeth to Him good.

For all the blessings of civil and religious liberty which we enjoy under an equal and benign administration, we desire to send up our thanks to the Ancient of days, the great Preserver of men, beseeching Him that the angels who conducted our forefathers through the wilderness into the promised land may graciously conduct you through all the difficulties and dangers of this mortal life; and when, like Joshua, full of days and full of honors, you are gathered to your fathers, may you be admitted into the heavenly paradise to partake of the water of life and the tree of immortality.

Done and signed by order of the Hebrew Congregation in New-port, Rhode Island. Moses Seixas, *Warden* [10]

Newport, *August 17, 1790*

3. WASHINGTON'S REPLY
TO THE HEBREW CONGREGATION
IN NEWPORT, RHODE ISLAND [11]

Gentlemen: While I received with much satisfaction your address replete with expressions of esteem, I rejoice in the opportunity of assuring you that I shall always retain grateful remembrance of the cordial welcome I experienced on my visit to Newport from all classes of citizens.

The reflection on the days of difficulty and danger which are past is rendered the more sweet from a consciousness that they are succeeded by days of uncommon prosperity and security.

If we have wisdom to make the best use of the advantages with which we are now favored, we cannot fail, under the just administration of a good government, to become a great and happy people.

The citizens of the United States of America have a right to applaud themselves for having given to mankind examples of an enlarged and liberal policy—a policy worthy of imitation. All possess alike liberty of conscience and immunities of citizenship.

It is now no more that toleration is spoken of as if it were the indulgence of one class of people that another enjoyed the exercise of their inherent natural rights, for, happily, the Government of the United States, which gives to bigotry no sanction, to persecution no assistance, requires only that they who live under its protection should demean themselves as good citizens in giving it on all occasions their effectual support.

It would be inconsistent with the frankness of my character not to avow that I am pleased with your favorable opinion of my administration and fervent wishes for my felicity.

May the children of the stock of Abraham who dwell in this land continue to merit and enjoy the good will of the other inhabitants; while every one shall sit in safety under his own vine and fig tree and there shall be none to make him afraid.

May the father of all mercies scatter light, and not darkness, upon our paths, and make us all in our several vocations useful here, and in His own due time and way everlastingly happy.   G. Washington

4. WASHINGTON'S REPLY [12]
TO THE HEBREW CONGREGATIONS
IN THE CITIES OF PHILADELPHIA, [13] NEW
YORK, [14] CHARLESTON, [15] AND RICHMOND [16]

Gentlemen: The liberality of sentiment toward each other, which marks every political and religious denomination of men in this country, stands unparalleled in the history of nations.

The affection of such a people is a treasure beyond the reach of calculation, and the repeated proofs which my fellow-citizens have given of their attachment to me and approbation of my doings form the purest source of my temporal felicity.

The affectionate expressions of your address again excite my gratitude and receive my warmest acknowledgement.

The power and goodness of the Almighty, so strongly manifested in the events of our late glorious revolution, and His kind interposition in our behalf, have been no less visible in the establishment of our present equal government. In war He directed the sword, and in peace He has ruled in our councils. My agency in both has been guided by the best intentions and a sense of duty I owe to my country.

And as my exertions have hitherto been amply rewarded by the approbation of my fellow-citizens, I shall endeavor to deserve a continuance of it by my future conduct.

May the same temporal and eternal blessings which you implore for me, rest upon your congregations.   G. Washington

5. WASHINGTON'S REPLY [17]
TO THE HEBREW CONGREGATION
OF THE CITY OF SAVANNAH [18]

Gentlemen: I thank you with great sincerity for your congratulations on my appointment to the office which I have the honor to hold by the unanimous choice of my fellow-citizens, and especially the expressions you are pleased to use in testifying the confidence that is reposed in me by your congregations.

As the delay which has naturally intervened between my election and your address has afforded me an opportunity for appreciating the merits of the Federal Government and for communicating your sentiments of its administration, I have rather to express my satisfaction rather than regret at a circumstance which demonstrates (upon experiment) your attachment to the former as well as approbation of the latter.

I rejoice that a spirit of liberality and philanthropy is much more prevalent than it formerly was among the enlightened nations of the earth, and that your brethren will benefit thereby in proportion as it shall become still more extensive; happily the people of the United States have in many instances exhibited examples worthy of imitation, the salutary influence of which will doubtless extend much farther if gratefully enjoying those blessings of peace which (under the favor of heaven) have been attained by fortitude in war, they shall conduct themselves with reverence to the Deity and charity toward their fellow-creatures.

May the same wonder-working Deity, who long since delivered the Hebrews from their Egyptian oppressors, planted them in a promised land, *whose providential agency has lately been conspicuous in establishing these United States as an independent nation,* still continue to water them with the dews of heaven and make the inhabitants of every denomination participate in the temporal and spiritual blessings of that people whose God is Jehovah.[19]

G. Washington

6. JEFFERSON'S [20] REPLY TO ADDRESS OF THE DANBURY BAPTIST ASSOCIATION, 1802 [21]

Believing with you that religion is a matter which lies solely between man and his God, that he owes account to none other for his faith or his worship, that the legislative powers of government reach actions only, and not opinions, I contemplate with sovereign reverence that act of the whole American people which declared that their legislature should "make no law respecting an establishment of religion, or prohibiting the free exercise thereof," thus building a wall of separation between church and state. Adhering to this expression of the supreme will of the nation in behalf of the rights of conscience, I shall see with sincere satisfaction the progress of those sentiments which tend to restore to man all his natural rights, convinced that he has no natural right in opposition to his social duties.[22]

7. JOHN ADAMS TO MORDECAI M. NOAH,[23] 1818[24]

Quincy, July 31, 1818

Sir: Accept my best thanks for your polite and obliging favour of the 24th, and especially for the discourse[25] inclosed. I know not when I have read a more liberal or more elegant composition.

You have not extended your ideas of the right of private judgment and the liberty of conscience, both in religion and philosophy, farther than I do. Mine are limited only by morals and propriety.

I have had occasion to be acquainted with several gentlemen of your nation, and to transact business with some of them, whom I found to be men of as liberal minds, as much honor, probity, generosity and good breeding, as any I have known in any sect of religion or philosophy.

I wish your nation may be admitted to all the privileges of citizens in every country of the world. This country has done much. I wish it may do more; and annul every narrow idea in religion, government, and commerce. Let the wits joke; the philosophers sneer! What then? It has pleased the Providence of the 'first cause,' the universal cause, that Abraham should give religion, not only to Hebrews, but to Christians and Mahometans, the greatest part of the modern civilized world.   John Adams[26]

8. JOSEPH MARX[27] TO JEFFERSON, 1820[28]

Richmond 3d July 1820

Sir: I avail myself of the conveyance afforded me by Governor Randolph[29] to transmit and to request your acceptance, of the Volume containing the proceedings of the Sanhedrin, convened by order of the Emperor Buonaparte.[30]

Should any part of their Deliberations, or Sentiments expressed by any Member of that Body, tend to confirm the liberal and enlightened views, expressed by yourself, of that persecuted Race, when last I had the pleasure of an interview, it will prove to me a source of high gratification. I am with Sentiments of profound Respect Sir Your most Obedient Servt.   Joseph Marx

Thomas Jefferson Esqr

9. JEFFERSON TO JOSEPH MARX

Th: Jefferson presents to Mr. Marx his compliments & thanks for the Transactions of the Paris Sanhedrin, which he shall read with great interest, and with the regret he has ever felt at seeing a sect, the parent and basis of all those of Christendom, singled out by all of them for a persecution and oppression which prove they have profited nothing from the benevolent doctrines of him whom they profess to make the model of their principles and practice.

He salutes Mr. Marx with sentiments of perfect esteem and respect.[31]

Monticello, July 8, 20

10. JEFFERSON TO JACOB DE LA MOTTA,[32] 1820 [33]

[September 1, 1820]

Th. Jefferson returns his thanks to Dr. De La Motta for the eloquent discourse on the Consecration of the Synagogue of Savannah, which he has been so kind as to send him. It excites in him the gratifying reflection that his country has been the first to prove to the world two truths, the most salutary to human society, that man can govern himself, and that religious freedom is the most effectual anodyne against religious dissension: the maxim of civil government being reversed in that of religion, where its true form is "divided we stand, united, we fall." He is happy in the restoration of the Jews, particularly, to their social rights, and hopes they will be seen taking their seats on the benches of science as preparatory to their doing the same at the board of government. He salutes Dr. De La Motta with sentiments of great respect.

11. JAMES MADISON TO JACOB DE LA MOTTA, 1820 [34]

To Doc[to]r de la Motta

Montpellier Aug: 1820

Sir

I have received your letter of the 7th inst. with the Discourse delivered at the consecration of the Hebrew Synagogue at Savannah, for which you will please to accept my thanks.

The history of the Jews must for ever be interesting. The modern part of it is at the same time so little generally known, that every ray of light on the subject has its value.

Among the features peculiar to the political system of the U. States is the perfect equality of rights which it secures to every religious sect. And it is particularly pleasing to observe in the good citizenship of such as have been most distrusted and oppressed elsewhere, a happy illustration of the safety and success of this experiment of a just and benignant policy. Equal laws protecting equal rights, are found as they ought to be presumed, the best guarantee of loyalty, and love of country; as well as best calculated to cherish that mutual respect and good will among citizens of every religious denomination which are necessary to social harmony and most favorable to the advancement of truth. The account you give of the Jews of your Congregation brings them fully within the scope of these observations.

I tender you, Sir, my respects and good wishes.   James Madison

Dr. de la Motta

II

Variations in State Constitutions, 1789-1840

Unfortunately, the state constitutions of the early national period do not present as clear a picture as that of the federal Constitution. There was not, at this time, any provision of the federal organic law that required, or could be interpreted as requiring all state constitutions to be brought into conformity with that of the central government. Because there was no such requirement and the tradition of state independence was far stronger in the older states than the newly-acquired federal loyalties, especially those states which had had constitutions prior to 1789, when the federal Constitution was formulated, tended to preserve older discriminatory provisions from colonial times. Some of the state constitutions were internally inconsistent, granting complete religious freedom in one clause, usually in their "bill of rights," but in another clause requiring a religious test oath for public office. In some cases, notably in the New England states, established churches were continued well into the nineteenth century, whereas other states made no provision whatsoever for any form or vestige of establishment. It is interesting to note that many of the state constitutions, even, in some instances, those that restricted office-holding to Christians or still further limited the right to hold office to Protestants, nevertheless contained a specific provision forbidding members of the clergy to hold office. The following documents are clauses from state constitutions illustrating these various types.

12. MARYLAND STATE CONSTITUTION, 1776 [35]

Article XXXIII. That, as it is the duty of every man to worship God in such manner as he thinks most acceptable to him: all persons, professing the Christian religion, are equally entitled to protection in their religious liberty; wherefore no person ought by any law to be molested in his person or estate on account of his religious persuasion or profession, or for his religious practice; unless, under colour of religion, any man shall disturb the good order, peace or safety of the State, or shall infringe the laws of morality, or injure others, in their natural, civil, or religious rights; nor ought any person to be compelled to frequent or maintain, or contribute, unless on contract, to maintain any particular place of worship, or any particular ministry; yet the Legislature may, in their discretion, lay a general and equal tax, for the support of the Christian religion; leaving to each individual the power of appointing the payment over of the money, collected from him, to the support of any particular place of worship or minister, or for the benefit of the poor of his own denomination, or the poor in general of any particular county; but the churches, chapels, glebes, and all other property now belonging to the church of England, ought to remain to the church of England forever. And all acts of Assembly, lately passed, for collecting monies for building or repairing particular churches or chapels of ease, shall continue in force, and be executed, unless the Legislature shall, by act, supersede or repeal the same: but no county court shall assess any quantity of tobacco, or sum of money, hereafter, on the application of any vestrymen or church-wardens; and every encumbent of the church of England, who hath remained in his parish, and performed his duty, shall be entitled to receive the provision and support established by the act, entitled "An act for the support of the clergy of the church of England, in this Province," till the November court of this present year, to be held for the county in which his parish shall lie, or partly lie, or for such time as he hath remained in his parish, and performed his duty.

Article XXXV. That no other test or qualification ought to be required, on admission to any office of trust or profit, than such oath of support and fidelity to this State, and such oath of office, as shall be directed by this Convention, or the Legislature of this State, and a declaration of a belief in the Christian religion.

13. NORTH CAROLINA STATE CONSTITUTION, 1776 [36]

Article XXXI. That no clergyman, or preacher of the gospel, of any denomination, shall be capable of being a member of either the Senate, House of Commons, or Council of State, while he continues in the exercise of the pastoral function.

Article XXXII. That no person, who shall deny the being of God or the truth of the Protestant religion, or the divine authority either of the Old or New Testaments, or who shall hold religious principles incompatible with the freedom and safety of the State, shall be capable of holding any office or place of trust or profit in the civil department within this State.

Article XXXIV. That there shall be no establishment of any one religious church or denomination in this State, in preference to any other; neither shall any person, on any pretence whatsoever, be compelled to attend any place of worship contrary to his own faith or judgment, nor be obliged to pay, for the purchase of any glebe, or the building of any house of worship, or for the maintenance of any minister or ministry, contrary to what he believes right, or has voluntarily and personally engaged to perform; but all persons shall be at liberty to exercise their own mode of worship: *Provided,* That nothing herein contained shall be construed to exempt preachers of treasonable or seditious discourses, from legal trial and punishment.

14. NEW YORK STATE CONSTITUTION, 1821 [37]

Article VI. Members of the legislature and all officers, executive and judicial, except such inferior officers as may by law be exempted, shall, before they enter on the duties of their respective offices, take and subscribe the following oath or affirmation:

"I do solemnly swear [or affirm, as the case may be] that I will support the Constitution of the United States, and the constitution of the State of New York; and that I will faithfully discharge the duties of the office of ——— according to the best of my ability."

And no other oath, declaration, or test shall be required as a qualification for any office or public trust.

Article VII, Section 3. The free exercise and enjoyment of religious profession and worship, without discrimination or preference, shall forever be allowed in this State to all mankind; but the liberty of conscience hereby secured shall not be so construed as to excuse acts of licentiousness, or justify practices inconsistent with the peace or safety of this State.

Article VII, Section 4. And whereas the ministers of the gospel are, by their profession, dedicated to the service of God and the cure of souls, and ought not to be diverted from the great duties of their functions; therefore, no minister of the gospel, or priest of any denomination whatsoever, shall at any time hereafter, under any pretence or description whatever, be eligible to or capable of holding any civil or military office or place within this State.

15. MASSACHUSETTS STATE CONSTITUTION, 1780 [38]

Part One, Article II: It is the right as well as the duty of all men in society, publicly, and at stated seasons, to worship the SUPREME BEING, the great Creator and Preserver of the universe. And no subject shall be hurt, molested, or restrained, in his person, liberty, or estate, for worshipping GOD in the manner and season most agreeable to the dictates of his own conscience; or for his religious profession of sentiments; provided he doth not disturb the public peace, or obstruct others in their religious worship.

Part One, Article III: As the happiness of a people, and the good order and preservation of civil government, essentially depend upon piety, religion, and morality; and as these cannot be generally diffused through a community but by the institution of the public worship of GOD, and of public instructions in piety, religion, and morality: Therefore, to promote their happiness, and to secure the good order and preservation of their government, the people of this commonwealth have a right to invest their legislature with power to authorize and require, and the legislature shall, from time to time, authorize and require, the several towns, parishes, precincts, and other bodies politic, or religious societies, to make suitable provision, at their own expense, for the institution of the public worship of GOD, and for the support and maintenance of public Protestant teachers of piety, religion, and morality, in all cases where such provision shall not be made voluntarily.

And the people of this commonwealth have also a right to, and do, invest their legislature with authority to enjoin upon all the subjects an attendance upon the instructions of the public teachers aforesaid, at stated times and seasons, if there be any on whose instructions they can conscientiously and conveniently attend.

Provided, notwithstanding, that the several towns, parishes, precincts, and other bodies politic, or religious societies, shall, at all times, have the exclusive right of electing their public teachers, and of contracting with them for their support and maintenance.

And all moneys paid by the subject to the support of public worship, and of the public teachers aforesaid, shall, if he require it, be uniformly applied to the support of the public teacher or teachers of his own religious sect or denomination, provided there be any on whose instructions he attends; otherwise it may be paid towards the support of the teacher or teachers of the parish or precinct in which the said moneys are raised.

And every denomination of Christians, demeaning themselves peaceably, and as good subjects of the commonwealth, shall be equally under the protection of the law: and no subordination of any one sect or denomination to another shall ever be established by law.

Chapter VI, Article I: Any person chosen governor, lieutenant-governor, councillor, senator, or representative, and accepting the trust, shall, before he proceed to execute the duties of his place or office, make and subscribe the following declaration, viz.:

"I, A.B., do declare, that I believe the Christian religion, and have a firm persuasion of its truth; and that I am seised and possessed, in my own right, of the property required by the constitution, as one qualification for the office or place to which I am elected."

16. TENNESSEE STATE CONSTITUTION, 1796 [39]

Article XI, Section 3: That all men have a natural and indefeasible right to worship Almighty God according to the dictates of their own consciences; that no man can of right be compelled to attend, erect, or support any place of worship, or to maintain any ministry against his consent; that no human authority can in any case whatever control or interfere with the rights of conscience; and that no preference shall ever be given by law to any religious establishments or modes of worship.

Article XI, Section 4: That no religious test shall ever be required as a qualification to any office or public trust under this State.

Article VII, Section 7: The legislature shall pass laws exempting citizens, belonging to any sect or denomination of religion the tenets of which are known to be opposed to the bearing of arms, from attending private and general musters.

Article VIII, Section 1: Whereas the ministers of the gospel are, by their professions, dedicated to God and the care of souls, and ought not to be diverted from the great duties of their functions; therefore no minister of the gospel, or priest of any denomination whatever, shall be eligible to a seat in either house of the legislature.

Article VIII, Section 2: No person who denies the being of God, or a future state of rewards and punishments, shall hold any office in the civil department of this State.[40]

III

Local Courts and Sabbath Laws,

1793-1833

It must not be forgotten that between the areas of federal and state jurisdiction there was still room for a large measure of local autonomy, and that it was at the local level that ordinances unfavorable to Jewish equality frequently appeared. This distinction between constitutional theory and local actuality is demonstrated especially in legal processes that involved the difference between Jewish and Christian observance of the Sabbath. Despite all constitutional indications to the contrary, in these Sabbath-observance cases custom and tradition were cited by presiding judges in a fashion that clearly implied that the United States was a Christian country. In 1817, in Pennsylvania, for example, the state Supreme Court affirmed a conviction against Abraham Wolf for "having done and performed worldly employment on the *Lord's* day, commonly called Sunday," in spite of the fact that the defendant was a professing Jew. The Supreme Court of South Carolina, in 1833, rejected the plea that Sunday laws contravened the federal Constitution and upheld the conviction of Alexander Marks under an ordinance of the Town Council of Columbia, South Carolina. The judicial interpretation given to local law in cases of this sort inevitably led the Jews (and, later, the Seventh Day Adventists) to be singled out as the most conspicuous violators of a custom that was regarded as implicit in the American tradition. Since the moral codes of both Judaism and Christianity stemmed from the same biblical source, difficulties did not arise on the moral level but on the level of custom. Sunday observance laws, even where they were less stringent than the "blue laws" of post-Puritan New England,[41] unintentionally introduced a hardship into the economic life of Jews who observed the seventh day for the sake of their own religious beliefs and were asked also to abstain from business on the first day of the week out of deference to their neighbor's religious beliefs. Indeed, since the courts themselves conducted business on Saturday, a Jewish litigant or witness might well find himself called to testify on his day of rest. As early as 1793, in Pennsylvania, a Jewish witness was fined £10 for refusing to testify on Saturday. Again in 1831 in the same state, the Supreme Court decided that the conscientious scruples of a Jew against appearing in court to attend to the trial of his cause on the Jewish Sabbath were no ground for postponing the judicial process.

17. STANSBURY VS. MARKS, PENNSYLVANIA, 1793 [42]

In this cause (which was tried on *Saturday*, the 5th of April) the defendant offered *Jonas Phillips*,[43] a Jew, as a witness; but he refused to be sworn, because it was his *Sabbath*. The Court, therefore fined him £10; but the defendant, afterwards, waiving the benefit of his testimony, he was discharged from the fine.

18. THE COMMONWEALTH VS. ABRAHAM WOLF, [44] PENNSYLVANIA, 1817 [45]

Charged on oath of *James Pusey* with having done and performed worldly employment on the *Lord's* day, commonly called *Sunday*. Warrant issued 29th *July*, 1816. And now *eodem die* defendant brought; be it remembered, that defendant being brought, confesses the fact, and alleges that he is a Jew by persuasion. And it is considered and adjudged by me, *Samuel Badger*,[46] one of the aldermen of the city of *Philadelphia*, that the said Abraham, according to the form of the act of assembly in such case made and provided, be convicted and he is hereby convicted of having done and performed worldly employment or business, not being a work of necessity or charity, on the *Lord's* day, commonly called *Sunday*. And I, the said alderman, do, therefore adjudge him to pay a fine of four dollars, which sum, by so doing and performing, he hath forfeited, to be distributed as the act of assembly directs. . . .

Phillips,[47] for the defendant, took the following exceptions to this conviction.

1. That the conviction does not state the debt to have been due in the city of *Philadelphia*.

2. That it does not state when the work was done.

3. That it does not state the particular kind of work that was done.

4. That there is no original conviction under the hand and seal of the magistrate; the proceedings being merely certified to be an extract from the magistrate's docket.

5. That the suit should be a *qui tam* action.[48]

6. That those who profess the Jewish religion, and others who keep the seventh day as their sabbath, are not within the meaning of the act of assembly inflicting the penalty. . . .

Yeates, J.[49] It was the obvious intention of the legislature, when they introduced into the 4th section of the law for the prevention of vice and immorality, passed 22d *April*, 1794, a form of conviction of the offences therein specified, to guard against reversals for want of technical niceties. . . .

But it has been objected, that those who profess the Jewish religion, and others who keep the seventh day as their sabbath, are not within the meaning of the act inflicting the penalty. That such people are comprehended within the general terms of the law, "any person," is not denied. But it is said, that such construction interferes with the 3d section of the 9th article of the state constitution, and is over-ruled thereby. The section runs thus: "All men have a natural and indefeasible right to worship Almighty God according to the dictates of their own consciences. No man can of right be compelled to attend, erect, or support any place of worship, or to maintain any ministry, against his consent. No human authority can, in any case whatever, control or interfere with the rights of conscience. And no preference shall ever be given, by law, to any religious establishments or modes of worship."

The defendant's counsel has not contended, that the prohibition of work on *Sunday*, immediately opposes the received doctrine of the Jews, as disclosed in the five books of *Moses:* but has asserted, that there may be persons of that religious persuasion, who may suppose, that the command in the decalogue, "six days shalt thou labour, and do all that thou hast to do," imperiously binds them to work six days in each week; and firmly believing *Saturday* to be the day set apart for rest, they can only cease to work on that day, consistently with their ideas of religious duty. It has also been urged, that there may be others who may make it a point of conscience to show, by plain, open, unequivocal acts, that the Christian institution of *Sunday* is abhorrent to their minds.

To this we answer, that we have never heard of the fourth commandment having received this construction by any persons who profess to believe either in the Old or New Testament. And that the Jewish Talmud, containing the traditions of that people, and the Rabbinical constitutions and explications of their law, asserts no such doctrine. The true meaning of the command is uniformly supposed to be, that we should abstain from our usual labour the one seventh part of our time, and devote the same to the worship of the Deity, and the exercises of our religious duties. Upon this subject the sense of the adherents to the *Mosaic* dispensation is strongly evinced by the religious holidays which they keep at the proper seasons. . . . The invaluable privilege of the rights of conscience, secured to us by the constitution of the Commonwealth, was never intended to shelter those persons, who, out of mere caprice, would directly oppose those laws, for the pleasure of showing their contempt and abhorrence of the religious opinions of the great mass of the citizens.

We have not the slightest difficulty in affirming the conviction of the defendant. . . .

19. TOWN COUNCIL OF COLUMBIA VS. DUKE AND MARKS, 1833 [50]

On the 18th day of July last, the Intendant and Wardens of Columbia passed an Ordinance, so much of what as is complained of by the applicants is in the following words, viz.:

"That immediately after the passing of this Ordinance, if any merchant, store-keeper, grocer, shop-keeper or keeper of a porter or drinking house, or keeper of a confectionary shall open their store for the transaction of business on Sunday, or are convicted of selling to negroes on that day within the town, shall be subject to a fine of $12 for every such offence." . . .

The relators rely, principally on the 1st section of the 8th article of the Constitution of this State. . . . The earnestness and confidence with which they have insisted that they are protected by the Constitutional provision, have induced me to consider it attentively. But I am wholly unable to discover its application in this instance. It cannot be pretended that this ordinance interferes with "the free exercise and enjoyment of religious worship," or that it makes any "discrimination" or "gives any preference"—or that "all mankind" are "not allowed" all that was intended to be secured by the Constitution. The ordinance neither exacts nor imposes any religious duty or obligation. It requires no sacrifice on the part of any one, unless closing their doors and suspending their business (of which I will speak presently) be so considered. It is general in its character, and therefore every class of citizens is embraced "without discrimination or preference." It enjoins no profession of faith, demands no religious test, extorts no religious ceremony, confers no religious privilege or "preference." The error consists in supposing that this regulation of the Corporation gives a "preference," or makes a "discrimination" in favor of all who conceive it to be a duty to keep this day holy; and while one of the relators contends that it does no violence to religion to keep open shop and sell on that day, the other, who is an Israelite, denies that it is the true Sabbath. . . .

Now if the Ordinance in question required either of the relators to observe Sunday as a sacred day, or to conform to the notions of others as to its holy character, then it would be giving a "preference," or making a "discrimination" in contravention of the Constitution. But it is manifest that the nearest approximation which this Ordinance makes to religion or religious subjects, is to be found in the probability of its securing very partially to those, who do observe that day, an undisturbed and quiet performance of what they conceive an imperative obligation. That those who do thus worship are entitled to this protection, and that the council have authority to secure it to them, I shall not stop to illustrate. . . .

If society, by one consent, or by law, designate any day of the week as one of leisure and rest and on which all the ordinary and laborious occupations and pursuits of life are suspended, the recurrence of that day necessarily throws upon the community, for the time, servants, apprentices and other laborers, ready to embrace every opportunity which presents the means of indulgence. To lessen these temptations or render such as do exist as innoxious as possible, is a duty incumbent on all the municipal authorities, paramount to all considerations of the exclusive interest of any individual or class of individuals. And if it be called a restraint on individual or personal liberty in not allowing every one to pursue his own interest, as it may be presented, the answer is, it is a restraint which the benefit of society imposes, and the right to impose it has been yielded by the individual himself—or, in other words, it is one which those "in whom all power is originally vested" (among whom he is himself numbered) have prescribed for the common benefit. No member of society has the right to pursue any trade, occupation or pursuit from which society suffers a positive injury or is exposed to imminent danger; and it is for those in authority to decide on the policy of prohibiting or removing such evils, when the case presented is within their jurisdiction. . . .

20. JUDGE GIBSON'S [51] OPINION ON OBJECTIONS TO TRIAL ON SATURDAY, PENNSYLVANIA, 1831 [52]

The religious scruples of persons concerned with the administration of justice will receive all the indulgence that is compatible with the business of government; and had circumstances permitted it, this cause would not have been ordered for trial on the Jewish Sabbath. But when a continuance for conscience' sake is claimed as a right, and at the expense of a term's delay, the matter assumes a different aspect.

It never has been held except in a single instance, that the course of justice may be obstructed by any scruple or obligation whatever. The sacrifice that ensues from an opposition of conscientious objection to the performance of a civil duty, ought, one would think, to be on the part of him whose moral or religious idiosyncrasy makes it necessary; else a denial of the lawfulness of capital punishment would exempt a witness from testifying to facts that might serve to convict a prisoner of murder, or, to say nothing of the other functionaries of the law, excuse the sheriff for refusing to execute one capitally convicted. That is an exemption which none would pretend to claim, yet it would inevitably follow from the principle insisted on here. Indeed a more apposite instance of conflict betwixt religious obligation and social duty, can hardly be imagined. Rightly considered, there are no duties half so sacred as those which the citizen owes to the laws. In the judicial investigation of facts, the secrets of no man will be wantonly exposed, nor will his principles be wantonly violated; but a respect for these must not be suffered to interfere with the operations of that organ of the government which has more immediately to do with the protection of person and property; the safety of the citizen, and the very existence of society, require that it should not. That every other obligation shall yield to that of the laws, as to a superior moral force, is a tacit condition of membership in every society, whether lay or secular, temporal or spiritual, because no citizen can lawfully hold communion with those who have associated on any other terms, and this ought, in all cases of collision, to be accounted a sufficient dispensation to the conscience. I therefore entirely dissent from the opinion of the Mayor's Court of New York, in the case which has been cited. No one is more sensible than I of the benefit derived by society from the offices of the Catholic clergy, or of the policy of protecting the secrets of auricular confession. But considerations of policy address themselves with propriety to the legislature, and not to a magistrate, whose course is prescribed, not by discretion, but rules already established. On this subject I expressed my sentiments somewhat more at large in Lesher *v.* The Commonwealth, 17 S. & R. 160, and I am for setting aside this nonsuit, certainly not for any supposed interference with the rights of conscience.[53]

IV

The Right to Elective Office, 1809

The anomalous position in which the disadvantages resulting from state constitutions and local statutes placed the Jews [54] led, in two cases, to overt attempts to find remedies. One of these, in North Carolina, concerned the right of an individual, Jacob Henry,[55] to hold a seat in the House of Commons to which he had been elected in 1809. Mr. Henry had also been elected in the previous year, but at that time his right to sit had not been challenged. North Carolina was one of the states whose constitution, unrevised since 1776, contained conflicting provisions. One article granted complete freedom of religion; another required all state officials to be theists and Protestants and to accept the divine authority of both Old and New Testaments. As a Jew, Jacob Henry could not conscientiously conform to the latter provision. When the challenge was raised, Henry was allowed the privilege of addressing the House. His speech on this occasion, a minor masterpiece, was included in several early collections of American oratory. When he had concluded, the House affirmed his right to be seated and, by implication, the right of other Jews to hold office as members of the legislature; this decision, however, did not apply to other offices in the state.[56] Nor did North Carolina act immediately to alter the constitutional provision that had made the challenge possible. In 1835, when a convention was held for the purpose of revising the North Carolina constitution, there was an interesting discussion on the question of changing the Test Oath clause. In the course of this debate, reference was made to the Henry affair, but the general question of Jewish rights did not arise. Amid loud paeans of praise for freedom, the recommended changes in the article in no way altered the status of Jews, but did extend the test oath so that all Christians might be eligible for state office.[57] Not until 1868, in a Reconstruction convention, was the

Constitution of North Carolina finally revised to allow the eligibility of Jews for state office.

21. JACOB HENRY'S SPEECH, 1809 [58]

I certainly, Mr. Speaker, know not the design of the Declaration of Rights made by the people of this State in the year 1776, if it was not to consecrate certain great and fundamental rights and principles which even the Constitution cannot impair; for the 44th section of the latter instrument declares that the Declaration of Rights ought never to be violated, on any pretence whatever; if there is any apparent difference between the two instruments, they ought, if possible, to be reconciled; but if there is a final repugnance between them, the Declaration of Rights must be considered paramount; for I believe it is to the Constitution, as the Constitution is to law; it controls and directs it absolutely and conclusively. If, then, a belief in the Protestant religion is required by the Constitution, to qualify a man for a seat in this house, and such qualification is dispensed with by the Declaration of Rights, the provision of the Constitution must be altogether inoperative; as the language of the Bill of Rights is, "that all men have a natural and inalienable right to worship ALMIGHTY GOD according to the dictates of their own consciences." It is undoubtedly a natural right, and when it is declared to be an inalienable one by the people in their sovereign and original capacity, any attempt to alienate either by the Constitution or by law, must be vain and fruitless.

It is difficult to conceive how such a provision crept into the Constitution, unless it is from the difficulty the human mind feels in suddenly emancipating itself from fetters by which it has long been enchained: and how adverse it is to the feelings and manners of the people of the present day every gentleman may satisfy himself by glancing at the religious belief of the persons who fill the various offices in this State: there are Presbyterians, Lutherans, Calvinists, Mennonists, Baptists, Trinitarians, and Unitarians. But, as far as my observation extends, there are fewer Protestants, in the strict sense of the word, used by the Constitution, than of any other persuasion; for I suppose that they meant by it, the Protestant religion as established by the law in England. For other persuasions we see houses of worship in almost every part of the State, but very few of the Protestant; so few, that indeed I fear that the people of this State would for some time remain unrepresented in this House, if that clause of the Constitution is supposed to be in force. So far from believing in the Thirty-nine Articles, I will venture to assert that a majority of the people never have read them.

If a man should hold religious principles incompatible with the freedom and safety of the State, I do not hesitate to pronounce that he should be excluded from the public councils of the same; and I trust if I know myself, no one would be more ready to aid and assist than myself. But I should really be at a loss to specify any known religious principles which are thus dangerous. It is surely a question between a man and his Maker, and requires more than human attributes to pronounce which of the numerous sects prevailing in the world is most acceptable to the Deity. If a man fulfills the duties of that religion, which his education or his conscience has pointed to him as the true one, no person, I hold, in this our land of liberty, has a right to arraign him at the bar of any inquisition: and the day, I trust, has long passed, when principles merely speculative were propagated by force; when the sincere and pious were made victims, and the light-minded bribed into hypocrites.

The purest homage man could render to the Almighty was the sacrifice of his passions and the performance of his duties. That the ruler of the universe would receive with equal benignity the various offerings of man's adoration, if they proceeded from the heart. Governments only concern the actions and conduct of man, and not his speculative notions. Who among us feels himself so exalted above his fellows as to have a right to dictate to them any mode of belief? Will you bind the conscience in chains, and fasten conviction upon the mind in spite of the conclusions of reason and of those ties and habitudes which are blended with every pulsation of the heart? Are you prepared to plunge at once from the sublime heights of moral legislation into the dark and gloomy caverns of superstitious ignorance? Will you drive from your shores and from the shelter of your constitution, all who do not lay their oblations on the same altar, observe the same ritual, and subscribe to the same dogmas? If so, which, among the various sects into which we are divided, shall be the favored one?

I should insult the understanding of this House to suppose it possible that they could ever assent to such absurdities; for all know that persecution in all its shapes and modifications, is contrary to the genius of our government and the spirit of our laws, and that it can never produce any other effect than to render men hypocrites or martyrs.

When Charles V., Emperor of Germany, tired of the cares of government, resigned his crown to his son, he retired to a monastery, where he amused the evening of his life in regulating the movements of watches, endeavoring to make a number keep the same time; but, not being able to make any two go exactly alike, it led him to reflect upon the folly and crimes he had committed, in attempting the impossibility of making men think alike!

Nothing is more easily demonstrated than that the conduct alone is the subject of human laws, and that man ought to suffer civil disqualification for what he does, and not for what he thinks. The mind can receive laws only from Him, of whose Divine essence it is a portion; He alone can punish disobedience; for who else can know its movements, or estimate their merits? The religion I profess, inculcates every duty which men owes to his fellow men; it enjoins upon its votaries the practice of every virtue, and the detestation of every vice; it teaches them to hope for the favor of heaven exactly in proportion as their lives have been directed by just, honorable, and beneficent maxims. This, then, gentlemen, is my creed, it was impressed upon my infant mind; it has been the director of my youth, the monitor of my manhood, and will, I trust, be the consolation of my old age. At any rate, Mr. Speaker, I am sure that you cannot see anything in this Religion, to deprive me of my seat in this house. So far as relates to my life and conduct, the examination of these I submit with cheerfulness to your candid and liberal construction. What may be the religion of him who made this objection against me, or whether he has any religion or not I am unable to say. I have never considered it my duty to pry into the belief of other members of this house. If their actions are upright and conduct just, the rest is for their own consideration, not for mine. I do not seek to make converts to my faith, whatever it may be esteemed in the eyes of my officious friend, nor do I exclude any one from my esteem or friendship, because he and I differ in that respect. The same charity, therefore, it is not unreasonable to expect, will be extended to myself, because in all things that relate to the State and to the duties of civil life, I am bound by the same obligations with my fellow-citizens, nor does any man subscribe more sincerely than myself to the maxim, "whatever ye would that men should do unto you do ye so even unto them, for such is the law and the prophets."

V

The Maryland "Jew Bill,"
1818-1819

A second *cause célèbre* arose over the attempt to remove test-oath provisions from the constitution of the State of Maryland, and thus to enable the handful of Jews in that state to serve in public office or to engage in the practice of law. This was a long and bitter fight, and one of the few occurrences in the life of the Jews of America in the early national period that has been adequately studied by historians. The story begins in 1797. In that year, and annually for several years thereafter, Solomon Etting [59] of Baltimore petitioned the state legislature for the elimination of the constitutional discrimination against the Jews. In every instance his petition was rejected, in the end so decisively that Etting grew discouraged and gave up his annual petitioning. In 1818, however, Thomas Kennedy,[60] a freshman legislator from Washington County in western Maryland, a devoted follower of Jeffersonian principles, took up the cause and asked leave to bring in a bill for relief of the Jews. This so-called "Jew bill" was prepared by a committee of three and introduced by Kennedy, but it did not pass at this time. The Democratic-Republican (Jeffersonian) press, not only in Maryland but also in neighboring states, regarded the defeat of Kennedy's bill as a shocking defeat for the ideal of a free America.[61]

22. J. I. COHEN [62] TO E. S. THOMAS,[63] 1818 [64]

Balt Dec 16, 1818

E. S. Thomas, Esq.,
Annapolis, Md.
Dear Sir:
    Noticing the proceedings of the present legislature of Md., I

observe a committee has been appointed in the house of Delegates to bring in a Bill "to extend to persons professing the Jewish Religion the same civil privileges that are enjoyed by other religious sects" and that yourself with Mr. Kennedy by whom the motion was made and Mr. Breckenridge [65] compose that committee.

Having the pleasure of a personal acquaintance with you I am induced from the importance of the subject to address you.

You cannot be aware Sir from not having felt the pressure of religious intolerance, of the emotions excited in the breast of an Israelite whenever the theme of liberty of conscience is canvassed. The subject of religion being the nearest and most vital to the soul of every sectarian it awakens every spark of feeling in support of those unalienable rights which the very nature of man forbids a transfer. On the question of the extension of religious freedom to any sect or denomination, the Jew feels with solicitude for a Brother sufferer and with the anxiety of him for whom the subject is intended particularly to operate, exults in his success or sinks deeper than before with the pangs which oppression have thrown over him, and in a tenfold degree bends him below his former station.

Judge then Sir how alive to the lightest sound in a prospect of relief from the shackles of temporal jurisdiction towards the enjoyment of rights in common with his fellowmen is the soul of a man heretofore deprived of those privileges, all the dormant faculties of his mind are then elicited and he experiences sensations only felt by those similarly situated and which in extent cannot be comprehended by those who always possessed those privileges and being thus in possession have never had cause to feel the want of.

The motion of Mr. Kennedy at the same time that it reminds us of the indignity of our situation in the States also brings to mind the many blessings our profession enjoys in this country of liberty— that by the Constitution of the United States an Israelite is placed on the same footing with any other citizen of the Union and can be elevated to the highest station in the gift of the government or in the people such toleration is duly appreciated. On the other hand we are not insensible of the protection in our persons and property even under the laws of Maryland still as those obnoxious parts of its Constitution were produced only in times of darkness and prejudice why are they continued as blots on the present enlightened period and on the honor of the State in direct opposition also to the features and principles in the Constitution of the United States.

I can scarcely admit a doubt that on a moment's consideration and reflection a change will be made as the Prayer of Justice and reason.

The grievance complained of and for which *redress* is asked is that part of the Constitution of Maryland, which requiring a declaration of belief in the Christian Religion prevents a Jew accepting any office his fellowmen might elect him to or think him deserving the enjoyment of. He is thus incapacitated because he cannot *abjure* the principles instilled in him of worshipping the Almighty according to the dictates of his own conscience and take an oath of belief in other tenets as if such declaration of Belief made him a better man or one more capable of exercising the duties of the office which the want of that declaration would deprive him of because he maintains his unalienable rights with a steadfast and upright hand. Because he cannot consent to act hypocritically he is deemed unworthy to be trusted and to be as it were disfranchised, thus incapacitating on the very grounds that ought to entitle him to confidence in the discharge of any duty he might be called upon to perform *viz:* a complete independence and unbiased judgment formed on the broad foundation of moral *rectitude*.

To you I'm sure I need not point out the effects resulting from an equal enjoyment of civil rights instead of being borne down by a state of despondency and consequent inaction, those talents idle which otherwise would prompt every effort to a spirit of ambition exhibiting the appreciation of his standing as a Freeman and observing the contrast with that when fettered by temporal authority.

In times of peril and war the Jews have borne the privations incident to such times and their best exertions have been given to their utmost, in defense of the common cause. See the Israelite in the ranks of danger, exposing his life in the defense of the Country of his adoption or of his nativity and then ask the views of the man in such exposure—the cause alone—he bears the brunt of the battle and the toils of the day with the knowledge of having discharged his duty; he retires with the pleasing consolation of mental correctness and the silent approbation of his own conscience. Here he rests, having attained the summit of his expectations. Sensible of his worth, his Commander would offer him promotion the honorable and only boon a Soldier aspires to. He cannot, vain are his wishes. The State under whose banners he has fought and bled debars him its acceptance. Here Sir, is an evidence of the injustice of the act of the Constitution, and the effect perhaps of that inaction which I have noticed above.

Still stranger tho are the cases requiring the decision of a Jury, look there at the situation of a man professing the Jewish Religion. I wish not to be understood that he could not obtain justice, such is not my meaning, but he is to be judged by men whom perhaps prejudice might influence in their verdict and the very course of justice be *impeded* by mere caprice incident to strong individual feeling.

By the present system a Jew is deprived of a seat in that body where by a liberal construction of matters and circumstances and a free interchange of sentiment on the broad basis of both Jewish and Christian doctrine to "do unto others as you would have others do unto you" might those prejudices be combatted and justice satisfied in its strictest sense. I cannot name the unworthy equality a Jew is placed on trial by Jury. On this great question of right, the guarantee of Freedom and political liberty I will leave you to judge as a legislator and an American Freeman.

Your attention I need not solicit on this occasion, being satisfied of the liberality of your views and the pleasure it would afford you in the opportunity of *redressing* the grievances of your Constituents. A bill relating to an equality of rights intended for the present purposes was reported in the Senate of Maryland during the Session of 1816 and was not acted upon. I do not know why. I confidently trust however that the present legislature will take up the subject with the consideration it merits.

Whatever may be the fate of the proposed bill permit me to request, if not improper that the Ayes and Nays be taken and placed on record on the general question as well as on any previous one, which might involve such general question or be indicative of its final result.

Before I conclude I would remark that previous to my commencing this letter a friend in this city applied to me for such papers as I had in my possession in any way relating to the object proposed by Mr. Kennedy's motion—these I gave him, I would have been glad to have forwarded to you with this but as I learn they will be laid before the committee, it will answer the same purpose as you will then have an opportunity of examining them.

I am, Dear Sir, Yours with great Respect, (*signed*)

J. I. Cohen.

23. REPORT OF THE SELECT COMMITTEE, 1818 [66]

The committee appointed to consider the justice and expediency of extending to persons professing the Jewish Religion, the same privileges that are enjoyed by Christians, have taken the same into their serious consideration, and ask leave to report:

That with respect to the justice of the case submitted to their consideration, your committee thinks there can be no question: in society, mankind have civil and political duties to perform, but with regard to religion, that it is a question which rests, or ought to rest, between man and his creator alone; there is no law can reach the heart—no human tribunal that has a right to take cognizance of this matter.

But, taking this subject up in a religious point of view, your committee would appeal with confidence to the authority of the christian religion itself, contained in the gospel, and the epistles, as a system that instead of persecution and proscription, breathes in every sentence and in every line, peace and good will to all mankind. . . .

It is in the interest and it ought to be the wish of every religious sect among us to see all political distinctions for ever abolished. Under the constitution of the United States, the most perfect freedom is allowed in this respect, and it is surely inconsistent, it is surely strange, that a Jew who may hold a seat in Congress, who may even be raised to the highest and most honourable station in the universe, the chief magistrate of a free people, cannot hold any office of profit or trust under the constitution of Maryland.

In three-fourths, or more, of the other states, particularly in all those whose constitutions have been recently formed, free un-restrained freedom of religious opinion is enjoyed; mankind are improving in the arts and sciences, the stock of knowledge is fast increasing. Shall we not also improve in the arts of government; and shall Maryland—shall that very state which was originally settled by Catholiks, by those, who in their turn had been proscribed and prohibited from making settlements in Virginia, and whose first founder, Sir George Calvert, was almost even denied the right of hospitality in that now hospitable state, except he would take the oath of supremacy and of allegiance. Shall Maryland, which ought to lead the van in the glorious cause of freedom, civil, political and religious, be the last to adopt a system which the other states in general, and which the United States have adopted.

Shall your committee be told, that however just it may be to abolish all distinctions among religious sects, yet that it is inexpedient to make innovations on the constitution of Maryland. This is the language of prejudice, this savours too much of that narrow doctrine so often used in other countries by those who are styled legitimate monarchs, and by their adherents. Our own government, from its very foundation, was an innovation; the declaration of Independence was an innovation; the reformation of Luther was an innovation; and to use the language of the eloquent Gerald, who fell a victim to tyranny, Christianity itself was an innovation.

Maryland possesses numerous advantages over many other states. Blest with a fruitful soil; with numerous navigable streams; with a noble bay, the wonder and admiration of the world, with situations for sea ports in abundance; it is therefore her interest to draw men of enterprise and of capital to her shores. The tide of emigration which is now flowing fast to the west, has already taken from Maryland many of her best and most industrious citizens, and although we need not hold out inducements to emigrants, we ought to let it be known that in Maryland, men enjoy civil and religious liberty, in as great a degree, as they do in any other state in the Union.

Your committee, therefore, are unanimously of opinion, that it is just, that it is expedient, that Jews and Christians should be placed on an equal footing in regard to their civil rights and privileges. That the adoption of this measure is recommended by reason as well as by scripture; stronger arguments are surely unnecessary. The mists of ignorance and of superstition are passing away at the approach of the sun of liberty; they are scarcely seen in the other states; let them no longer cast a gloom over our beloved Maryland, let their baneful influence be felt no more; let them vanish forever.

Your committee therefore beg leave to report a bill, entitled, "An act to extend to the sect of people professing the Jewish religion, the same rights and privileges that are enjoyed by Christians." All which is respectfully submitted By order,

J. W. Preston, Clk.

24. THE FIRST FORM OF THE "JEW BILL," 1819 [67]

To extend to the sect of people professing the Jewish Religion the same rights and privileges that are enjoyed by Christians.

WHEREAS, It is the acknowledged right of all men to worship God according to the dictates of their own consciences. And whereas, it is declared by the thirty-sixth section of the bill of rights of this state, "That the manner of administering an oath to any person ought to be such as those of the religious persuasion, profession, or denomination of which such person is one, generally esteem the most effectual confirmation by the attestation of the divine Being. And whereas, religious tests for civil employment, though intended as a barrier against the depraved, frequently operate as a restraint upon the conscientious; and as the constitution of the United States requires no religious qualifications for civil office, Therefore,

Sec. 1. *Be it enacted, By the General Assembly of Maryland,* That no religious test, declaration or subscription of opinion as to religion, shall be required from any person of the sect called Jews, as a qualification to hold or exercise any office or employment of profit or trust in this state.

Sec. 2. *And be it enacted,* That every oath to be administered to any person of the sect of people called Jews, shall be administered on the five books of Moses, agreeably to the religious education of that people, and not otherwise.

Sec. 3. *And be it enacted,* That if this act shall be confirmed by the General Assembly, after the next election of delegates, in the first session after such new election, as the constitution and form of government direct; that in such case, this act and the alterations and amendments of the constitution and form of government therein contained, shall be taken and considered, and shall constitute and be valid as part of the said constitution and form of government, to all intents and purposes, any thing in the declaration of rights, constitution and form of government contained, to the contrary notwithstanding.

Sec. 4. *And be it enacted,* That the several clauses and sections of the declaration of rights, constitution and form of government, and every part of any law of this state, contrary to the provisions of this act, so far as respects the sect of people aforesaid, shall be, and the same is hereby declared to be repealed and annulled on the confirmation hereof.

25. A NOTE FROM KENNEDY TO JEREMIAH SULLIVAN, 1819 [68]

Annapolis Jan 12th 1819

Dr Sir,

This day the Jew Bill was called up but postponed at the request of some of its friends. It is made the order of the day for to morrow. It will likely come on then, yet some wish a postponement again. I am for acting on it.

Do pray see Mr Winchester him and Genl Winder ought both to be here on its getting to the Senate. And be assured there is no time and no votes to lose. I am anxious and feel more than it is right to express. Prejudice, Prejudice is against the Bill and you know prejudice has many votaries. Good night. If you are not on to morrow I will write you again to morrow night

truly yours

Tho: Kennedy

26. THE MARYLAND "CENSOR" [69]

We are truly mortified that the bill for extending to the Jews, civil rights enjoyed by other citizens of the state, has been rejected in the house of delegates of this state by a vote of 50 to 24. We regard this odious constitutional proscription, on account of difference of religious tenets, as a disgrace to the state and the times. A libel upon the christian religion, a much greater dishonor to those who advocate it, then to those against whom it is directed.

It is contrary to every idea of genuine republicanism to say, that, although the people might wish to select a Jew for office, they shall not be allowed to do so. . . . They may, and do, fight our battles to the last drop of their heart's blood, yet are they shut out from the jury box, the bar, and the bench. What bigotry! How contemptible must we appear in the eyes of our more enlightened sister states! Who shall boast that the age of fanaticism and bigotry has passed! [70]

27. THE PHILADELPHIA "AURORA"

The Legislature of Maryland have recently decided, by a large majority, that Jews shall not enjoy, in that state, an equality of political rights with other denominations of persons. It is remarkable, and indeed disgraceful, that such a measure should be adopted in one of the republics of America, at a time when even the bigoted monarchs of Europe are removing those lines of religious distinction which are inconsistent with a sincere devotion to the Almighty Father of all. When such proceedings once begin, there is no calculating where they will stop: if the Legislature of Maryland have the right to disfranchise any portion of the freemen of that state, because they believe in the God of Abraham, Isaac, and Jacob, they may next decide which of the various sects are the *true* Christians, and disfranchise all the rest. We had considered the erection of the elegant Unitarian church, in Baltimore, an honorable evidence of the liberality of a state first settled by a particularly tenacious sect; we now find, however, that the honor belongs to Baltimore alone; and it will not surprise us, should the

Unitarians ere long be politically excommunicated by the *liberal* and *enlightened* Legislature of Maryland, in the nineteenth century, because they, too, believe in the same God.[71]

28. THE PHILADELPHIA "FREEMAN'S JOURNAL"

It is with much regret we observe the illiberal principles which have pervaded the Legislature of Maryland, in rejecting the bill, commonly called the Jew Bill, which went to put the descendents of Abraham, as regarded their civil rights, on the same footing with those *who go under the name of Christians*. In Maryland, a Jew cannot hold any office whatever. These things ought not to be in this country, the asylum of the oppressed. As the press has deservedly a great influence on the public mind, we hope our brother editors in Maryland, several of whom we know personally, and others from report, to be men of high and liberal minds, will not suffer this matter to rest, but will endeavour to have it raised at the next session.[72]

29. THE CHARLESTON "SOUTHERN PATRIOT"

But it may be said that when we speak of *distinctions* we should turn our attention at home, and look at the conduct of Maryland, who appears to have caught the spirit of the German governments. Yes, it may be said, as a reproach to our country, the people of Maryland permits a civil proscription to stand in their constitution to the dishonour of our age—to the disgrace of their own state. . . . Our National charter, our various state constitutions, contain no such feature of bigotry and intolerance. Sentiments of liberality and toleration have not penetrated the bosoms of a portion of the American people, who yet boast of their *equal privileges*. Equality, in their political creed, means the enjoyment of civil rights by the most numerous part of the people only, and their denial to those who are few in number. If this odious clause of the constitution of Maryland be not expunged how can any of her citizens boast, without a blush, of living under liberal institutions, that confer on all equal privileges? With what argument could any one of them meet a subject of one of those European governments, whose narrow policy and bigoted spirit, their own state has so well emulated, who may be disposed to ridicule the pretensions of Maryland to the possession of a free constitution? Could he reply that in granting equality of civil privilege, we mean to include those only who possess our religious faith? Could such an absurdity be employed by any one of common sense in a liberal age? Yet such is the *practice* of Maryland. Hasten citizens of Maryland! and blot from your charter this disgraceful feature! Cease to perpetuate distinctions that do not belong to an enlightened and liberal era, and cannot belong to a country, distinguished for its freedom, and whose national charter places all on the same footing.[73]

VI

Roman Catholics
and the "Jew Bill," 1819-1823

Maryland was originally, in the seventeenth century, a proprietary colony under a Roman Catholic proprietor. Although the state had long lost its special character as a refuge for English Roman Catholics, the nature of the original settlement was such that many of the influential families in Maryland were Roman Catholic, a situation unlike that in any other of the seaboard states. When the "Jew Bill" was defeated in 1819, Mordecai Noah's newspaper, the *National Advocate* of New York, suggested editorially that the defeat was due to Roman Catholic opposition. J. I. Cohen, Jr., of Baltimore, who was in a far better position than a New York newspaper to know what had actually occurred, immediately wrote a letter, reprinted below, denying that there had been significant Roman Catholic pressure.

Indeed, when the Bill was presented and passed on first reading in the 1822–23 session of the state legislature, it was again supported by Roman Catholic members of the House. Unfortunately, one of the non-Catholic advocates of the Bill, former Governor W. G. D. Worthington,[74] used the expression "monkish superstition" in one of his speeches, and some Catholic feelings were raised by this expression. Charles Carroll [75] of Carrollton, one of the signers of the Declaration of Independence and Maryland's most distinguished Catholic citizen, had to intervene to prevent this unfortunate phrase from being used to defeat Worthington's bid for reelection later in 1823.

30. J. I. COHEN, JR.,
TO MORDECAI M. NOAH, 1819 [76]

Baltimore, Feb., 2nd, 1819.

M. M. Noah, Esq., New York.
Dear Sir:

I have duly noticed in the "National Advocate" [77] the remarks on the failure of the Jew Bill before the Legislature of this state in that part bearing on the Catholics on the supposition of their influence in the rejection of the bill permit me to say is not so. I think your impressions are incorrect. My opinion is founded on the liberal expressions of sentiments by the Catholics within the Circle of my acquaintance in this City and who are among the principal of that religious sect in this State and on the regret evinced on the failure of the attempt. In the Senate on Gen. Winder's motion, Mr. Taney, a catholic,[78] addressed that body in eloquent strains in favor of abolishing test oaths universally and in fact if the members of our legislature could have brought themselves to have acted independently, without having the fear of losing their election before their eyes, and had followed the honest dictates of their consciences no doubt the bill would have passed, but in lieu of being entirely divested of politics, contrary to expectations, it assumed that aspect, and if you will recollect the very slender federal [79] preponderance in the political affairs of Maryland you will with me see the cause of the rejection of the Bill. But the prospects of Jews in Md: are brighter than ever before, and in the Senate had the motion *been special* instead of for universal toleration it might have succeeded, several members voting in the negative, who would have given an affirmative had the object been special, tolerating the Jews, the motion in the Senate on the Score of general abolition of tests, was made contrary to our express wish, we wanted it on *our special right and no other* and on the results of the question as taken we were not surprized. The Editors of the public papers in this City are all very favorably disposed towards the rights we demanded, and you will bear in mind that notwithstanding this being a state of Catholic settlement *and this city an Archbishopric,* not a syllable against the bill was even noticed or published during the whole time the result was pending, or before or since. The Fed. Gazette has received a communication addressed to the editor of the National Advocate with a view of correcting the impressions under which the editor has made his remarks. I mentioned to Mr Gwynn [80] that no doubt by this time you might have been informed of the mistaken grounds of rejection and as soon as time would permit, notice no doubt would be made of the same, and that the Editor of the Advocate would certainly prefer doing so voluntarily, than it should be elicited by any public address to him. In the mean time therefore the Gazette has merely announced the receipt of the communication and "*for want of room*" it will be left out untill there may be no necessity of its appearing in consequence of an explanation which *may anticipate* the communication. I have thought proper thus to notice the circumstance's to you, leaving it entirely to act as your own opinion may point out, before concluding permit me to mention the pleasure given here on perusing the remarks on the condition of the Jews and the question generally, with the exception of that part relative to the Catholics.

Yours very sincerely,   J. I. Cohen, Jr.[81]

31. TO THE ROMAN CATHOLIC VOTERS [82]

One of your best friends begs leave to advise you of a trick got up to beguile you in the election of this day—A detestable and mischievous handbill has been circulated through the city, for the low purpose of exciting your religious feeling to influence the election. By '*Monkish Superstition*' Mr Worthington meant no more than I would by '*Cameronian Bigotry*' or '*Vandal Oppression*'. It is the abuse of the Christian religion, and not its administration by any sect, that liberal men would deprecate. Mr Worthington is a liberal man, as may be seen by the following card, composed and read by him on the hustings on Saturday evening last.

Carroll

32. A CARD

W. G. D. Worthington, respectfully greeting his Roman Catholic
fellow citizens of Baltimore, has, with great pain, understood
from various sources, that a part of his address at the Monument
Square, on Friday evening has been misconceived by some persons
present.[83] Mr W. now declares, that he never meant the slightest
irreverence of your venerable church, its head, or any of its members. On the contrary he intended then, and does now positively
promulgate, his highest reverence for, and confidence in, the purity
of the religion of the Gospel, whether administered by Roman
Catholics, or other orthodox Christians.

Baltimore, Oct. 4th., 1823

VII

The "Christian Ticket" Defeats Kennedy, 1823

When Thomas Kennedy tied his political fortunes to the "Jew Bill," he created a situation in which his political opponents, the Federalist party, in Washington County, Maryland, were encouraged to use the appeal to religious prejudice. The party struggle in Maryland was keen; in the state as a whole, the Federalists had a very slight edge.[84] Normally, Washington County in the Piedmont area would be counted in the Jeffersonian (Democratic-Republican) column. By calling himself the head of the "Christian ticket" and denouncing Kennedy as the head of the "Jew ticket," Kennedy's opponent, Benjamin Galloway, was able to swing the voters to his support and the defeat of Kennedy, and thus, temporarily, to win Washington County for the Federalists. The election handbill reprinted below shows how Galloway's religious appeal was phrased, in the attempt to keep Kennedy out of the session at which the "Jew Bill" would come up for its second, confirmatory, vote.

33. ELECTION HANDBILL, 1823 [85]

To the Christian Voters of Washington County, State of Maryland:

Highly respected fellow-citizens:

Venienti Occurrite Morbo.

Oppose the threatened disorder.

I am as decidedly opposed now to the confirmation by the next General Assembly, as I was during the late session of the present one, to the passage of the Act, which has been published for your serious consideration, bearing on its front the insidious title 'an act to extend to all the citizens of Maryland the same civil right and religious privileges that are enjoyed under the Constitution of the United States.'

Messrs. Thomas Kennedy, Keller and Drury, who zealously supported said act, at the last session, have lately presented themselves to your view in public prints, as candidates for your votes at the approaching election, with sanguine expectations (no doubt) of success. It was not, believe me, fellow-citizens, my intention to have again appeared before you as a candidate for a seat in the General Assembly, having arrived at the advanced age of three score years and ten; but, as to retreat at so very important a crisis might be considered by you as desertion, should you be disposed to elect me as one of your delegates to the next General Assembly, I will most unquestionably serve as such, and I will, in that event, vote in point blank opposition to the confirmation, as I did at the late session, to the passage of said (in my judgment) highly exceptionable act; and which I hold to be no more nor less than an attempt to undervalue, and, by so doing, to bring into popular contempt, the Christian religion.

Preferring, as I do, Christianity to Judaism, Deism, Unitarianism, or any other sort of new fangled ism, I deprecate any change in our State government, calculated to afford the least chance to the enemies of Christianity, of undermining it in the belief of the people of Maryland. What could not heretofore be effected by Hooke, it seems, is now attempting to be done by Crooke.

Yours respectfully,   Benjamin Galloway

Hagerstown, Washington County,
Maryland, Aug. 18, 1823.

VIII

An Appeal by the Jews
of Maryland, 1824

During the years from 1818 to 1823 in which the "Jew Bill" was
being pressed by Kennedy and his fellow Jeffersonians, the Jews
of Maryland seem not to have played a public role in stimulating
interest in their cause. Yet in 1824 when the "Jew Bill" was up
for confirmatory action without Kennedy's being seated in the
legislature, a "memorial," or petition, was submitted by the Jews
on their own behalf. A word of clarification, perhaps, is necessary
to explain why a bill passed in the 1822–23 session had to come
up again in the 1823–24 session. When a constitutional change was
at issue, as it was in the "Jew Bill," the Maryland laws required
that the bill embodying the constitutional change had to be passed
at two successive sessions of the legislature. If it were not so passed
on second reading, the bill was held to be completely defeated;
and its advocates had to start campaigning for its passage all over
again. It may well be that, while the Jews of Maryland felt it
desirable to stay out of the battle for first passage, they realized
the need for bringing all pressure to bear on the legislature for
the confirmatory passage of the bill in which they were so deeply
interested.

34. PETITION OF MARYLAND JEWS, 1824 [86]

To the Honorable the General Assembly of Maryland.
   The Memorial of the subscribers, Citizens thereof,
RESPECTFULLY REPRESENTS:
   Your Memorialists are of that class of the Citizens of Maryland,
long subjected to the pressure of political disqualifications, by the
operation of a religious test in the Constitution of the State; and
they approach your Honorable Body with this their prayer, that

an Act passed the 29th of January 1823 "to extend to all the citizens of Maryland the same civil rights and religious privileges that are enjoyed under the Constitution of the United States," may be confirmed at the present session, becoming thereby part of the Constitution.

Your Memorialists, feeling it incumbent on them at this stage of the proceeding, address themselves on the subject, to your Honorable body, in the honest confidence, which the American is educated to entertain in his fellow citizens, and in the legislative guardians of his rights. It is not their wish, to obtain from your honorable body, a grant of exclusive privilege; because such a privilege would be hostile, not only to the principles of our institutions, but to the express provisions of that charter which we have all alike, sworn to support: but it is equal rights which they petition; their voice is not raised in favor, but in opposition, to exclusive privilege; they ask an equality of rights with their fellow citizens. If the disqualifications under which they labor, were imposed as the penalty of law for civil delinquencies, for habits of social intemperance, or a disregard of the obligations of religion, they would blush to murmur; but it is, as they humbly apprehend, the retribution for a too honest perseverance in conscientious faith, unmindful of political disqualifications, of social inconvenience, and of individual contumely: and this same manly and virtuous constancy, which, exerted in the cause of their Country; would entitle them to be honored as patriots, exposes them to proscription, when exercised in the service of the acknowledged God. They firmly flatter themselves, and have at length some reason to believe, that your enlightened Councils will suffer no longer, those strange anomalies to endure, that the period has arrived at last, when conscience and reason, the peculiar gifts of an Omnipotent benevolence, will be respected, and persecutions be abandoned to the Inquisitor and the Bigot. Are their doctrines immoral? They are the foundation of the general faith. Are they dangerous? It is no part of them to work conversions. Are they new? Ancient as the revelation of Almighty truth. Your memorialists, with all humility, are at a loss to understand what there is so peculiarly exceptionable in these their tenets, as to have induced a solitary, but persevering departure, from the sublime system of our American political jurisprudence: why even at this moment, when the whole American pulse throbs with indignation, at the civil and religious proscriptions, renewed and asserted in the old world, the good people of Maryland alone, should find it necessary or expedient, to continue for a moment, the disqualification of any class of their fellow Citizens. Your Memorialists beg leave to remind your Honorable Body, that the honors of office in our happy Republic, are not assumed, but conferred; not usurped by guilty ambition, but bestowed directly or indirectly, by popular confidence; that to disqualify any class of your citizens, is for the people to disqualify themselves: can it be necessary, can it be wise or politic at this day, for the people to disqualify themselves on the score of opinion only, from consulting merit in the selection of their public servants? . . .

As fellow citizens of Maryland, as Brethren of the same human family; for the honor of the State, for the great interests of humanity; your Memorialists humbly pray at your hands, that the Bill before you may be confirmed.

IX

The "Jew Bill" Is Finally Passed, 1826

The forces of the Democratic-Republican party were only temporarily halted by the second defeat of Kennedy's "Jew Bill." Even Kennedy himself, after but one session in retirement, was triumphantly reelected to carry his bill, in slightly revised form, at the 1824–25 session, and to lead it to confirmatory passage early in the 1825–26 session. Fortunately, Solomon Etting, whose early efforts to improve the position of Maryland's Jews had been unheeded, was still alive to receive congratulations on the happy outcome, thirty years after his first petition. More than this, Etting and J. I. Cohen were, at the first opportunity, elected to serve on the Baltimore City Council and Etting was elected president of one of its branches. Thus, the long agitation was resolved in a victory for the friends of liberty and a personal triumph for Solomon Etting.

35. FINAL FORM OF THE "JEW BILL," 1826 [87]

Sec. 1. Be it enacted by the General Assembly of Maryland, that every citizen of this state professing the Jewish Religion, and who shall hereafter be appointed to any office or public trust under the State of Maryland, shall in addition to the oaths required to be taken by the constitution and laws of the State or of the United States, make and subscribe a declaration of his belief in a future state of rewards and punishments, in the stead of the declaration now required by the constitution and form of government of this state.

Sec. 2. Be it enacted, that the several clauses and sections of the declaration of rights, constitutional and form of government, and every part of any law of this state contrary to the provisions of this act, so far as respects the sect of people aforesaid, shall be, and the same is hereby declared to be repealed and annulled on the confirmation hereof.

Sec. 3. And be it enacted, that if this act shall be confirmed by the General Assembly of Maryland, after the next election of delegates in the first session after such new election as the constitution and form of government directs, in such case this act and the alterations of the said constitution and form of government shall constitute and be valued as a part of the said constitution and form of government to all intents and purposes, anything therein contained to the contrary notwithstanding.

36. BENJAMIN C. HOWARD [88] TO SOLOMON ETTING, 1826 [89]

Annapolis Jany. 5th. 1826

Dear Sir

The Jew Bill passed the House this morning, having previously passed the Senate. The Act of last session is therefore confirmed and I give you my hearty congratulations thereon. Tyson [90] made a beautiful & able argument upon it. It was the best speech I ever heard him make. I held myself ready to reply to any one who might take the field against him but no one stepped forth in such a miserable cause. I thought it therefore unnecessary to come out. The stain upon the Constitution of Maryland is blotted out forever, for in the march of the human mind it is impossible to recede.

Accept my sincere congratulations and believe me

Yours truly,   Benjn C Howard

37. NEWSPAPER CONGRATULATIONS, 1826 [91]

The Jews. Though a little paragraph complimentary to ourselves, as citizens of Baltimore, was prepared for the press last week, it was accidentally omitted. We intended to have said, that, at the late election for members of our city council, two gentlemen of the Jewish persuasion were chosen by the suffrages of a large part of the citizens of their several wards, Messrs. S. Etting and J. I. Cohen. They are such as we would (in the language of Henry the IV.) introduce, either to the friends or the enemies of our city. They are the first Jews ever elected by the people to office in Maryland, being until lately denied the rights of citizens, by the constitution of the state. Mr. Etting has been elected president of the first branch of the city council.

X

Sensitivity to
Anti-Jewish Expressions,
1832-1835

For all the legal and judicial problems that arose in the years of
the early national period, the Jews of the United States made a
place for themselves in American life and were, by and large,
welcomed in that place by their non-Jewish fellow-citizens. There
was, of course, a certain amount of casual anti-Jewish sentiment
expressed; the creation of a new nation does not immediately re-
make human nature. We can point to only a few explicit statements that might have aroused Jewish resentment. The Jews were
not numerous, and whatever theological odium there was seems
to have been directed more against Roman Catholics than against
Jews. Indeed, even the attacks on the Catholic Church were negli-
gible compared with the flood that came about the middle of the
nineteenth century. Another sort of anti-Jewish reference that we
might expect to find would be with respect to the sharp trading
of Jewish peddlers; here, too, fairness demands the statement that
these references are no more biting than references to Yankee
peddlers. "The whole race of Yankee peddlers, in particular," wrote
the anonymous author of *Men and Manners in America*,[92] "are
proverbial for dishonesty. These go forth annually in thousands to
lie, cog, cheat, swindle. . . . In this respect they resemble the
Jews, of which race, by the by, I am assured, there is not a single
specimen to be found in New England." The relative absence of
occasion for its exercise did not in the least abate Jewish sensitivity,
as the exchange of letters between Solomon Etting and Henry
Clay, printed below, illustrates.

38. PETTY ANTI-SEMITISM, 1835 [93]

I continued my peddling until January 1835, when one evening, in deep snow and quite frozen I came to Easton, a pretty little town in Delaware, and entered an inn. A number of guests sat around the glowing stoves; and as they saw me enter, a pale and snow-covered merchant, a feeling of compassion must have come over them, for nearly every one bought something of me; and thus even in the evening, I did some good business, after I had run about the whole day in terrible winter weather, earning scarcely enough for a drink.

While preoccupied with my business, I was watched by an oldish-looking, occasionally smiling, but apparently unconcerned man behind the stove. He allowed me to finish the business in peace but then he got up, tapped me on the shoulder and bade me follow him. Out of doors his first question was whether I had a trade-license for peddling? I still felt so strange in America, and he spoke in so low a voice that I did not understand him and, therefore, looked at him in astonishment. My long, ten-days-old beard struck him, and he asked me further whether I was a Jew. He did not want to believe me when I denied it. Fortunately, I had with me the passport of my homeland, which I presented to him. Now he grew somewhat better disposed, looked at me sympathetically and said: "Since I see that you are an honest Protestant Christian I shall let you go, although I am losing twenty-five dollars through it. I have no kind feelings for the Jews, and were you one of them, I would not treat you so gently. If I wanted to arrest you, you would have to pay 50 dollars fine or, until you were able to raise it, you would have to go to jail, and half the fine would be mine. Still I shall forego that; but you better give up your trade and look for another one. Sooner or later you will be caught and then you'll be out of luck."

39. SOLOMON ETTING TO HENRY CLAY,[94] 1832 [95]

Balto July 15. 1832

Dr Sir

You know that I am your friend, and therefore I write to you freely. Several of the religious Society to which I belong, myself included, feel both Surprised and hurt by the manner in which you introduce the expression "the Jew" on debate in the Senate of the United States, evidently applying it as a reproachful designation of a man whom you considered obnoxious in character and conduct.

I do not know the person you allude to, the term "the Jew" *as used by you,* is considered illiberal. If therefore you have no antipathy to the people of that religious Society, I can readily believe you will have no objection to explain to me by a line, what induced the expression. I am, With Respt & Esteem

Your Obt. St So Etting

Hon H Clay
U.S. Senate Washington

40. CLAY'S REPLY TO ETTING, 1832 [96]

Washington 16th July 1832.

My Dear Sir.

I regret extremely to perceive, from your letter of yesterday, that you have thought it possible that a remark of mine applied to a subordinate officer of the customs, who was in attendance here, was liable to an unfavorable interpretation in respect to the Jews generally. Nothing could have been further from my intention. The remark was intended to describe a person and not to denounce a Nation. It was strictly moreover, defensive. Some of my friends who were in the Senate had been attacked by Genl. Hayne,[97] as I thought, rudely for the assistance which they had rendered about the Tariff. In reply I said that they were not the only persons attending on that object; but that, on the other side, Moses Myers (or Myer Moses, for I do not yet know his proper designation) [98] had been summoned by the Secy of the Treasury and might be seen daily skipping about the house, and I proceeded to describe his person &c.

I Judge of men not exclusively by their Nation, religion &c, but by their individual conduct. I have always had the happiness to enjoy the friendship of many Jews, among whom one of the Gratz's of Lex'n [99] formerly of Philadelphia stands in the most intimate and friendly relations to me. But I cannot doubt that there are bad Jews as well as bad Christians and bad Mahometans.

I hope my dear Sir that you will consider this letter perfectly satisfactory.

With much regard   I am truly Yrs   H. Clay

Solomon Etting Esq.

XI

Jews Prominent in
Public Life, 1799-1830

The comparative openness of American life led to the Jews appearing in public life in a wide range of functions. These positions were held and services rendered without regard to the insignificant pressure that the Jews as a group might conceivably exert. In 1828, referring to Mordecai M. Noah, James Fenimore Cooper noted that, "The sheriff of the city of New York, an officer elected by the people, was, a few years ago, a Jew! Now all the Jews in New York united, would not probably make three hundred voters." [100] Indeed, Jews were appointed to positions of responsibility and trust from the very beginning of national life. For example, Reuben Etting may have served in the office of the U.S. Marshal for Maryland in 1791 early in the Presidency of George Washington and he was officially appointed marshal by Thomas Jefferson in 1801.[101] Levi Sheftall of Savannah, Georgia, served as United States Military Agent, having the responsibility for the purchase and distribution of matériel and supplies in that state. His son, Moses Sheftall, was named Justice of the Inferior Court of Chatham County, Georgia, in 1817.[102] Solomon Bush, never financially secure after his Revolutionary service, was a perennial applicant for public position; shortly before his death he applied for appointment as Postmaster General. Many others might be named here, but their positions and services to the United States will be illustrated at other places in these volumes.[103] Here two instances of services of a less memorable character will be given: a letter from Paul Hamilton [104] to Lewis Levi, who had already done good service in the Treasury branch in Charleston, offering Levi a clerkship in the office of the Comptroller and Superintendent of Finance, and a letter to Samuel D. Ingham,[105] Secretary of the

Treasury, written by Solomon Etting in his capacity as chairman of the Infirmary Committee of the Baltimore City Council.

41. OFFER OF A GOVERNMENT CLERKSHIP, 1799 [106]

Mr Lewis Levi,
In particular care of Mr. Simons
Charleston

West Bank Decm. 30 1799

Sir:

Having been appointed by the Legislature Comptroller and Superintendent of Finance, I am in want of a Clerk to assist me in discharging the Duties of that office. Your known Integrity & Ability, accompanyed by an extensive experience in the Charleston Branch of the Treasury point you out as the Gentleman moist [sic] suitable to my aims; I therefore request that you'll consent to take part with me in that Business. I am willing to allow you a liberal Salary, which I have no objection to commencing immediately, because your closing with my proposal would prevent you from forming another connection and though my Duties do not (by Law) commence before the 1st of March ensuing, yet the intermediate time may be very properly, though not very busily fill'd up by preliminary arrangements of the Genl. Plan of Proceeding, in which your assistance would be valuable.

My receiving this appointment, brought me on the eve of my departure from Columbia, and not having leisure to write you on the Subject I delivered a message for you to some of my Charleston Friends, relative to my intended proposal which I hope and indeed doubt not you have receiv'd.

The attention necessary to my Country affairs prevent me at present from being in Charleston.

I however expect to be there in the beginning of the coming month (January), and if you accede to my proposal we can then close, in any satisfactory manner, an agreement. In the mean time I beg you'll favor me with a letter by the Jacksonborough Mail to inform me of particulars on your side to which I will return you an immediate answer.

With great esteem I remain Sir yr most obdt.   Paul Hamilton
Mr Levi

42. SOLOMON ETTING TO
SAMUEL D. INGHAM, 1830 [107]

Baltimore 14th. June 1830

Sir

By a note received from James Mosher Esqr of the 11th instant
I am asked as Chairman of the infirmary Committee to make a
proposition to the Treasury Department "Stating the price per day
or week at which the infirmary will accommodate the Sick Seamen,
and also the expense of interring in the Potters field (in the least
expensive manner) such as may die." The Baltimore Infirmary [108]
attached to the University of Maryland is an establishment belonging to the State, is under the management and direction of a board
of trustees The Governor of Maryland Ex Officio the President.
The immediate direction and control of the establishment is placed
under a committee of the board of Trustees, Weekly meetings are
held at the infirmary, and the house is daily visited by a member
of the Committee to see that nothing be neglected, which can
conduce to the Comfort of the patients.

The surgical and medical departments are conducted by the
professors. A medical & Surgical professor attend daily exclusive
of three young gentlemen *Resident Students*. The nursing is performed by eight Sisters of Charity from the house of St Joseph
at Emmetsburg (at a Salary of $42 each per Annum) One porter
and three Colored Women.

The Committee have conducted the establishment nearly 4 Years.
the charge for medical attendance, boarding, washing lodging
mending &c for patients in the public wards is $3 per week and
in same proportion per day, and $4 for a patient requiring a private
room. We did cherish the hope, that we would be enabled to
conduct the establishment at a price less than $3 per Week, but
experience has proved that with all proper economy it cannot be
done at a less rate to afford the necessary degrees of comfort and
consolation to the sick which humanity dictates, altho' the services
of the Committee of Trustees, the Professors and Students are

bestowed gratuitously. The Infirmary was originally established auxiliary to the Medical School of the University. Medical Students derive great advantage & information in witnessing the operations & attending Clinical Lectures. Provision, Medicine and all the necessaries secured for the Establishment are well selected and of the best quality, and no small matter (such as may be styled Nicknacks, or trifling delicacies) withheld which come within the desire of our poor sick fellow creatures. The charge for interment of the dead, I cannot exactly ascertain, as in most cases in the infirmary the dead are removed by their friends: The Sister Superior informs me the charge will be from 2 to 3 dollars, but not exceeding the latter.

The books of the Infirmary are kept in regular order, every day transaction shows for itself. Record is made of the date of each patients admittance, the age and place of nativity the time of discharge or death, with a Statement of the disease of which yearly reports are made by the Committee.

Upon application to Mr Mosher this morning, I am informed that the number of sick Seamen at present in the hospital is twenty, and that the number in general varies from fifteen to thirty and never exceeding that number

I may positively say, that we can accommodate thirty sick seamen in addition to the number of patients we generally have. We have comfortable accommodation for sixty patients. We do not admit the maniac or Lunatic or patients afflicted with malignant diseases, such are provided for in our state hospital.

Any information you may require on this occasion I will give to you with pleasure. If there be a disposition on the part of the Govt. to place the sick seamen at the Baltimore Infirmary, we will receive them, and be glad to be informed thereof as soon as convenient.

You may rest assured that if placed there they will be well attended and kindly treated.

I have the honor to be   Sir   With great respect   Your Obt Servt

(sigd)   Solomon Etting

The Hon'ble Saml. D Ingham
Secretary of the Treasury
United States

XII

Jewish Cadets and
Applicants at West Point,
1818-1828

A clear indication of the degree to which the Jews of America were accepted as equals by the general population is to be seen in the readiness with which Jewish applications for admission to the United States Military Academy (West Point) were granted. Traditionally the rank of officer in the military forces has been one of the strongest bastions of exclusiveness; yet a young Jew, Simon M. Levy,[109] was a member of the first graduating class of West Point in 1802. Unfortunately we have no further record of Levy's career. In 1819, Alfred Mordecai of Richmond, Virginia, and Warrenton, North Carolina, was admitted as a West Point cadet in June, 1819, at the age of 15 years and 5 months. At the time of his graduation, in 1823, Mordecai was the highest ranking student in his class and went on to a distinguished Army career, including a teaching position at the Military Academy. Edwin Warren Moise, whose letter of application is printed below, was all of twelve years old, at the time of his application; he was not admitted. As for Abraham C. Myers, the third of the candidates of whom the letters below speak, his warrant finally was approved. His greatest military distinction, however, came in rebellion against the government which had commissioned him, for like many other Southern officers in the Army of the United States, he gave his devotion to the Confederate cause in the Civil War.

43. JACOB MORDECAI [110] TO
JOHN C. CALHOUN, [111] 1818 [112]

Warrenton 13th January 1818

Sir

It is with reluctance I trouble you on the present Occasion as I sin against conviction Knowing your dislike to solicit appointments from Government the subject of the present application is a son named Alfred Mordecai [113] aged fifteen, well grown healthy constitution of moral Habits and good disposition his acquirements are I trust equal to lads of his age he is a good english Scholar has read the Latin & Greek classics has made considerable progress in the French language and lately commenced Euclid it is his wish to enter the Military Academy at West Point to effect this object I sometime in Dec addressed a letter to Genl. Swift [114] to which I have not recieved [sic] an answer if it is agreeable to you to make application in his behalf I believe you will have no cause to regret the agency you may have in his appointment. . . .

I am very respectfully   Sir Yr obt Sert   Jacob Mordecai

44. JACOB MORDECAI TO
THE WAR DEPARTMENT, 1818 [115]

Warrentown No Car 27th Octr. 1818

Dear Sir

I have no other apology to offer for addressing you than a parent's solicitude for the improvement of a Son whose welfare is deeply involved in the success of the application I venture to make. I am desirous of procuring his admittance into the military academy at West Point, his age about Fifteen his acquirements at least equal to lads of his age, he is well versed in Geography, a good english Scholar, has read the usual Greek & Latin authors, is a good French Scholar and has latterly been instructed in the mathematicks in which from the shortness of the time he has made little progress. His disposition is very good, of a studious habit, well grown, possesses a sound constitution, his moral character and deportment unexceptionable, his name Alfred Mordecai. Without the smallest claim for the favour I solicit I prefer making an application to you should I be so fortunate as to interest you in his favour. Have the goodness to address your letter to me in this place.

With great consideration I am   Sir   Your obet Sert

Jacob Mordecai [116]

45. EDWIN WARREN MOISE [117]
APPLIES FOR WEST POINT, 1823 [118]

Charleston S.Ca. Jany 27th 1823.

Respected Sir:

I hope your usual amiableness will induce you to pardon the liberty I have taken in thus addressing you, as I am induced to do so from the ardent desire that I have for becoming a member of the military Academy at West Point. I hope it is unnecessary to inform you, that the object of these lines is, respectfully but earnestly, to solicit, that you would be pleased to keep in mind the request of my beloved mother, on this subject, & not permit it to glide from your memory.

With sentiments of respect & esteem, your obedt. humble Servant,   Edwin Warren Moise

46. A LETTER OF SUPPORT
FROM STEEDMAN [119] TO CALHOUN, 1823 [120]

Washington May 7th 1823

Dear Sir

Permit me to recommend Master Edward Warren Moise, of Charleston So Carolina, for an appointment of Cadet in the Military Academy at West Point. Master Moise is of respectable connexions, but in Ordinary Circumstances. He is about Twelve years of Age and promises from Talents & general Conduct to be an usefull Member of Society.

I feel Satisfied that if his application should be so fortunate as to meet with Success, he will be among the number, who are distinguished for Talents & good Behaviour.

I have the Honor to be   With great Respect   Your Obt. Servt.

Charles Jno Steedman

The Honble John C. Calhoun
Secretary of War.

47. JOHN A. ALSTON [121] NOMINATES ABRAHAM C. MYERS, [122] 1828 [123]

Georgetown, South Carolina February 28th 1828

Dear Sir,

Mr Abraham C. Myers who is from one of the best families of our state & is the only son of the Hon: Abraham Myers [124] Intendant of this town a gentleman of weight & influence here and a warm supporter of the administration, is desirous of being appointed into the Academy at West Point. He has long flattered himself with prospects of admission & should he be disappointed would probably turn his attention to another pursuit unworthy of his talents & acquirements, which would be a loss to our country and a misfortune to his friends, it is to prevent this if possible, that I have presumed to take the liberty of intruding upon you & could you favor me in this matter I would be very much obliged to you. The Abilities & understanding of Mr Myers are eminently conspicuous. His moral character is a pattern highly worthy of imitation. He is in the strict sense of the phrase integer vita scelerisque purus. He has associated with those whose notice is sufficient to confer honor. Our representative Mr Mitchell [125] will doubtless take great pleasure in giving you further information about him. Notwithstanding my anxiety for his success I should not have ventured upon so bold a step as that of addressing you had I not had the pleasure of some acquaintance with you at College & moreover am aware of the regard you entertained for my deceased brother Joseph Alston. [126]

I have the honor to be, dear Sir, your Most Obedient servt

John A. Alston

To the Honorable Richard Rush [127]

48. ABRAM MYERS COMPLAINS
TO JAMES BARBOUR,[128] 1828 [129]

Georgetown South Carolina March. 7. 1828

To the Honorable James Barbour
Sir

I wrote you the 2nd february & I have not had a reply to it, presuming that it had not come to hand, I will recapitulate the Substance of it. the 12 Septr 1825 New Haven Connecticut, I wrote you enclosing a Certificate of the qualifications of my Son & requested you when the annual appointments were made for admission at West Point that my application should be taken into consideration. In April 1826 I read a letter from Col. Wm Drayton [130] a member of Congress to Mr Whitehurst, an extract of which letter was in these words 'Washington 6 april 1826 Sir, I this morning received a letter from the Secretary of War in reply to your application for admission at the Academy at West Point in which he says that he had directed the letter & recommendations in your favor to be put on file to be considered next year when the Selections will be made from the applicants to fill the vacancies which may occur in the interim at the Military Academy. Mr Ab. C. Myers of Georgetown has been appointed for the present year no vacancy exists as Mr D. W. Whitehurst supposes.' two years have passed away since this has occurred & my son has not received his warrant. I have waited patiently in expectation that justice would be done to him, but as yet it appears to be as far off as if he had not been appointed. As a member of the American family my pride in my government will not permit me to forbear any longer to express my sentiments & to appeal to you to measure out to my son that justice which belongs to the humblest citizen. The injury done in taking the appointment from my son & giving it to another is a public one, & they as well as myself will be interested in it. It is foreign to my intentions to reflect on your department but that some imposition has been practised upon it is manifest. the idea I have of an appointment is, that after it is once made it cannot be superseded unless for misconduct, in the present case there was no trial made, therefore there could be no misconduct. if after an appointment is made, the incumbent can be removed at the Will & pleasure of an individual, what security has a parent or Guardian that he is certain of obtaining a Warrant for his son or Ward the person appointed must have had sufficient recommendation previously to the appointment, & after it is once made I should think that it was permanent unless with the exception I have stated. I beg Sir, that I should be distinctly understood that I throw no censure on you under the impression that you were deceived. I think it fair & honorable that I should make known to you my sentiments on this occasion, trusting that you will do that justice to my son which comports with your high standing in the government. It is unnecessary for me to send you the qualifications of my son as they were before you in 1826 with the recommendation of the representative in Congress from this congressional District. If you should wish to know who I am I refer you to Judge Smith [131] & Col. Hayne,[132] Senators & Col Drayton representative in Congress, also Mr. Rush, Secretary of the Treasury although not personally known to him, he knows me by reputation.

I am Sir, with high respect   Yr Obdt Servt   Abram Myers

XIII

Pensions for Jewish Veterans of the Revolution, 1818-1821

In March, 1818, the Congress of the United States passed an act to provide pensions for needy veterans of the Revolutionary War.[133] There were some Jews among the applicants who were granted pensions under this act. It must be remembered that pensions were not provided for *all* veterans of the war for independence, but only for those who could prove to the satisfaction of the officers of the courts that they were truly in need. Thus, although these records tell us the two interesting stories printed below, they do not tell us about all Jewish veterans of the Revolution who were alive in the second and third decades of the nineteenth century.

49. ISAAC FRANKS'S
PENSION APPLICATION, 1818 [134]

City & County of Philadelphia, Ss.

On this eight day of April, in the year one thousand eight hundred & eighteen, Before me Joseph B Mc Kean,[135] Judge of the District Court for the City and County of Philadelphia, in the Commonwealth of Pennsylvania. Personally Appear'd Isaac Franks [136] of the same City, who being duly sworn, deposes and says, That He served in the War of the Revolution against the Common Enemy, as an Ensign in the Army on the Continental establishment above twelve Months without any intermission. That He enter'd the service in the Month of May or June 1776 and Joined Colo Leshers Regiment in the City of New York (his native City) as a Volunteer, That He was in the Battle of Long Island.

And in year 1777. He Joined the Quarter Masters Department at the Continental Village a fue [sic] miles above Peeks Kill, in the state of New York, as an Assistant Forrage Master, The Department

was under the Direction of Colo Hughes, D.Q.M. Genl. And in
January 1778. The Deponent was appointed, *Forrage Master,* And
in the spring of the same year (1778) was stationed at West Point,
as Forrage Master of the Garrison of West Point and its Depend-
ences; and so continewed for several years, untill the Month of January in the year 1781. when as an Ensign He Joined the Seventh
Massachusetts Regiment in the Army of the United States, then
stationed in the Garrison of West Point; and afterwards received
his Commission as Ensign in said Regiment dated the 12th. day
of March 1782. to take rank as such from the first day of January
One Thousand Seven hundred & Eighty one, the day He Joined
said Regiment and continewed in the service till about the Month
of June 1782, when the deponent resign'd, with the approbation of
the Commander in chief; through the interference of Docr. Samuel
Findley Surgeon of said Regimt, in consequence of being Afflicted
with the Gravel, which still occasionally greatly distresses him.
That by reason of his reduced Circumstance in life,[137] He is in need
of assistance from his Country for support, and that He never has
received or been allowed any pension by the laws of the United
States. That He is a native born, and yet a resident Citizen of the
United States, and now resident in the City of Philadelphia in the
Commonwealth of Pennsylvania.

Isaac Franks

50. JOHN WILLIAMS SUPPORTS ELIAS POLLOCK'S CLAIM, 1818 [138]

State of Maryland
City of Baltimore S

On this 15th day of August in the year of our Lord One thousand
Eight hundred and Eighteen personally appeared before me the
undersigned John Williams of the City of Baltimore aged Sixty one
years or thereabouts, who being by me duly sworn deposeth and
Saith, "that he knew Elias Pollock [139] now present and a resident
of the City of Baltimore who then passed by the name of Joseph
Smith,[140] to have been in Captain Joseph Marburys Company 3d
Maryland Regiment, Commanded by Colonel Mordeica [sic] Gist,

some time about the Month of May 1778, deponant belonging then
to Captain Samuel Griffith Company of said Regiment, marching
together from Baltimore to Philadelphia, lay there three months,
then joined the Northern Army, remained therein from 1778 to 1780.
Marched with him to the Southward under General Smallwood,
after which separated and does not recollect what became of him
until about 1786, when they again met in Baltimore—which above
described person (Joseph Smith) has ever since been known by
the name of "Elias Pollock:"   John Williams

Subscribed & Sworn   to before me one   of the Justice of the peace
in and for Balto. County   Tho Bailey [141]

51. THE CLAIM OF ELIAS POLLOCK, 1818

State of Maryland
City of Baltimore S

   On this Twentieth day of August in the year of our lord One
thousand Eight hundred and Eighteen personally appeared before
me the undersigned Elias Pollock of the City of Baltimore and
State of Maryland, aged Sixty three year and upwards as applicant
for a pension, under the late act of Congress, intitled "An Act to
provide for certain persons engaged in the land and naval service
of the United States during the Revolutionary War" and then and
there made the following declaration on Oath by me administered,
to him on the five books of Moses he being a Jew. "that he enlisted
on or about the Month of May 1778 at Baltimore, by the *name
of Joseph Smith,* was marched to, and mustered at Philadelphia
in June same year into Capt. Joseph Marbury's Company 3d. Maryland Regiment Commanded by Col Mordeica [sic] Gist, there
Remained and performed duty for Six Months (say til after Christ-
mas) then marched to Bondsbrook, New Jersey, and there went into
Winter Quarters, Remained until the beginning of May 1779, from
thence marched to Buttermilk Falls, on the North River, after
which during the summer was in several expeditions particularly
the taking of Stoney point, assisted in building four forts on the
North River viz No. 1. 2. 3 & 4, the ensuing Winter was placed
into the Adjutants guard, wintering at Morris Town, during which

was on several expeditions with Col Lee Hart under Lord Sterling on Staten Island after which Returned to Morris Town, and on or about the 15 Apl 1780 left there for Charleston S.C, but before they arrived, was engaged on the 18 Aug. 1780 in the battle of Camden when Gates was defeated, deponant wounded in the side, and taken prisoner, carried to Charleston and from thence sent as a prisoner of War to St. Augustine East Florida, remained there until news of peace, then sent to Hallifax and liberated. Returned to Baltimore, that his name hath never been placed on any pension list, therefore hath none to relinquish and from his reduced Circumstances needs the Assistance of his Country for support.

[signed "Elias Pollock" in Hebrew script]
Subscribed & Sworn   before me   NBrice C J Bo Cy Ct [142]

Schedule, viz:

(F.)

My property consist of Two Common Table, One old Desk, Seven chairs, Some trifling articles of Crockery ware and Kitchen furniture. The whole worth about Twenty Dollars say $20.00 That my family Consists of a wife named Rebecca aged about fifty three years, now nearly helpless, two daughters under twelve years of age, and there are also with me and have heretofore been dependnt on me for Support, a daughter and her two infant children who were deserted by the husband and father and now left destitute.

I formerly manufactured *Black Balls* on an extensive Scale by which and other small trade had supported myself & family with a Comfortable home, but in consequence of becoming *Bondsman* for another have had my House, Furniture and property of every kind seized and Sold under *Fieri Facia,* leaving me in such a state of *penury* as to be absolutely unable to Support myself or family without the benefit of my Revolutionary pension, or from private or public charity, particularly as I labour under Severe affliction from a *Rupture* Occasioned by hardships & Cold experienced while in the army of the U.S. and from a Bayonet wound received at the Battle when I was taken prisoner, usually called Gates' defeat.

[signed "Elias Pollock" in Hebrew script]
Sworn to and declared on the 18th day of June 1821 in Open Court   Th. Harwood Clk [143]

XIV

Jewish Law and American Law, 1831

There is no record of conflict between Jewish law and American law during the fifty years of American Jewish history represented in this volume. Indeed, on one occasion, in South Carolina in 1802, a civil court limited the fine in a case of assault to the nominal sum of one dollar because the Hebrew congregation in Charleston had already punished the guilty party.[144] Thus the civil court took notice of the operation of a justiciary procedure in the Jewish synagogue even though this procedure had no official sanction. Apparently, too, the authorities of the State of New York, in 1831, were interested in the legal status of the marriage contract (*Ketubah*) used in the Jewish community. Israel B. Kursheedt,[145] reputedly the most learned Jew in America at this time, was asked for information about the precise nature and the limitations of the obligations entered into in a *Ketubah*. With his reply to this inquiry, Kursheedt submitted a translation of the contract in the marriage of Lucius Levy Solomons [146] to Selina Seixas [147] in 1824.

52. I. B. KURSHEEDT TO GEORGE SULLIVAN,[148] 1831 [149]

New York Aug 23rd 1831

To George Sullivan Esqr.

Dr Sir

In compliance with the request contained in your note of 15th Inst. I have examined the several works which treat of the *written Marriage Contract* and its obligations and shall state briefly the result of this examination.

Like instruments have been in use since the Compilation of the Babylonish Talmud in the 4th Century. The contract of Mr L

Solomons to Selina daughter of Gershom Seixas is duly executed. *This Contract* is payable before any debt or debts contracted prior or subsequent thereto. But All *Bonds* given prior thereto, take precedence thereof. Debts must be paid before heirs inherit. Neither wives nor daughters are heirs. Property may be disposed of by will to the entire disherison of the heirs, but not to the prejudice of *this contract.* This is but a trifling recompense, when we consider that the husband is sole heir to the wife; and that she can hold no separate property, during coverture.

I subjoin a note of two cases reported in Eben Ezer, the work of next authority to the Talmud. A Woman consented to the sale of real Estate to A. A thereunder purchased of her husband sold to B. B took possession. The husband died and the woman demanded payment of her contract from B. on the ground that her consent to A would not endure to B. And so it was held, B being decreed to satisfy her demand. The other case stands thus. A bond was given bearing the same date as the Marriage contract. The husband died without sufficient to discharge both. They were held payable rationally.

I must remark that I have used the term "bond" in the sense of a contract written, signed and acknowledged, but not sealed as in the laws of this country. The Jews have never used, nor recognized the use of seals, in their transactions, except in compliance with the laws of other nations, to whom they have been subjected.

Permit me to express my thanks for the very polite terms in which you have thought proper to communicate your enquiries and to conclude with assurances of the high respect of Dr sir   Your very Obt sert   I. B. Kursheedt

53. A TRADITIONAL
MARRIAGE CONTRACT, 1824 [150]

On the fourth day of the week, on the second day in the month of Nissan, in the year of the Creation of the World Five Thousand five hundred and eighty four, as we compute here in the City of Philadelphia in America

Whereas Lucius Levy Solomons, asks the maiden named Selina, the daughter of Mr. Gershom Seixas (blessed be his memory) of

New York, to be his lawful wife, according to the laws of Moses
and Israel, and promises her, that "I will maintain, support, and
sustain thee, and will provide for thee, in all circumstances, and
situations agreeably to the laws of the Jewish Nation, which regard
the support, maintenance, and faithful protection of the wife, and
that I will give thee, the dowry of a virgin which these laws estimate
at two hundred zuzim and to which you are entitled by the Jewish
laws, Furthermore that I will maintain, respect, provide for, and
protect you, and will cause you to be respected in all things, according to the manners of the world," and hereto the said Selina consented, and she became his wife.

The portion which she brought from her mother's house, whether
in silver or in gold, in ornaments or wearing apparel, in household
furniture, or beds & bedding, is valued at four hundred and fifty
pounds, and the said Lucius L Solomons, adds hereto, from and out
of his own estate, the sum of four hundred and fifty pounds, making
the whole amount of this marriage contract nine hundred pounds.
And the said Lucius L Solomons declares and says that "the risque
and obligation of this written marriage contract, this portion and
the addition thereto, hereinbefore mentioned I will take upon myself
and my heirs after me, and I will, and do bind myself and my heirs
after me, to cause the same to be faithfully discharged from and
out of all and every manner of temporal estate, and possession,
which I now have and possess, or which I may hereafter acquire
or possess. Whether it be property on risque, or property free from
risque, All and every Kind is hereby pledged, secured, and promised
to, and for the payment, satisfaction, and discharge of this written
marriage contract, this portion and the addition thereto "and even
to the apparel which covereth my person, it is bound herefor, and
from this date forever."

The risque, effect and force of this written marriage contract, and
of this portion and the addition thereto, the said Lucius L Solomons,
the groom, takes upon himself, and acknowledges this instrument
to possess the force of all like marriage Contracts, given to the
daughters of Israel, agreeably to the orders of our wise men; and
further that this Instrument shall not be considered as merely
formal, but hereby the said Lucius L Solomons, the groom, promises
the said Selina, the daughter of Gershom, to fulfill, all herein

written, and above specified, and the whole is hereby established ratified and confirmed

Witnesses (*signed*)
⎧ Saml Hays [151]
⎨   (*signed*) Lucius Levy Solomons Groom
⎩ H Marks [152]

Levi Phillips [153]
officiating at the Nuptial Ceremony

I certify that I have translated the annexed marriage certificate or contract, from the Rabbinical Hebrew of the one written on parchment and hereunto appended

That the date upon which the said instrument was executed was (as therein expressed) correspondent to the thirty first day of March One Thousand eight hundred and twenty four. And that the form of the said instrument is the same as used by & among all Jews throughout the world, and that Such Certificates or Contracts are indispensable with them, to their entrance into the married state, and likewise take precedence of all other Contracts, Claims, Wills, or writings of every description, and are considered and held from the dates thereof forever binding and irrevocable—

The term "property on risque" used in the foregoing, signifying such as is in its nature perishable or transitory, and that of "Property free from risque," that which is more stable & certain,

In Witness whereof I hereunto sign my name in the City of New York the tenth July 1831   IBKursheedt

XV

A European View of
American Jews, 1796

Both Jews and non-Jews in Europe followed with attention the grant of full citizenship to the Jews of America. Even before 1789, Moses Mendelssohn [154] had noted actions of the Continental Congress that seemed inconsistent with what he regarded as America's basic philosophy.[155] The course of debate over the Maryland "Jew Bill" attracted attention in Europe. H. M. Brackenridge's speech was translated into German; W. G. D. Worthington himself wrote, in his own copy of the English pamphlet publication of the address, that a Rabbi had told him that the speech was translated into Hebrew.[156] There was, in short, a European interest in America and the American Jews.

The situation of the Jews in America entered largely into the debates in the Dutch National Assembly, in 1796, at The Hague, on the question of full emancipation for the Jews of Holland. The extracts below are from the speeches of, first, an advocate, and second, an opponent, of Jewish emancipation. It should be noted that both speakers refer to the Jews of America. What "famous and authentic document" Lublink De Jonge referred to, we do not know. The population figures that he cites are most inaccurate. More important, his argument tries to have it both ways; there are, he says, very few Jews in the United States—true, though not as few as he thought—and Jewish lack of interest in political matters is "proved" by the fact that only a very few of the 500 Jews of his estimate held government positions. How many government officials could there have been, in 1793 or 1796, in any group of 500 Americans or Dutchmen?

54. DEBATE ON EMANCIPATING
THE JEWS OF HOLLAND, 1796 [157]

Hahn: [158]

As we know, the Jewish population of this country [Holland] does not exceed fifty thousand souls. Many of them are unable to comprehend the benefits of freedom. But some of them are intelligent enough to cherish liberty, and these constitute a very ethical and proper element of our population.

Consider, my lords, and you people of Batavia! Consider the justice of the thing and the good that will come to us and our nation if we emancipate the Jews. I need not take up your time in trying to prove my assertions. It is well known how the emancipation of the Jews in France and North America has contributed to the progress and prosperity of these countries. . . . As to the apprehension of some that the Jews would flock to our country in large numbers if they were granted citizenship, the fear is groundless. Such an argument can be advanced only by persons who would like to see the Jew remain in his past state of subjugation. In reality, however, there is no basis for such an assumption. North America and France might well serve as an example. The Jewish emancipation there has caused no large influx of Jews to these countries.

De Yong: [159]

In answer to the speaker who quoted the Jewish emancipation in America and France as evidence in favor of the Jews, I will simply say this: The present state of affairs in France makes it impossible for us to investigate the matter thoroughly and to get authentic information about the condition of the Jews there. Still less is it possible for us to gain a true knowledge concerning the Jews of North America, as to whether they have been conducting themselves properly, or as to whether they have really contributed to the prosperity of their fellow citizens, or as to whether they have taken an active interest in the government of the country. In all these matters, I say, we are but too little informed to judge clearly.

On the other hand, I should like to call your attention to a famous and authentic document which was sent from the city of New York in September 1793. In this document it is stated that all the Jews of North America number about five hundred. Of these, two hundred and fifty reside in New York City. But there are very few, indeed, who occupy official positions in the government. In fact, one Jew was chosen to fill the office of, what they call, alderman, and he declined to serve.

XVI

American Jews Look at
American Jewry, 1798-1826

The Jews in America were well aware of their happy lot in their adopted country. They lost no occasion to affirm their devotion to the land that had given them the opportunity to participate so fully in all aspects of life, while maintaining their religious integrity. The selections below, excerpted from speeches by Gershom Mendes Seixas [160] and Mordecai Manuel Noah,[161] and from a special memorandum written by Isaac Harby [162] are good illustrations of the grateful sense of belonging that was characteristic of the Jews of the United States in the early national period.

55. G. M. SEIXAS DISCOURSE, 1798 [163]

It hath pleased God to have established us in this country where we possess every advantage that other citizens of these states enjoy, and which is as much as we could in reason expect in this captivity, for which let us humbly return thanks for his manifold mercies, and sincerely pray for a continuance of his divine protection: Let us not be deficient in acknowledging his power and his goodness, and with one heart supplicate him to promote the welfare of these states, the United States of America; to grant wisdom, knowledge and understanding to the rulers and administrators of the government, and enable them to persevere in the paths of rectitude, so as to procure peace and safety to the citizens, both in their persons and their properties; that every man may sit under his own vine and under his own fig-tree, when ye shall have beaten your swords into plough shares and your spears into pruning hooks.

The many marvellous deliverances that we have experienced since the time of our redemption from Egypt, are manifest evidences of our being under the providential care of the God of Israel; for "had it not been that the Lord was on our side," where should we have been now? Perhaps not in existence (as a peculiar people among all nations); for of all the ancient nations that were famous in the world at the time of our being settled in our own land, there is none remaining but us, who I am confident are reserved to answer the particular purpose of infinite mercy. He it was who led our fathers through the Red Sea on dry land: He it was who fed them with manna in the wilderness for forty years: By his direction they were settled in the holy land: He it was that destroyed the enemies of our faith, and subdued those that rose up against us, and he it is who hath preserved us alive, even as at this day.

For all those benefits, what can we return but an humble acknowledgement of our dependance on him, and by a steady observance of his holy law, endeavor to retain his protection and mercy; for we know ourselves to be deficient in good works; but, as it is said in Jer. ch. 14, "Oh Lord, though our iniquities testify against us, do thou it for thy name's sake, for our back-slidings are many. We have sinned against thee," and again it is said in holy writ, "He who confesseth and forsaketh his sins shall have mercy."

56. MORDECAI M. NOAH ADDRESS, 1818 [164]

Let us turn, then, from Europe and her errors of opinion on points of faith, to contemplate a more noble prospect. OUR COUNTRY, the bright example of universal tolerance, of liberality, true religion, and good faith. In the formation and arrangement of our civil code, the sages and patriots whose collected wisdom adopted them, closed the doors upon that great evil which has shaken the old world to its centre. They proclaimed freedom of conscience, and left the errors of the heart to be judged at that tribunal whose rights should never have been usurped. Here, no inequality of privileges, no asperity of opinion, no invidious distinctions exist; dignity is blended with equality, justice administered impartially: merit alone has a fixed value; and each man is stimulated by the same laudable ambition—an ambition of doing his duty, and meriting the good will of his fellow citizens. Until the Jews can recover their ancient rights and dominions, and take their rank among the governments of the earth, this is their chosen country; here they can rest with the persecuted from every clime, secure in person and property, protected from tyranny and oppression, and participating of equal rights and immunities. Forty years of experience have tested the wisdom of our institutions, and they only will be surrendered with the existence of the nation.

Let it not, however, be said, that because there are no laws which fetter the conscience, or religion incorporated in the government, that the people are insensible to the obligations of religious worship. I have been in many parts of the globe, and I may safely aver, that this is the only country where religion flows in one pure, broad, rapid stream, supported by the intelligence of the people, and the liberality and toleration which are always the effect of moral and enlightened habits. We have only to fear the effects of too great a zeal, which, in mistaking the salutary principles of religion, may render crooked the fair and noble path of toleration. It is incumbent on us who enjoy blessings in this country which are denied to many of our brethren throughout the world, to render ourselves worthy of equal rights by duly estimating their importance, and enlightening the mind, so as to be fully sensible of the nature and value of those privileges. The means are within our reach. It is a system of sound education, alone, which tends to strengthen the faculties, improve the morals, and unfold the intellectual powers of man. To rescue our fellow creature from a state of ignorance, to enlighten his understanding, to render him sensible of the benefactions of his God, to excite that laudible ambition, that spirit of emulation, that noble and elevated disposition which the cultivated and accomplished mind is capable of attaining, are the most pleasing, the most rational efforts of a benevolent heart. As education, therefore, is the mean by which these great objects are to be attained, they can never cease to be of the highest and most interesting importance to the Jews. It has hitherto been too much neglected throughout the world; and this neglect has tended to increase the evils, and augment the portion of intolerance to which our nation has been subjected. We have a long list of illustrious philosophers and moralists who have enlightened and advanced the early ages of our history. Modern times have produced many learned and scientific

Jews, but a more general dissemination of learning is called for. We have genius and talent amongst us, which only wants exertion to develope itself. . . .

After forming the minds, and enlightening the intellect of children, the next duty is to place them on the road to solid independence, by a selection of such pursuits as may comport with their abilities, inclination, and fortune. Not in dragging out a life of restless wanderings and migrations, in emasculating their minds, and cramping their energies in those crooked paths of traffic, miscalled commerce; but by giving them a lasting fortune, in causing them to be taught a useful branch of labour, in founding and perpetuating a spirit of industry in the attainment of some mechanic art, in giving them to know that Providence has bestowed health and vigour upon them for active purposes. Such measures tend to incorporate the Jews among the class of useful, frequently the most wealthy citizens, and to give a tone and character to the rights and liberty which they enjoy. Agriculture, in the early periods of our history, was the general and favourite pursuit. The wealth of the patriarchs was their flocks; the wine, the corn, and oil were the fruits of their husbandry. Since the dispersion of the Israelites, this useful branch of labour has been abandoned, not from inclination, but from a want of participation in those rights assigned to the cultivators of the earth. These rights *we* fully possess, and no occupation brings with it health and profit, purity of manners, integrity and independence, equal to agriculture. It is the cradle of virtue, and the school of patriotism. The hardy yeoman, strengthened and invigorated by agricultural pursuits, is the sure guardian and protector of his country.

While our attention is thus directed to means calculated to promote our temporal felicity, and to insure, in due time, our everlasting reward, we may calculate upon the friendly protection and zealous cooperation of every liberal and tolerant man, without reference to his faith. Whatever may have been the persecutions of the Jews, there is no disposition on the part of civilized powers to revive those acts of cruelty which, for centuries, stained their annals, and defaced their religion. The light of learning has exhibited the errors of the past. The justice and mercy now established —the morality and good faith now encouraged and promoted, are sure guarantees for the future. Instead of whips and chains, blows, and contumely, we have the olive of peace extended to us; and we now have only to combat the errors of education—the prejudice of other religions. Let reason be free, and those errors and prejudices are harmless. Still it could be wished that less asperity of opinion flowed from the ministers of a religion, mild, persuasive, and tolerant. From their pulpits they should call for blessings on the Jews, founders of religion, and of that morality which all civilized nations adopt, as temporal and eternal guides; and they should never forget, that every reflection on the existence and religion of the Jews, is a direct censure on that God whom we all acknowledge, and who, in his mercy and divine will, has thought proper, thus far, to cherish and protect us. We never arraign the faith of others— let none then arraign our faith. If we require light, we must receive it from heaven—not from earth; not from the divisions and contentions of sectarians. We never can go wrong when we acknowledge one God; and we may fatally err in dividing his attributes. The religion of the Jews requires no defence; it speaks for itself; it is the religion of nature—the religion of reason and philosophy. The word of God has been transmitted to us by our illustrious legislator; and his prophesies, in part, have been so fully and completely substantiated, as to leave no room to doubt the issue.

57. ISAAC HARBY'S MEMORANDUM, 1826 [165]

The number of the Jews in the United States it is difficult to arrive at with any precision. Such are the influence of habit and time, that while in the *old world,* under innumerable exactions and disqualifications, there are *six millions* of Israelites, there are in these happy United States, not more than *six thousand.* I arrive at this conclusion, rather from comparative corollaries, than from any given and accurate *data.* Neither Ramsay,[166] Mellish,[167] Morse,[168] Bellamy,[169] nor any other writer, pretending to *enumerate* various religious classes, has thrown one spark of light upon the subject. In the New England States there cannot be more than three or four hundred in all; in Pennsylvania, about that number; in New York, about nine hundred and fifty; in Virginia, about four hundred; in South Carolina, about one thousand two hundred; in Georgia, about four hundred; in Florida, thirty or forty; in Louisiana, about one hundred; and making a large allowance for the scattered and unknown, I think six thousand the *maximum.*

Emigration is not so great now as it was formerly, except to New York. South Carolina had formerly the largest number of emigrant Israelites. Charleston alone had a congregation of six hundred. I think that Charleston has been stationary, in this respect, for the last twenty years, and that the city of New York certainly equals it, and soon will double it.

Men, who reflect, go anywhere in pursuit of happiness. The immediate ancestors of the most respectable Jews in these United States came, some for the purposes of commerce, others for the more noble love of liberty, and the majority for both. In Georgia and in South Carolina, several honorably bore arms in the revolutionary war. My maternal grandfather contributed pecuniary aid to South Carolina, and particularly to Charleston, when besieged by the British. My father in law was a brave grenadier in the regular American Army, and fought and bled for the liberty he lived to enjoy, and to hand down to his children. Numerous instances of patriotism are recorded of such Israelites.

As to the descent of the Jews of the United States, they are principally German and English; though South Carolina has a portion of French and Portuguese. My ancestors came originally from Barbary, where my father's father enjoyed a post of honor in the palace of the emperor of Morocco, that of Royal Lapidary. He fled to England, and married an Italian lady. My father left England for Jamaica before he was twenty years of age. He afterwards settled in Charleston, and I think I may say, was among the first to set an example to his Jewish brethren, of giving a liberal education to their children.

XVII

An American Christian View
of the Jews of America, 1812

The most useful contemporary general review of the position of
the Jews in America was written by a Christian lady, reputedly the
first professional woman writer in America, Hannah Adams.[170]
Brought up by a bookish and impractical father and never in robust
health, she developed an early interest in the comparative study
of religion.[171] The first fruit of this study was *A Dictionary of All
Religions and Religious Denominations*, first published in 1784, and
later several times reprinted in augmented editions. Like many other
histories written at this time, Miss Adams's work was a compilation
of materials from various sources. The article "Jews" in her *Dictionary*,[172] while it is objective and sympathetic, shows only a superficial
acquaintance with its subject. The Jews of the United States are
twice referred to: in one place, an estimate of their number at 3,000
is given,[173] and, in another place, while discussing the generally
improved condition of the Jews in the late eighteenth and early
nineteenth centuries, Miss Adams commented that "In the United
States of America they have never been persecuted, but have been
indulged in all the rights of citizens." [174]

When a later attempt to improve her financial situation by writing
an American history for schools led to controversy with the geographer, Jedidiah Morse,[175] Miss Adams, always shy, decided to write
a history of the Jews, feeling certain that in this field she would
be able to do her work without interference. In her *History of the
Jews*,[176] Miss Adams gives evidence of the use of a larger number
of sources than in her earlier *Dictionary*.[177] In addition, her work
shows that she received help from the Abbé Gregoire [178] and from
her young patron, the Reverend Joseph S. Buckminster,[179] as well
as from letters and memoranda prepared for her use by Jewish
correspondents. In the *History*, a long chapter is devoted to the

Jews in the New World, including Surinam and Jamaica as well as the United States of America.[180] A German translation of Miss Adams's *History of the Jews* was published at Leipzig, 1820; the section dealing with the Jews of America was reprinted several times.[181] This was the source of much European interest in American Jewry; thus Hannah Adams, seeking merely a quiet and lady-like way to support herself, succeeded in transmitting a sympathetic view of the Jews of the United States, supplementing an already existent concern among both Jews and liberal non-Jews in Western Europe.[182]

58. FROM HANNAH ADAMS'S "HISTORY OF THE JEWS"

Preface [183]

The history of the Jews since their dispersion has been but little investigated even by the literary part of the world, and is almost entirely unknown to the general mass of mankind. The design of this work, including the introduction, is to give a brief sketch of their situation, after their return from the Babylonian captivity, to the nineteenth century. The compiler is sensible, that the subject is not calculated to engage the attention of those readers whose object is merely amusement. Instead of a narration of new and entertaining events, they will find a tedious succession of oppressions and persecutions, and probably turn with disgust from the gloomy picture of human guilt and wretchedness.

To the speculative and inquisitive part of mankind the subject must, however, appear more interesting. The history of the Jews is remarkable, above that of all other nations, for the number and cruelty of the persecutions they have endured. They are venerable for the antiquity of their origin. They are discriminated from the rest of mankind by their wonderful destination, peculiar habits, and religious rites. Since the destruction of Jerusalem, and their universal dispersion, we contemplate the singular phenomenon of a nation subsisting for ages without its civil and religious polity, and thus surviving its political existence.

But the Jews appear in a far more interesting and important light when considered as a standing monument of the truth of the christian religion; as the ancient church of God to whom were committed the sacred oracles; as a people selected from all nations to make and preserve the knowledge of the true God. To them the gospel was first preached, and from them the first christian church in Jerusalem was collected. To them we are indebted for the scriptures of the New, as well as of the Old Testament. To them were given the spirit of prophecy, and power of working miracles. From them were derived an illustrious train of prophets and apostles. To use the language of an inspired writer, "To them pertaineth the adoption, and the glory, the service of God, and the promises, and of them, as concerning the flesh, Christ came." . . .

To the intelligent and well informed the difficulty of collecting the history of a people so little known, particularly in this country, during the last and present century, wholly from desultory and unconnected materials, will appear obvious. The compiler can only say, that however deficient and ill arranged her history may be, she has spared no exertions in her power to collect authentic documents, and has used them to the best of her ability. But while she relies on the candour and indulgence of the publick, she cannot forbear to express the warmest gratitude to those respectable gentlemen whose generous patronage has enabled her to devote her time to literary pursuits.

Chap. XXXIV [184]

The Jews have never been numerous in New England; but among those who settled in the colonies some have been distinguished for the respectability of their characters. Judah Monis,[185] a Jewish convert to the christian religion, was admitted a publick teacher at Harvard University. He is stated to have been a native of Algiers, who probably received his education in Italy, though we know nothing of him till his arrival in this country. But after he came to Boston he seems to have been soon invited to fill the office of Hebrew instructer in the university, where he was settled March 27th, 1722. Before he could be admitted, it was rendered necessary by the statutes, that he should change his religion, which he professes to have done with perfect disinterestedness, though he continued till his death to observe the seventh day as the sabbath.

From the address delivered upon the occasion by the Rev. Dr. Coleman of Boston,[186] it may be suspected that doubts were entertained of the sincerity of his declaration. The expressions, "Is your heart with God?" "We cannot be content with good professions," &c. &c. shew no very strong confidence in his integrity. However, it is certain he always sustained an unblemished character, and was well contented with his condition. He married at Cambridge; and when death deprived him at a very advanced age of the society of his wife, he resigned his office, and retired to Northborough where he resided with her relations. He died at 1764, at the age of eighty one years, forty of which he spent in his office.

Monis bequeathed a small sum to be distributed among seven clergymen then living in the vicinity, and left a fund, the interest of which was to be divided among ministers in indigent circumstances; and the remainder of his estate, which was considerable, he gave to the relations of his wife. His printed works are, a discourse delivered at his baptism; one entitled "the truth," another, "the whole truth," and a third "nothing but the truth," and a Hebrew grammar.

Previous to the American revolution, while the Jews convened at their synagogue in Rhode Island, the late president Stiles [187] commenced an acquaintance with Haijim Carigal,[188] a rabbi who had lately arrived in the city. "Having travelled very extensively in the eastern world, and being a man of observation, learning, and intelligence, his conversation was highly entertaining and instructive. He was born at Hebron, and educated there and at Jerusalem. He had travelled all over the Holy Land, and visited many cities in Asia and Europe. The doctor was greatly delighted with his society, and had frequent intercourse with him for the purpose of acquiring the pronunciation of the Hebrew; of ascertaining the meaning of ambiguous expressions in the original of the Old Testament; of learning the usages of the modern Jews; of conversing on past events relating to this extraordinary nation, as recorded in sacred history; and of tracing its future destiny by the light of prophecy. They cultivated a mutual friendship when together, and corresponded in Hebrew when apart."

The rabbi, not long after his arrival, attended his worship by agreement, and heard him discourse in an affectionate manner on the past dispensations of God's providence towards his chosen people; on his promised design of rendering them an exalted nation in the latter day glory of the Messiah's kingdom; and on the duty of Christians, and of all nations, to desire a participation in their future glorious state.

"So catholick was the intercourse between this learned Jew and learned Christian, that they often spent hours together in conversation; and the information which the extensive travels of the Jew enabled him to give, especially concerning the Holy Land, was a rich entertainment to his christian friend. The civilities of the rabbi were more than repaid. The doctor very frequently attended the worship of the synagogue at Newport, not only when rabbi Carigal officiated, but at the ordinary service before his arrival, and after his departure."

With six other rabbis of less eminence he became acquainted, and showed them every civility, while he maintained a friendly communication with the Jews in general in Newport. Such rare and unexpected attentions from a christian minister of distinction could not but afford peculiar gratification to a people, conscious of being a proverb and bye word among all nations. To him they accordingly paid every attention in return, and expressed peculiar pleasure in admitting him into their families, and into their synagogues.

Dr. Holmes [189] in concluding this account judiciously remarks, that "this civility and catholicism towards the Jews is worthy of imitation. It is to be feared that Christians do not what ought to be done towards the conversion of this devoted people. While admitted into most countries for the purpose of trade and commerce, instead of being treated with that humanity and tenderness which christianity should inspire, they are often persecuted and condemned as unworthy of notice or regard. Such treatment tends to prejudice them against our holy religion, and to establish them in their infidelity."

A respectable rabbi [190] of New York has given the following account of his brethren in the United States.

"There are about fifty families of Jews in New York, which, with a number of unmarried men, make from seventy to eighty subscribing members to the congregation *Sherith Israel,* which is incorporated by an act of the legislature of the state, empowering all religious societies to hold their property by charter, under the direction of trustees chosen annually by the communicants of the society, according to certain rules prescribed in the act. . . .

"In Philadelphia there may be about thirty families of Jews. They have two synagogues, one for those who observe the Portuguese customs and forms of prayer, and the other for those who adhere to the German rules, customs, &c.; neither of them are incorporated. There may be about from eighty to one hundred men, in the whole state of Pennsylvania, who all occasionally attend the synagogues in Philadelphia. . . ."

A more particular account of the Jews in South Carolina has been given by one of the principal members [191] of their congregation in the capital of the state, the substance of which is as follows.

"The first emigration of the Jews to Charleston took place long before the revolution. The spirit of commerce can never be extinct in them; and their wealth increased with their numbers, which were augmented from time to time, both by marriages, and acquisitions from Europe. The present number of Jews may be estimated about a thousand. Charleston alone contains about six or seven hundred individuals.

"The present number of Hebrews in the city are chiefly Carolinians, the descendants of German, English, and Portuguese emigrants, who, from the civil and religious tyranny of Europe, sought an asylum in the western world. While the contest for freedom and independence was carried on, the majority distinguished themselves as brave soldiers and gallant defenders of the cause of a country which protected them. This spirit still actuates them; and as it is but natural that a people, who for ages have groaned under the impolitic barbarity and blind fanaticism of Europe, should inhale the breath of freedom with delight, the Hebrews in this city pay their hearty homage to the laws, which guarantee their rights, and consolidate them into the mass of a free people.

"The religious rites, customs, and festivals of the Jews are all strictly observed by those of this nation in Charleston; but ameliorated with that social liberality, which pervades the minds and manners of the inhabitants of civilized countries. Indeed the seats in a Jewish synagogue are often crowded with visitors of every denomination. The episcopal functions are now discharged by the Rev. Ca[r]valho,[192] late professor of the Hebrew language in the college of New York. . . .

"The institutions which the Jews have established in Charleston, are chiefly religious and charitable. They have built an elegant synagogue; and what strongly exhibits the liberality of the city is, that the Roman Catholick church is directly opposite to it. They have also societies for the relief of strangers, for attending the sick, and for administering the rites of humanity, and burial to the dying and the dead. The most modern institution is a society for the relief of orphans. The capital is already considerable, and it is yearly increasing. The children receive every advantage which is necessary to enable them to be well informed and honourable citizens of their country."

In Richmond, (Virginia) there are about thirty Jewish families, who are now building a synagogue; but they are not as yet incorporated. The number of unmarried men is unknown, though there may be about an hundred scattered throughout the state, who are and will become members of the congregation. At Savannah in Georgia there are but few Jewish families, who assemble at times, and commune with each other in publick prayers. The United States is, perhaps, the only place where the Jews have not suffered persecution, but have, on the contrary, been encouraged and indulged in every right of citizens.

The Jews in all the United States, except Massachusetts, are eligible to offices of trust and honour; and some of them in the southern states are in office. They are generally commercial men, and a number of them considerable merchants.

Part Two
Economic Life

In the 1790s, the population of the United States was primarily involved in agriculture. Approximately 90 percent of the working population was to be found on the farms and only about 10 percent in trade and commerce. At this time, manufacturing was largely carried on in the home workshops of small entrepreneurs, working themselves, with perhaps an apprentice or two and a handful of employees. This domestic manufacturing occupied the time and the productive effort of a relatively small number of Americans. When Alexander Hamilton, as Secretary of the Treasury in the administration of President George Washington, prepared and submitted his celebrated "Report on Manufactures," it was in the hope of stimulating a greater diversity of pursuits and thus enabling the new United States of America to develop a more balanced and self-sufficient economy.

Occupationally, the Jews in the United States were not distributed in the same manner as the population in general. Very few earned their living in agriculture; most were occupied in trade, commerce, and related activities. The chief ports of the young country were Boston, Newport, New York, Philadelphia, Baltimore, Richmond, Norfolk, Charleston, and Savannah. With the exception of Boston, where only an occasional Jewish inhabitant is recorded before the late 1830s, and Newport, where the early Jewish community was broken up by the Revolution, the major ports were the cities of Jewish concentration. In addition to the involvement in foreign trade that these locations suggest, Jews living in these commercially vital cities were vendue masters (auctioneers), small manufacturers, especially in the metal trades, and retail shopkeepers.

In foreign trade, R. G. Albion described the decade from 1783 to 1793 as "one of the dreariest in the annals of American commerce."[1] It was the first experience that American merchants had of what it meant to be no longer part of the British imperial system.

American ships were excluded from many rich ports where previously they had been welcomed. As a result, American shippers
were seeking new markets and trying to subsist, meantime, on short-
haul carrying. Even here, part of the difficulty was that so much
of the none-too-abundant mercantile capital of the time was tied
up in the long-range attempt to open Far Eastern trade that the
smaller operator found himself constantly pressed for credit. After
1793, the situation improved for the English and French were at
war, and the American shippers were able to profit from the national
neutrality.[2]

Not least of the advantages to the young American nation from
the opening of war between the French and the English was that,
because of the widespread sympathy for France (partially destroyed after the XYZ Affair in 1797), America's neutral ports were
used for the outfitting, supply, and repair of French ships. This
rewarding activity was carried on although it was illegal under the
terms of the neutrality act of 1794.[3] In addition, American merchants acted as prize masters for ships captured by privateers of
the warring nations as well as outfitters to the privateers and the
regular naval vessels. Jewish traders profited by these circumstances
as did their non-Jewish competitors. Moses Myers [4] of Norfolk, for
example, was a very prominent Jewish merchant. He had many
excellent business connections in the West Indies and in Europe as
well as with men of prominence in mercantile activities in Philadelphia—men like Stephen Girard.[5] A substantial part of his business, carrying on well into the early decades of the nineteenth century, consisted of acting as outfitter and prize master. His success
in carrying on this kind of business was recognized by his official
appointment, in 1795, as agent of the French Republic at Norfolk.[6]

Not all Jewish commerce was international. Goods, once imported, had to be sold or exchanged for pelts and other commodi-
ties. In pursuing this mercantile phase of economic activity, the
Jews of America began to disperse into the smaller towns and villages; first to towns like Lancaster, Pennsylvania, jumping-off places
for the westward migration that was already beginning to be revealed as the pattern of American life, and then, as time went on
and settled towns appeared where there had been only a frontier,

to nascent communities—like Pittsburgh, Pennsylvania; Lexington, Kentucky; Cincinnati, Ohio; Fort Wayne, Indiana; and Fort Smith, Arkansas. In the parent cities and even more in these smaller and newer communities, we can seldom identify Jews as of one business or another. Many of them took part in a variety of economic activities and thus helped in the building of the great heartland of the United States, the middle west.

The persistence of close family ties and of established friendships (illustrated in the documents of Part Three) had an important though secondary economic function. In the years before wire services made extensive coverage of commercial news possible, both family and business correspondence was used for the transmitting of commercial "intelligence." This was particularly the case with respect to dealings in perishable cargoes, notably in the trade with the West Indies.[7] This part of the trade of the United States was carried to a great extent by the ports from Philadelphia south to Charleston and, to a lesser degree, Savannah. The Jews of these cities were involved along with their non-Jewish fellow-merchants, and many details of current prices are incorporated into letters exchanged on other subjects. During the period when the American role in the West Indian trade was large, Charleston was the most thriving Jewish community in the United States.[8] As the importance of this trade diminished, the Charleston Jewish community lost much of its strength.

Again, during the period of embargoes and Non-Intercourse Acts,[9] in the years before the War of 1812, the relations between the United States and both England and France were strained.[10] Looking forward to an easing of tensions, American commercial houses like that of Moses Myers in Norfolk[11] maintained contacts with English firms by means of letters, often addressed to branch offices outside of the home country, assuring the English business houses that when political conditions again permit, they will reestablish their dealings. One letter of 1810, from Moses Myers and Son to the English firm of Gibson and Company, announces that John Myers, Moses's son, who had been taken into partnership in 1809,[12] was soon to visit England and the Continent, and that while in England he would try to formalize the business relationship.[13]

This letter also includes, as part of its commercial intelligence, reference to the decline in tobacco prices, and thus presages the rise in importance of cotton in the southern economy.[14]

The roles played by Jews in these multifarious aspects of trade and commerce prepared some of them for service to the nation in public positions related to economic life: as Indian agents, military agents, consuls, weighers, customs inspectors and collectors, treasury agents, auditors, marshals, and other similar capacities. In some cases, these governmental positions were undertaken to bridge over periods of general depression or personal financial stringency. In others, they were part-time occupations carried on simultaneously with other businesses. In only isolated instances, were there Jews who made government service their career.

One of the important needs of the American economy in the early days, as has been suggested above, was for expansion capital to build the country's economic growth. By involvement in commerce, the Jews played their proportionate part in capital accumulation. They entered into the promotion of lotteries, which, in the days before the multiplication of joint-stock enterprises, was one of the accepted methods of raising capital. Later, they engaged in commercial banking. Jews invested in government notes and bonds, and thus aided their country in obtaining needed capital sums. In the smaller communities especially, Jewish merchants were among the investors in local banks. Foreign Jewish bankers, like the Rothschilds, and their American agents and counterparts—Phillips and Company of Philadelphia and the Cohens of Baltimore—tried to become, and in some cases did become officially designated fiscal agents for the United States, as the Rothschilds did in the matter of the French Spoliation Claims in the late 1830s.

Throughout this period, many Jews either newly-arrived in America or lacking the support of a well-established family business began their commercial careers as peddlers. As the rate of immigration stepped up in the 1830s, an increasing number of German-Jewish immigrants were to be found on the road as peddlers. The increasing manufacturing developments in the New England area led Yankee peddlers to withdraw from their earlier preeminence in this type of economic activity, and some of those who stepped in to replace them were Jews. Some Jewish peddlers graduated upward into the ranks of storekeepers, and, still later, became bankers or department store owners; many, of course, were less successful. The mobility and fluidity that characterized the expanding American economy created many opportunities for thrifty, hardworking Jews to improve their worldly position, though not everyone took advantage of the opportunities that came his way. It is easy, in the light of the conditions that generally prevailed through the American economy, to understand why Jews made a close identification of their material welfare with the growth of the country.

In this early national period, Jewish economic opportunity was, indeed, tied closely to the general health of the American economy. Every breeze that rippled the surface of American life was felt by the Jewish segment. Wars and threats of war, depressions and financial panics, land speculation booms, Indian affairs, the moving frontier, and slavery all had their repercussions in the microcosm that was the economic life of America's Jews.

XVIII

Mercantile Conditions, 1791

Spermacetti candles [15] were one of the by-products of the whaling industry. Moses Michael Hays [16] was ready to take a fair quantity at a reasonable price, to be paid three months after delivery, or later. These terms indicate how the shipper, who was himself starved for capital, was nonetheless forced to extend credit to his customers. Finally, it should be noted that even for the short haul from Providence to Boston there were alternatives to sea transportation, so here, too, the ship owners were at a disadvantage.

59. M. M. HAYS TO CHRISTOPHER CHAMPLIN,[17] 1791 [18]

Boston Nov 12th 1791

[M]r Chris Champlin
Dear Sir

I thank you very much for your kind attention in enquiring of Capt. Handy respecting the spermacitea Candles, I would not by any means choose to make purchase of any. but the very best Quality. any other would not answer my Purpose. if Capt. Handy will take two Shillings & fourpence per pound. for the forty Boxes of Good Quality, you speak of. I will take them & pay him in Three months. and interest after That Time, if delayed. if my Terms are acceded to. Capt. Aiken is a Comeing Round and will take them on freight. if not they can come some other way from Providence. Mrs. Hays with me salutes your worthy Lady with very cordial affection; & was rejoyced to hear, she has reacht her Habitation in safety

And am very respectfully Dr Sr yr mo: ob: M M Hays

XIX
Rental Property, 1794

The following lease, in which Mary Habacker rented a "messuage," or dwelling, in Philadelphia from Solomon Lyon,[19] its owner, is a characteristic legal document, of which a great many are extant. Its form needs no comment. The content is interesting, first, as indicative of the sort of property, in the very heart of Philadelphia, that a well-to-do Jewish shopkeeper could own;[20] and, second, for the fact that Solomon Lyon is described in the document by the title "gentleman,"[21] an indication of social and economic status. Incidentally, the lease reflects one of the economic difficulties of the period, that of establishing a uniform monetary standard for the various states. The rental fixed herein is in terms of the currency of Pennsylvania. Three years earlier, in 1791, Alexander Hamilton had recommended the establishment of a mint and a national coinage system. Although his recommendations were accepted, it was not until the discovery of gold in California, in the 1840s, that Hamilton's proposals for a standard were effective in eliminating foreign and local money from circulation. The final solution did not come until after the Civil War.[22]

60. SOLOMON LYON, INDENTURE, 1794 [23]

This Indenture made the twenty eighth Day of April in the year of our Lord One thousand seven hundred and Ninety four between Solomon Lyon of the City of Philadelphia Gentleman of the one part and Mary Habacker of the same place Widow of the other part Witnesseth that the sd. Solomon Lyon for and in Consideration of the Payment of the Yearly Rent and performance of the Covenant and Agreement herein after mentioned and reserved which on the part and behalf of her the sd. Mary Habacker are is or ought to be paid observed performed and kept Hath granted, demised set and to farm Let and by these presents Doth grant, demise set and to farm Let unto the sd. Mary Habacker A certain three Story Brick Messuage or Tenement and Lot or piece of Ground Situate on the West Side of Fourth Street from the River Delaware between Vine and Sassafras Street in the sd. City.[24] lately Occupyd by Doctr. Frederick Ruhe together with all the Appurtenances thereunto belonging To have and to Hold the sd Messuage or Tenement and Lot or piece of Ground hereby demised with the Appurtenances unto the sd Mary Habacker her Executors, Administrators and Assigns from and after the first day of May next and for and during and unto the full end and term of One Year thence Next ensuing and fully to be Compleat and ended Yielding and Paying therefore unto the sd. Solomon Lyon his Executors, Administrators and Assigns the Yearly Rent or Sum of Sixty Pounds Lawful Money of Pennsylvania in equal Quarterly payments that is to say the Sum of fifteen Pounds on the first days of May, August, November and February. . . .

And the sd Mary Habacker paying the aforesaid Yearly Rent in Manner aforesaid and Observing and Performing the Covenants and Agreements herein before mentioned, shall and Lawfully may during the sd Term hereby demised freely peaceably and Quietly, have hold Occupy and enjoy the same without the Lawful Let Suit Trouble hindrance or Molestation of him the sd Solomon Lyon his Executors, Administrators or Assigns or of any other persons whatsoever In Witness whereof the sd Parties have hereunto set their hands and Seal interchangeable the Day and Year first above written.   Mary Habacker

Sealed & Delivered in the presence of us
Hilary H Baker [25]
Christopher Baker

XX

Jews in the Copper Trade, 1794

Congressional acceptance of Hamilton's 1791 proposal for establishing a mint and a national coinage [26] created a market for copper as well as for the precious metals. There were, however, only a few small mines, like the Schuyler Copper Mine,[27] to supply both the needs of the treasury and the needs of the shipbuilders, who lined their ships with copper as protection against rats. Since these mines could not provide enough, much of the needed copper had to be imported. As early as 1800, President John Adams sent Senator Tracy [28] of Connecticut as far west as Michilimackinac to look for sources of copper. But it was not until the 1820s that large copper deposits were discovered on the Upper Peninsula of Michigan and more than twenty years elapsed before these new mines went into production and the early mines were finally supplanted. Meantime, it is interesting to note the participation of Jews in the copper trade, as revealed in the letter printed below and by the importance of the New Jersey firm of Harmon Hendricks and Co.[29]

61. JACOB MARKS TO
ALEXANDER HAMILTON, 1794 [30]

The Hon. Alexander Hamilton Esq.[31]
Sir

The Directors of the Mine commonly called Schuyler Copper Mine take the liberty of informing the secretary to the Treasury that they have raised sufficient oar [ore] the [to] enter into Contract for the delivery of 50 Tons Refined Copper by the last of May next.

If you have not already orderd the Quantity which is required for the Mint we beg to be favoured with the preference of Your Command. Your Answer will ob[l]ige us

Your sinceer friend & obedient Humble S.   Jacob Marks Co.[32]

XXI

Holdings of a Vendue Master,

1797

Jacob Jacobs [33] was a successful vendue master (auctioneer) in Charleston. His will indicates what the rewards of success in this occupation were at the close of the eighteenth century. He owned a good deal of city real estate, a number of slaves, horses and carriages, much personal property, and notes and bonds. Altogether, while one does not get an impression of fabulous wealth there seems to be no doubt that Jacobs had accumulated a substantial fortune. It is worthy of notice that such a large part of Jacobs's investment was conservative rather than speculative in character.

62. WILL OF JACOB JACOBS, 1797 [34]

In the Name of God, Amen. I Jacob Jacobs of the City of Charleston, in the State of South Carolina Vendue Master, being of sound and disposing Mind, Memory and Understanding do this twenty fourth day of June in the Year of our Lord One thousand seven hundred and Ninety-Six, Make, publish and declare this my last Will and Testament in manner and form following, that is to say: First, I will that all my just Debts and Funeral charges be fully paid, as soon as may be after my decease, by my Executors herein after named. Item I give unto the Synagogue in Charleston of which I am a Member [35] the Sum of Ten Pounds. Item I give unto my Sister Rachael Jacobs [36] the Sum of Twenty five Pounds to be remitted to her in Great Britain free of all deductions by my Executors herein after named, as soon as may be after my decease. Item I give unto my Brother Samuel Jacobs [37] the Sum of Ten pounds, To my Sister in law Phila Nunes [38] I give the Sum of Twenty Pounds, And my Will is that the said several pecuniary Legacies shall be paid free from all deduction whatever. Item my Will is, and I do hereby give unto my Friend Gershon Cohen [39] of the City of Charleston aforesaid, my gold Stock Buckle, Silver Shoe Buckles and Stone Knee Buckles. Item I give and bequeath unto my dearly beloved Wife Katey Jacobs [40] all my Household and Kitchen Furniture, Plate, China, Stock of Liquors, Horses, Carriages, Monies, Bonds, Notes, and Book Debts whatsoever and wheresoever absolutely for ever, subject nevertheless to the several Devises and Bequests herein before by me made and given. Item I give and devise unto my said dearly beloved Wife Katey Jacobs during her Widowhood and no longer all those my Negro and other Slaves named Toby, Scipio, Jack, Jenny with her three Children Peter, John and Eve, and Flora with her two Children Rachael and Lucy and all the other Slaves that I may be possessed of, at the time of my death. And from and immediately after the death or Marriage of her my said Wife, which may first happen, then my Will further is, and I do hereby direct, enjoin, authorize and empower my Executors herein after named, or such of them as shall take upon themselves the burden and execution of this my Will, to expose to Sale and sell either at public or private Sale, each, every, and all of the said Negro, and other Slaves, with the Issue of the Females, herein before given unto my said Wife, and the money arising from the Sale of the said Slaves, to be placed out at Interest, and secured with a Mortgage of real Estate, and also good and Sufficient personal Security.[41] And the Proceeds arising from the Sale of the said Slaves to be equally divided share and share alike between each and every of the Children (if more than one) of my Friends Gershom and Rebecca Cohen [42] of Charleston aforesaid, the Share of Proportion of each Child (if more than one) to be paid over and given up, on it's attaining the Age of Twenty one Years (if a Male, or if a Female) the Age of Twenty One Years, or day of Marriage which shall first happen. Item I give and bequeath unto my said Wife during her Widowhood and no longer the full and absolute use, Occupation Possession and enjoyment of all and every part and parcel of my real estates, Lands, Tenements, and Hereditaments whatsoever and wheresoever within this State and the State of Georgia without impeachment of Waste, and from and after her death or Marriage which may first happen, then my Will is respect of my Lands, Tenements, Hereditaments, and real

Estates in the State of Georgia aforesaid is, and I do hereby give
and bequeath the same unto Philip Cohen [43] and Jacob Jacobs
Cohen,[44] the two sons of Gershon and Rebecca Cohen, to hold the
same to them and each of them, and to have, take and receive the
Rents, Issues and Profits thereof, to them and each of them, and
their and each of their use and behoof equally during the term
of their natural Lives, and from and after the death of either of
them, then to the sole use, benefit and behoof of the Survivor of
them, and to his Heirs and Assigns absolutely for ever. Item my
Will in respect of my lot of Land situate in the City of Charleston
and which I purchased from Thomas Osborn [45] Esquire Sheriff of
Charleston District is, and I do hereby give and bequeath the same
after the death or Marriage of her my said dearly beloved Wife,
which may first happen, unto Philip Cohen the Son of Gershon and
Rebecca Cohen to hold the same to him, and to have and receive
and take the Rents, Issues and Profits thereof to him and his Heirs
for ever. Item my Will in respect of my Lot of Land Situate in the
City of Charleston lately purchased of Edward Lowndes [46] is and
I do hereby give and bequeath the same, after the death or Marriage of her my said dearly beloved Wife, which may first happen,
unto Philip Cohen and Abraham Serzedas Cohen [47] the two Sons of
Gershon and Rebecca Cohen, to hold the same, to them and each
of them, and to have take and receive the Rents, Issues and Profits
thereof to them and each of them, and to their and each of their
use and behoof equally during the term of their natural Lives, and
from and after the death of either of them; then to the sole use,
benefit and behoof of the Survivor of them, and to his Heirs and
Assigns absolutely for ever. . . . Item my Will in respect of my
Lot in Troot Street adjoining the aforesaid Lot No. containing
Thirty four feet front on the said Street, and one hundred and two
feet in depth, is, and I do hereby give and bequeath the same (after
the death or Marriage of her my said Wife which shall first happen)
unto the said Philip Cohen, and Hyam Cohen,[48] the two Sons of the
said Gershon and Rebecca Cohen, to hold the same to them, and
each of them, and to receive and take the Rents and Profits thereof
to them and each of them, and their, and each of their Use and
behoof equally during the Term of their natural Lives, and from
and after the death of either of them then to the sole use, benefit

and behoof of the Survivor of them and to his Heirs and Assigns absolutely for ever. And Lastly I do hereby Nominate, Constitute and appoint my said dearly beloved Wife Katey Jacobs Executrix, Joshua Ward [49] the elder Esqr. attorney at Law William Somarsal,[50] Esquire, Bennet Taylor,[51] Merchant, and Thomas Jones,[52] Esquire, the present President of the Bank of Carolina, Executors of this my last Will and Testament, being contained on four sides of one sheet of post paper, hereby revoking all other Wills by me heretofore made, and admitting this and this only to be my last Will and Testament. In Witness Whereof I have hereunto set my Hand and Seal, the day and Year first above written.   Jacob Jacobs Ls [53]

XXII

Report on the Petition of Simon Philipson, 1805

Simon Philipson,[54] a merchant of Philadelphia, was unfortunately sick in November, 1803, when a vessel on which he was shipping a cargo went through the Philadelphia Customs House. His illness continued for some time, and he was unable to file the document required to get his "drawback," or rebate on the charges paid to the Customs. This might have been a serious matter, for drawbacks were a part of a discriminatory system that was evolved for the protection of local interests in both coastal and oceanic shipping.[55] Merchants took advantage of this and similar devices to establish their enterprises on a profitable basis. Since the rebate was a federal matter, the only recourse that a merchant like Philipson had when he missed the proper date for claiming exceptions was to file a petition with the Committee on Commerce and Manufactures of the House of Representatives. The recommendation of this committee, embodied in a report like that printed below, was then acted upon by a committee of the whole House of Representatives, and, if this committee approved the report, the rebate was belatedly granted.

63. REPORT, 1805 [56]

The Committee of Commerce and Manufactures to whom were referred the petition of Simon Philipson, of Philadelphia, submit the following

REPORT—

The petitioner represents that on the 29th of November, 1803, he shipped a cargo on board the schooner Olive Branch, bound from Philadelphia to the West Indies, and that from sickness he was prevented from making the qualifications to his entry at the custom house, within the ten days required by law, and thereupon the collector refused to grant the drawback for that part of the cargo on which it was claimed. The petitioner applied within two days of the time, and he has fully proved to the committee that a severe and dangerous illness prevented him from giving his attendance at an earlier period.

Accompanying the petition is the attestation of T. Breithaupt [57] and Zachry Mossina, in which it is declared "that on or about the second day of December (1803) and until the eleventh of said month, they daily and severally visited Simon Philipson of the city of Philadelphia who was then confined to his bed and apparently dangerously ill, and that to their recollection the said Simon Philipson was between the fifth and eleventh of said month not expected to live," and Zachry Mossina further declares "that the said Simon Philipson repeatedly mentioned to him during his illness, a desire of going to the custom house to qualify to his entry about goods shipped by him on board the schooner Olive Branch to the West Indies, but observed to him that his situation would not permit him to leave his bed, on account of which he recollects perfectly well the said Simon Philipson expressed to him his uneasiness on account of his not being able to go to the custom house."

The collector for Philadelphia states, that he has no doubt the statement in the petition is correct, so far as relates to the transaction of the custom house, and adds, that Simon Philipson produced his affidavit taken before a notary public, stating that he had been four days of the time limited by law so much indisposed, that he could not leave his room, but the collector considering the law as positive, and vesting no discretionary power in him, he had refused the drawback.

After a considerate examination of this case, the committee are of opinion, that the petitioner is justly entitled to relief from Congress, and they do not hesitate to offer the following resolution.

Resolved, That the prayer of the petitioner is reasonable and ought to be granted.

XXIII

Legal Apprenticeship, 1810

Apprenticeship, while its major use was to train young boys in commercial or mechanical pursuits, was also used as one device for training for the professions. A young man preparing to be a lawyer might, in some instances, go to college and then "read" law; more often, he would be apprenticed to a lawyer for a period of three years, during which he would gain a practical, almost vocational, knowledge of the law. In the indenture reproduced below, a standard printed apprenticeship contract has been used, but some of the usual terms have been deleted, and an interesting special provision has been written in. Where, for example, the standard form reads, "Art, Trade, and Mystery," the word "Trade" has been cut out; so, too, have the usual provisions for the living accommodations of the apprentice; the deleted materials are here underlined. More interesting than what has been removed is what has been added; the non-Jewish lawyer Thomas U. P. Charlton,[58] who was taking on the Jewish apprentice, agreed that the boy was to be free of work on "the Jewish Sabbaths, or any other days consecrated to that religion." Thus the opportunity for religious observance was assured to Mordecai Sheftall[59] by legal contract.

64. MORDECAI SHEFTALL, INDENTURE,[60] 1810[61]

State of Georgia,
County County.
THIS INDENTURE Witnesseth, That Mordecai M, Sheftall, of the State, & County aforesaid, with the consent of his Father hath put himself, and by these Presents doth voluntarily, of his own free will and accord, put himself Apprentice unto Mr Thomas U. P. Charlton, Attorney at Law, to learn the Art, Trade, and Mystery, and after the Manner of Apprentices at Law to serve the said Thos U P Charlton from the date hereof, for and during, and until the full

End and Term of three years next ensuing. During all which Term, the said Apprentice his said Master faithfully shall serve; his Secrets keep; his lawful Commands every where readily obey: he shall do no Damage to his said Master: nor see it done by others, without giving Notice thereof to his said Master: he shall not waste his said Master's Goods, nor lend them unlawfully to any: he shall not commit fornication, nor contract Matrimony within the said Term: at Cards, Dice, or any other unlawful Game he shall not play, whereby his said Master may have Damage: with his own Goods, nor the Goods of others, without Licence from his said Master shall neither buy nor sell: he shall not absent himself Day or Night from his said Masters Service, without his leave; nor haunt Ale-Houses, Taverns, or Play-Houses; but in all Things behaving himself as a faithful Apprentice ought to do, during the said Term. And the said Master shall use the utmost of his Endeavours to teach, or cause to be taught or instructed, the said Apprentice, in the Trade or Mystery of the Law Profession—And and procure and provide for sufficient Meat, Drink, Lodging, and Washing, fitting for during the said term of

the said Thomas U. P. Charlton, convenants and agrees not to require the said Mordecai Sheftall, to attend to any business or to do, or perform any thing appertaining to the study or profession of Law, on the Jewish Sabbaths, or any other Days consecrated to that religion.[62] And for the true Performance of all and singular the Covenants and Agreements aforesaid, the Parties bind themselves each unto the other, firmly by these Presents.

IN WITNESS WHEREOF, the said Parties have interchangeably set their Hands and Seals hereunto. Dated at Savannah the eleventh Day of June in the Year of our Lord one thousand eight hundred and ten and in the 34 Year of the Independence of the United States of America.   Mordecai M Sheftall

Sealed and Delivered in the Presence of

Levi S. DLyon [63]

                                        Thos U P Charlton
                                        Moses Sheftall

XXIV

The Indian Trade, 1811-1813

Jacob Marks, whom we have already met [64] as a dealer in copper and other metals in the 1790s, later entered the business of supplying trading goods for the Indian market. This was apparently a venture at wholesale; Jacob Marks does not appear as one who traded directly with the Indians. He seems, rather, to have furnished goods to the Office of Indian Trade for later use by the actual traders. The letter to Marks from J. Mason,[65] Superintendent of Indian Trade, printed below, reveal the pettiness of the detail with which the Superintendent had to concern himself; it also suggests that Marks was not above padding his accounts when it suited his purposes to do so, and that Mason kept his eyes open for even the smallest items of overcharge.

Levi Sheftall [66] of Georgia also served both the Office of Indian Trade and the War Department. When he died, his sons Benjamin [67] and Mordecai [68] tried to straighten out his accounts with both government offices. From the correspondence printed below it appears that Levi Sheftall had money due him from the Office of Indian Trade and owed money to the War Department; the War Department accountant was pressing for payment, while Mason, as Superintendent of Indian Trade, wanted all details of Sheftall's account with his office cleared up before he paid over the balance to the War Department. The documents are interesting both as an indication of the confusion into which Levi Sheftall had gotten his affairs and as a revelation that even in the early years of the United States the bureaucratic temperament was at work.

65. JOHN MASON TO JACOB MARKS, 1811 [69]

Office Indian Trade
Georgetown 10 April 1811

Jacob Mark Esq.
New York
Sir:

Your favours of the 14, 15 & 26 February and 6th inst have been duely received & would have been replied to sooner but for the great pressure of business in this office for some time past. The goods shipped by you for this office pr the Schooner Greyhound have been received. On opening some of them were found of rather inferior quality particularly the Siamoise, many pieces of which were entirely deficient as to pattern and much inferior to the samples furnished you from this office I have however determined on taking the whole as they will answer tolerably well for Indian trade.

The 400 td Beads which you offer I cannot think of purchasing at the price you quote say 90 Cts p td. If you can put them at 38 Cts p td for the white and 40 Cts p td for the other colors, I have no objection to taking them these are precisely the prices paid for the parcells out of which the samples were furnished you from this office.

As to the mock garnets if our understanding respecting the Bunches is the same I will take them at your prices for each number say for No. 2, 13 Cts; No. 3, 16 Cts & No. 4, 20 Cts p Bunch. A Bundle or paper contains 5 Bunches each Bunch contains 10 masses or smaller Bunches, each mass or smaller Bunch contains 12 Strans. It is for each Bunch of 10 masses or 120 Strans that I will give the price stated above against each number.

I must beg leave to remark that some of the charges on your Invoice appear exorbitant for instance $15 for effecting an insurance which only amounts to $46.25 & $4.50 for drayage & Porterage of 8 Packages which were not large & by no means weighty, were I to allow these charges they would certainly be rejected at the Treasury. I hope therefore that you will think it reasonable to strike out the former altogether & to reduce considerably the latter charge. The amount for your account when these deductions are made will be paid at the time stipulated say first June next.

I am & &   J M[ason] [70]

66. J. MASON TO WILLIAM SIMMONS, 1813 [71]

Indian office
2d Feby 1813

Willm Simmons Esq
Accot War Department
Sir: I return you herewith the letter to you of 21 Jany from Mr. Ben: Sheftall sent over yesterday. The late Mr. Levi Sheftall rendered his accounts to this office last up to 31st Decr 1808 making a Bala due him of $1027.22 ¾ by a letter of the 26 Jany 1809 from Mr. Ben: Sheftall and before the accounts were examined I was informed of his Fathers death, and about same time was requested by the Secretary of War not to pay over such balance as might be due his estate untill his accounts were settled at the War Dept.

On 31 May following I wrote Mr. Mordecai Sheftall (who had addressed me during the previous month on the subject of these accounts as one of his fathers executors and pressed a remittance of the Balance) stating certain errors and deductions to be made in some of the accounts—and explanations wanted in others—and informing him of the request from the Secretary of war & giving him permission when these errors and overcharges were corrected to draw for the Balance in favor of the War Dept. In June of same year he acknowledged the receipt of my letter and promised to enquire into the accounts and inform me. I heard no more from either of these Gentlemen untill this fall and winter by letters of 28 Oct & 16 Decr 1812 Mr. Ben Sheftall states generally that unable to discover any errors and unwilling to make the deductions proposed he begs I will pay the Balance originally stated by his father over to you, neither of which letters have yet been answered. I have been thus particular Sir to Shew that Mr. Sheftall had no authority for stating as he does in his letter to you that the sum of which he speaks constitutes an acknowledged Balance due from this office.

I have now again reveiwd [sic] his accounts, and make a balance due the estate of the late Levi Sheftall of 947.26 $ for which sum I will pay the draft of his executors in your favor on their sending me a general acquittance, as I shall this day write Mr. B. Sheftall and send him a statement of the manner in which I have settled the account.[72] It is due to them in the present stage of the business to inform you that of the deductions made from the account here of the late Mr. Sheftall, are $37.47½ deducted from an account original of which I send you in which charges for Cherokees annuity were blended with those for Indian trade and with which annuities I had at that time nothing to do—since if they are allowable to him, it must be from the Indian Department [73] or some quarter other than [this] office—as this voucher however is requisite to be retained here for that part I pay on it, you will please return it, or if wanted for the Indian Department a copy certified by you will do.

I am & &   J M[ason]

67. JOHN MASON TO BEN SHEFTALL, 1813 [74]

Indian office
2d March 1813

Mr. Ben Sheftall
Savannah Ga
Sir: Being called on by Mr. Simmons the accountant to do so, I have this day paid to the War Dept $947.26 being the balance due from this office to the estate of the late Mr. Sheftall as per my letter to you of 2d ulto.

Notwithstanding the account has been closed you will be pleased on receipt of this to send me a draft in favor of the accountant of the War Department drawn on myself for the above named sum— with "a certificate under seal from the proper court or office that the drawer or drawers of the Bill have been qualified as executors." [75]

I am & &   J. M[ason] Supt

XXV

Effects of the War of 1812, 1812-1814

The War of 1812 was not sought by commercial interests in the United States. Its coming completed the shutting-down of mercantile activity that had been begun by the Non-Importation Act of 1806 and the Embargo of 1808.[76] The index of business activity fell in 1812 to 1814 almost as low as it had in 1808; meantime, wholesale prices rose to a sharp inflationary impetus as the result of an increase in the price of imported goods; this was followed by a rise in transportation costs and in production costs for domestic goods which led, in turn, to price increases not as great as those for imports. The capital needs of the government as well as those of private business led to excessive expansion of credit and to a tottering financial structure. The letters printed below illustrate in small part the reflection of these general conditions in the business activities of American Jewish merchants.

68. RICHARD LEAKE [77] TO DR. MOSES SHEFTALL,[78] 1812 [79]

Philadelphia July 29. 1812

Dear Sir

I wrote you from New York immediately on our arrival and from this on the 16th. inst. enclosing J. Cuylers Bill of Exchange protested—which beg you to collect & with any money you can get from the Negroes remit as when this reaches you they will owe about six weeks wages—and this will lay me under a very particular obligation. We are now living in our own house—a rented one observe at $380 in So. 7th. between Chesnut & Market St. New & decently furnished

Upwards of 160 Privateers have sailed from this & other No[rther]n ports. Captures arrive daily. The war is getting popular spite of the Essex Junto.[80] Have our heroes returned from Augustine. The grateful plaudits of an approving Country wait them. If you can, you ought to make a short trip here just to see Society on a grand Scale.[81]

Do you know that we never are sensible of our attachment to a place till we have left it. Having as yet had no letter from you am quite anxious to have that pleasure. Believe me when I say I truly desire not only to see one but to see you all. My time yet hangs heavy nothing to do and having been so often at the Northward it has lost its novelty. We saw in N.Y. all your friends, except the Jacobs: whose residence was too remote from where we staid to call. We sent yr. Sisters letter & Mrs Leake writes to her with this.

It is said by a recent arrival that in consequence of the distress at home and the clamours of her starving manufacturers and distressed population, the new English ministry have on the 17th. June promised or pledged themselves to a repeal of the orders in Council.[82] Should this prove true it may pave the way to an early adjustment of the differences unhappily subsisting between the two Countries. And the approaching Session of our national Legislature unite, if it is possible to unite the discordant materials of all parties in one common Country. Attacks on the federal presses in Balto continue to be made by the people, in a late one 2 of the assailants were mortally wounded. Dr. Gale & Mr. Williams.

Mr. P & Lady & Mrs. Solomon & sister are well.[83]

Mr Cuylers draft being protested was a disappointment I did not calculate on and hope it will be duly taken up. Please give my Compts & best regards to Mrs. Sheftall. yr Mother & Sister and let me hear of Mordecai.[84] Mrs L unites with me in the warmest wishes for your welfare & happiness & begging you to believe that I am yr friend

Rich. Leake [85]

Dr. Moses Sheftall Sav

Mrs. Leake as well as myself request to be very particularly remembered to your brother Sheftall. & Miss Abigail S. & Mr. & Mrs Delyon & family.

If you can sell Phillis for $300. do it.

69. ROBERT FULTON [86] TO
SOLOMON ETTING, [87] 1814 [88]

New York Nov 26th 1814

Solomon Etting Esq
Dear Sir

Yesterday morning I received your favor of 22 In' And am happy to learn that you have at Baltimore many conveniences for constructing a steam Vessel of War. In placing the funds at the disposal of the United States what is the amount? is it $150000 for her hull and machinery or 225,000 for her total outfit?

In such a work one or two load of my Models must be sent from hence for the castings. One of the Messrs Browns must go to superintend the construction of the hull he having the required experience. Also some of my workmen to construct the Boilers and Machinery Are those arrangements to be left to the secretary of the navy and to me, or is your committee to treat with me on this subject?

What will be the cost of copper per pound for her boilers? 25 tons will be required?

What the price of wrought Iron shafts per pound weighing from 500 lb to $2\frac{1}{2}$ tons?

What the Cylender and hollow castings per pound from 500 lb to $2\frac{1}{2}$ tons each?

How much solid casting such as wheels pinions, beams & Pillow blocks per pound.

How much per pound for brass castings such as Valves Valve seats and gudgion boxes.

On your intended steam Vessel of war I have not yet heared from the Secretary of the Navy.

I am Sir very respectfully   Your most Obedient

Robert Fulton [89]

XXVI
Lotteries, 1815-1819

During the first third of the nineteenth century, lotteries were a fairly common method of raising capital.[90] The purchaser of a lottery ticket gambled on winning a prize; the lottery advertisement reproduced below indicates that there were a number of prizes, and that some of these were rather substantial, up to $20,000. The sponsor of the lottery gained capital in the form of the "house" percentage of the money raised by the sale of tickets. There are said to have been two hundred lottery offices in Philadelphia alone. Lotteries were held for all sorts of worthwhile causes, such as the Erie Canal, Union College (Schenectady, N. Y.), and various synagogues.[91] There were, inevitably, some fraudulent schemes that developed, and some lotteries that were honestly started failed to sell enough tickets to enable payments of the announced prizes to be made. Different states disagreed on the permissibility of lotteries; as a result, at least one case that reached the Supreme Court —Cohens v. Virginia (1820) [92] dealt with lotteries.

70. LOTTERY ADVERTISEMENT, 1815 [93]

Grand National
Lottery,
Authorised

By an Act of Congress of the U. S.
For Washington Canal, positively to commence drawing in August next,
And will draw regularly 3 days in each
week, 600 numbers each day.

J. S. & D. SOLIS [94]
PRESENT TO THE PUBLIC THE FOLLOWING
SCHEME,

Which, perhaps is the most brilliant ever
before published in this country, and
presents more chances for obtaining capital prizes, viz.

[Details of the prizes are omitted.]

Tickets and Shares for Sale

By

J. S. & D. SOLIS,
AT THEIR HOUSES,
No. 22 & 24,
Third-street, between Market
& King streets,
WILMINGTON, (DEL.)
N. B. A premium given for Dollars,
Gold and small Silver.
June 20–4

71. TESTIMONY FROM A LOTTERY
LIBEL CASE, 1818 [95]

Eleazer S. Lazarus,[96] sworn. He has been a co partner with Mr.
Judah [97] in the lottery business since 1809. He knows of no particular intimacy between Mr. Judah and Mr. Sickles. The latter
came frequently to read the newspapers in their lottery office. Mr.
Sickles sometimes borrowed money of Mr. Judah, as well as of the
witness. The witness never knew, or heard, or entertained the
least suspicion of Mr. Judah having information from Mr. Sickles,
or any other person, respecting the day on which No. 3, in Med.
Sci. lottery No. 4, or No. 15,468, in 5th class of the same lottery,
would be drawn, until the report in circulation the day after the
drawing of the latter number. Mr. Judah showed to the witness
the anonymous letter which was spoken of in Mr. Judah's testimony
on Baldwin's trial, two days after the No. 15,468 was drawn, as
the witness thinks. He did not know the hand writing and never
saw it before that time to his knowledge. He does not recollect
that Mr. Sickles and Mr. Judah ever retired into the room back

of the office, to be alone, though they might have done so, as Mr. Judah frequently took persons there to speak to them on particular business, and the witness has also frequently done the same. He knew nothing of the insurance made by Thorne on No. 15,468, until after the number was drawn. If Mr. Judah wished to have a number underwritten on his own account, he would not, as a matter of course, tell the witness of it, nor would the witness inform Mr. Judah of the number of a ticket which he covered, as a matter of course. He had heard the day before Mr. Judah shewed him the anonymous letter, that Mr. J. had hit the offices to a large amount, and that they refused to pay. The day after he heard the reports, he met Mr. Judah, and asked him what the meaning of it was; he replied that he had hit the offices, and they refused to pay, from an idea that there was incorrectness about it. Judah said he was as innocent as a new-born infant. The witness asked him how he came to insure that particular number; when Judah immediately took out the letter, and said it was a letter which had been left at his house, and upon the information contained in it, he had taken that number. Mr. Judah was in the habit of effecting insurances in the former lottery every day, but the witness does not know that he had taken any number before in that lottery (No. 5). He does not recollect whether they took insurance on No. 3, in Med. Sci lottery No. 4, at their office. He recollects paying Mr. Brower, Mr. Burtus, and others, hits on some low numbers in that lottery, but does not recollect that No. 3 was one of them. He does not believe that insurance was ever effected on that number at their office to the amount of $7,000. He never had any intimation that the low numbers, or either of them, would not be drawn out of the wheel until near the end of the drawing, or at any other specified time during the drawing of that lottery, and was never informed that he might safely insure those numbers. He is not acquainted with Frederick Seely. Mr. Judah insured all the overplus that the several offices did not wish to risk. The witness has frequently had an opportunity of knowing the conduct of all the managers, and knows of nothing improper on the part of either of them; on the contrary, he has observed to Gen. Johnson, on some occasions, that he was more cautious and particular than he would probably have been on private transactions of business. The witness thinks that No. 3, in Med. Sci lottery No. 4, was one of the running numbers at their office, and was insured both by the partnership and by Mr. Judah, individually, to an average on the whole lottery, for from $800 to $1,100 per day. He does not recollect telling Mr. T. B. Jansen that he had known Mr. Judah to have made money by insurance out of doors whilst witness as one of the firm had sunk money by insurance in the same lottery. . . .

Mordecai Myers,[98] being sworn. Says, that he was auctioneer in behalf of the managers for the sale of the lottery tickets in the three last lotteries; was afterwards applied to by several persons who had purchased tickets at the managers sales, to re-sell their tickets. At the managers' sale tickets brought from $25 to $25 14. On the [   ] day of August, witness sold at the request of Solomon Seixas,[99] tickets to the amount of $779 62, the first sold for $24 50, and from that price to $23. On the 14th Sept. 1818, sold some tickets on account of David Gillespie. The highest price of some of them was $23 25; the lowest $22 87. The whole amount of this sale was $807 41. This sale was made under the following circumstances: tickets were selling in the Coffee-House under price, and Mr. Gillespie called on witness to go immediately to the Coffee-House and sell tickets for him at auction until he should be requested to stop the sale. The object of this was to drive away those who were selling tickets under the regular market prices. Witness called with Judah at Mr. Baldwin's on the afternoon of the day in which the publication headed "Citizen look out," appeared. Judah told Baldwin that he considered himself implicated in that publication to which Baldwin replied, that he did not think so, and added, that he had not the least intention of doing an injury to him. Nothing in the conversation conveyed the most distant idea that Judah would have been willing to give money in order to have the publication suppressed. Witness never, either at the request of Mr. Judah or of any other person, had any other conversation with Mr. Baldwin upon this subject, but has frequently spoken to him about it of his own accord.[100]

XXVII

Postwar Expansion and Depression, 1819

At the beginning of the nineteenth century, and especially after the War of 1812, there was a significant shift to manufacturing in the American economy. A major element in this new development was the emergence, especially in the New England states, of textile manufacturing—first of cotton goods and later of woolens. Much of the capital that was invested in the early industrial expansion had been acquired through mercantile activity. The Jews of the Middle States and the handful of New England Jews participated in this shift from trade to industry, often, as in the case of the petition printed below, in partnership with non-Jews.

This petition comes on the eve of the depression of 1819. It was in part the excessive overloading of the credit structure during the War of 1812 that was combined with a decline in the demand for foodstuffs for the export trade, over-investment and speculation in western lands, and a contraction in the money supply from 1817 that brought on the crisis two years later. Extant letters, not reproduced here, from Asher Marx [101] and his brother Joseph Marx [102] to Moses Myers illustrate not only the way in which Jewish businessmen were caught up in the depression but also the fact that the failure of one mercantile house might affect the fate of other Jewish firms with which the bankrupt house did business.[103]

72. PETITION FOR INCORPORATION, 1819 [104]

To the Honorable General Assembly of the State of Connecticut
  now in Session at Hartford in said State:
The Petition of Eben. Jesup, Lewis Raymond, & David Richmond of Fairfield in the County of Fairfield, Oliver C. Sanford of Weston in said County & Moses Judah [105] and Joseph Cornell of the City

& State of New York respectfully herewith: That your Petitioners have formed an association for the purpose of pursuing the manufactoring of Cotton & woolen fabrics in the Town of Norwalk in Fairfield County; that they have purchased an eligible situation & contemplate employing a large capital in said business & pray your Honours that they together with such persons as are or shall associate with them may be incorporated into a company under the name of the Richmondville Manufacturing Company [106] with such powers as shall be necessary for the well ordering of the business and concerns of the same; and with the privilege of doing business under an Act of incorporation granted by your Honours, whenever there shall be vested in said Company property to an amount deemed proper & reasonable and to be ascertained by your Honours, and your Petitioners as in duty bound will ever pray.

dated at Fairfield this 8th. day of May 1819

Signed   Ebeneser Jesup
Lewis Raymond
David Richmond
Oliver C Sanford
Moses Judah
Joseph Cornell

XXVIII
Pioneer and Indian Agent, 1820

For such Jewish pioneers as John Hays,[107] a variety of occupations was essential to enable them to establish their families on a firm financial footing. John Hays was basically a fur trader when he first settled in Illinois in the 1780s as an agent of a Canadian firm. Sometime about 1793, he settled in Cahokia, Illinois, as an independent fur trader, having served in the militia of St. Clair County from 1790. His land warrant payment for his military service enabled him to purchase a hundred acres of land; he farmed this land successfully. He held numerous public offices; for many years he was postmaster in Cahokia, a position that yielded him virtually no revenue, but put him in line for other paying positions. For twenty years, 1798–1818, he was Sheriff of St. Clair County. He was Collector of Internal Revenue for the Indian Territory from 1814. In 1821, shortly after the correspondence given below, he was formally appointed as Indian Agent at Fort Wayne,[108] and still later, from 1824, he was Receiver of Public Moneys at Jackson, Missouri.[109] He had married "a lady of excellent family" in Vincennes, Indiana; the couple had three daughters who inherited Hays's estate. Hays apparently retained his sense of Jewish affiliation, although his wife was not Jewish and his daughters married non-Jews. His life may be taken as typical of the small group of Jewish pioneers in the midwest.

73. INSTRUCTIONS TO JOHN HAYS, 1820 [110]

Detroit Oct. 11. 1820

Sir: Your several letters of October 1st have been received.

My letter to you of the 29th Ulto. will have informed you what is my opinion respecting the period when the compensation of Dr. [William] Turner shall cease & yours commence. If you or Dr.

Turner think my construction incorrect, I will request the decision of the Secretary of War.[111]

The articles of agreement, a copy of which you have transmitted, executed between Dr. Turner & Mr. Barber are certainly out of the ordinary course of business. I do not see the necessity of entering into formal contracts for the delivery of articles, which may be purchased at almost all times & places, so long before they are wanted. Nor do I recognize such a Contract as obligatory on the part of the United States.

After paying the Officers attached to the Agency, the residue of the sum appropriated for the expenditure of the Agent is at his discretion. That is, he is allowed to expend it upon such articles, as he may think best for the interest of the U. States, and for the Indians, and as are customary in our intercourse with them. Such quantity of provisions may be issued, agreeably to the instructions, as a sound discretion will warrant, and presents may under the same limitation be distributed. In fact the various contingent demands can neither be foreseen nor recapitulated, and in deciding upon & allowing them, the Agent must be guided by the law, the instructions & his own judgement. . . .

The sum demanded for building the Mills [112] for the Miamies is so great, that every proper caution should be used to prevent imposition. There is no doubt, but that Dr. Turner acted according to the best of his judgement in forming the contract. But I was not satisfied at first, nor am I now, that the sum is not much greater than it should be. The course you propose of inspecting the work is perfectly correct, but in selecting the persons, take particular care that they are not only competent to form a correct judgment, but independent enough to express it. Ideas are frequently too prevalent, that the U.S. cannot pay too much, and in any question between them and individuals, the estimates are rarely as low as they should be. You will not pay for the Mill finally, until the papers are transmitted here & examined.

Your opinions respecting the general impropriety of issuing Whiskey to the Indians correspond with my own. Exceptions of course must be admitted to the general principle of exclusion of which you must judge.

The accounts of Mr. Kercheval for goods given to the Indians are not sufficiently specifick. Instead of entering Merchandize only, he should charge the actual articles delivered. I will thank you to cause particular attention to be paid to this subject hereafter.

If you do not wish to appeal to the War Department on the subject of your salary, it will be necessary for you to transmit me with your next account, a statement of the time, when you commence the execution of your duties. You should in all cases for your own salary, make out an account with a receipt, as in other cases, except that the receipt should state that you have received the amount from the United States.

Contracts for provisions in cases, and in the manner stated in the instructions, are to be formed. That, that Dr. Turner entered into with Mr. Kercheval appears to be fair & reasonable and has my approbation.

I shall write to the War Department by this mail upon the subject of the annuities due to the Miamies.[113]

I must again repeat to you, that I do not consider the U.S. pledged for the full sum claimed for building the Mills for the Miamies. You must bear this in mind in all your proceedings upon this subject.

I am, Sir, Very Respectfully, Yr obt Serv't [114]

John Hays Esq
Ind. Agt Fort Wayne

XXIX

Commercial Instruction, 1825

This letter from Moses Lopez,[115] a New York merchant, to Stephen Gould,[116] his friend and agent in Newport, is typical of such documents of commercial instructions. Gould was told about care of property and collection of rents. There is incidental mention of problems of banking and the discounting of bills. Among the other duties that Gould was ready to undertake was to care for the building of the old synagogue in Newport.[117] The formality of appointing him as agent, however, had not been completed at the time, and Lopez was active in trying to have this agency confirmed.

74. MOSES LOPEZ TO STEPHEN GOULD, 1825 [118]

Newyork Decem 5th. 1825

Esteem'd Friend ⎱
Stephen Gould ⎰

 Capt. Lawton was the bearer of my last to you, about 5 or 6 weeks ago, who having always been punctual in the delivery of my former letters to you, have reason to presume it reached your hands at the time which if so, I anticipated the pleasure of soon after receiving an answer to it on the subject of the house. From the information given me in your last that it required some indispensable repairs before winter my Cousin Aaron Gomez [119] wrote you a few lines in my sd. letter desiring your immediate attention to the shingling of the roof. in particular & to repair only such other parts at present as would not admit of further delay to accomodate our Tenants leaving the rest for the spring or summer, which if my letter did not find the way to your hands I must conclude that nothing has been done & that it may now be too late in the season to begin any thing, should Manchester however think he can yet do it it must be on moderate terms considering the shortness of the days, leaving you to do the best bargin you can. The materials I doubt not you may obtain on a Credit no longer than till the work is done, when you can draw on my Cousin for the amount. of the whole expence including your Commission for the trouble of superintinding the business & the draft will be honorably paid which possibly Edward Lawton may take from you & give you the money then, as he did for me once. In a Conversation lately with my sd. Cousin on the subject of his late purchase of the house some Circumstance occurd to us Connected with our joint Concern in it which made us both think best to have that property at present convey'd to me & in Consequence of it he has authorised me to say to you that if the deed is not yet executed to have it drawn in my name to which you will be pleas'd to attend & to have it recorded before you send it, but if it is already in your hands let it remain so. Some Banks of other States having lately Faild, people here in general are unwilling to take any bills, but those of this City & as I have hitherto made out to pass the Bills of the Newport Bank [120] tho with a small discount I shall be willing to take them when you recived any money for me which please to mention to my friend Betsey Perry. In regard to the synagogue business it must remain this winter as it now stands, Keep the Keys in your hands & if you are not made the agent it will not be from want of exertion on my part to disappiont [sic] your opposers.

Tender mine & family's best regards to your Wife and all friends in general & Close with saying that a letter from you soon will be very acceptable to

Your sincere friend   Moses Lopez [121]

XXX

The Opening of New Trade
Areas, 1826

This letter, from David Nathans to his father, Isaiah Nathans,[122] illustrates the opening of new western areas for trade during the period after the depression of 1819, recovery from which did not come until after 1822.[123] In this case, it was Pittsburgh that provided the locale for the new ventures. At this time, Pittsburgh was just beginning its career as one of the centers of the iron trade, but it had not yet achieved the preeminence it was later to reach. It was a bustling river-port city, booming as a jumping-off place for migrants to the middle western frontier, after they had crossed the Alleghany Mountains. Western products reached Pittsburgh by river and were then hauled by land to the east, and especially to Philadelphia; the importance of this trade is seen from the fact that in 1820 as much as $18 million worth of goods were thus transshipped. It is interesting to note that at this early period Philadelphia merchants, including Jews, were already probing the region beyond the Alleghenies for trade opportunities. Soon afterwards many of these men found their road to fortune in the coal mines of western Pennsylvania.

75. DAVID NATHANS TO ISAIAH NATHANS, 1826 [124]

Pittsburgh July 7 1826

Ever Affectionate Parent
    With the most Lively sensations of pleasure I take up my pen to address you in the enjoyment of perfect health which I pray yourself and all the family may enjoy your affectionate letter I duly recived which afford more real gratification than I possibly can describe to give you a discription of my reception in this City

would defy my abilities Suffice it to say that the Greatest attention possible is paid to me I have visited the various manufactory Establishments about this place which is beyond human Conception my stay in this city will be longer than I expected there are several Lodges in this place [125] I expect to leave it in about a week for Mercer and Erie Countys from thence I turn towards home I expected to have written by Judge Shaler [126] who Left this place on Sunday last but concluded to defer it until the present I shall endeavour to pass through as fast as possible in order to get home by September. as I intend to write next week I will give you a full description of this place, the most Stirring and Lively City I ever visited Steam Boats factorys of all descriptions Stores and Warehouses equal to Philada you can scarcely imagine the Business that is done here I shall pay Strict attention to every thing that may be advantageous to you I am pleased to hear that Phillip is so attentive also of Francis improvement I intend to write to Brother Thomas Grand Secretary next week. I am in great haste as the mail is starting. . . .

I subscribe myself your   Affectionate Son   David Nathans

P S my Best respects to all enquiring friends I have seen many old acquaintances in this City. Ephraim Pentland [127] recorder of this City who carried me to school in my young days & ma others. One of the Andrews Passd through here for Philad I was at Washington [Pa.] therefore did not see him [128]

D N

XXXI
Business Difficulties, 1826

After the major depression of 1819, there was a slow economic recovery in the United States, with another slight downturn coming in the years 1825 and 1826. Mercantile houses, in the southern states especially, were so closely interlinked in their business relations that even a very slight recession could be the occasion of several local crises.[129] The letter below, written by Samuel Hays Myers [130] of Richmond, Virginia, to his uncle, Judah Hays,[131] pictures the effects of such business difficulties. The Cohens of Baltimore, originally from Richmond,[132] are mentioned as having lost a considerable amount in the failure of one of the largest mercantile houses in Richmond. Myers made an interesting distinction between a business failure in New York, "like the wreck of a vessel in the midst of the ocean the waves close over her, and there is an end," and a business failure in Richmond, "left high and dry on the shore where she stands a melancholy monument untill she drops to pieces plank by plank."

76. SAMUEL H. MYERS TO JUDAH HAYS, 1826 [133]

Richmond 11 August 1826

I arrived here my dear Uncle on Tuesday night last, and should have given you earlier notice of it, but I went out the next day to Mr Mordecai's,[134] & have just returned this morning. I had the satisfaction to find all at home well, with the exception of my aunt Katy who had been indisposed, but was convalescent & will I trust shortly be well. This City is full of gloom. The failure of Moncure R. & P. one of our largest houses produced a tremendous shock. Every body is crying out upon the times & you scarcely see a man who does not look absolutely poverty struck. Cohen came on here for the purpose of settling his affairs with the house I have mentioned. As well as I can ascertain he & his brothers are in from 16 or $20000 how much with the house in N. York I cant pretend to say. Yesterday there was a sale of some of the effects of this house & C. purchased at very high prices—say $20 for sugars other articles at a still higher rate, so that I presume he considered the debt bad enough. From the N. York house he said he expected nothing. A failure in N. York is like the wreck of a vessel in the midst of the ocean the waves close over her, and there is an end, but here it is as if she were left high and dry on the shore where she stands a melancholy monument untill she drops to pieces plank by plank. This is being rather poetical, but as I have not absolutely settled down into business,[135] I suppose I may be now and then indulged in a flight of fancy, at least I am sure you will indulge me. I trust however that I shall shortly be fixed in business. I long to be making an independence for myself. I long for it because as a man it is my duty, I long for it because I can not think of involving another in my fate untill I have reason to suppose it might be done without a diminution of personal comfort. You know my dear Sir to what I allude.[136]

Many affectionate enquiries have been made after you, and I am charged to send you many affectionate salutations. Will you be so good when you find it convenient to write as to detail your views of the Culture of the grape. I wish to explain the matter fully to my father [137] & Mr Mordecai. I trust your health improves

My love to Uncle B when you see him. If the Dr is with you I greet him most lovingly.

God bless you   Yr affecte Nephew   Sam. H. Myers [138]

XXXII

Tariff Problems, 1828-1839

Inevitably, as American Jews became involved in manufacturing
and in importing, they had questions to raise with respect to the
administration and the interpretation of the tariff acts.[139] The three
letters printed below raise three different problems in connection
with tariffs. The first letter from Joseph Gratz[140] to Secretary of
the Treasury Richard Rush,[141] concerns goods imported from India
for reshipment and sale in the West Indies. As shipped from India,
the goods were not well-packed for resale; if, however, they were
to be repacked in the United States, they would become liable for
full payment of duty. Gratz inquired about the possibility of having
the repacking done under customs supervision in order to avoid
the payment of extra duty. The second letter, from Benjamin
Gratz[142] to Samuel Ingham,[143] raises a question on protective
tariff, involving an interpretation of the tariff of 1828. As a manu-
facturer of cotton bagging (used for baling cotton), one of the
protected items of American manufacture, Gratz was disturbed
to see competitive fabrics being imported where the specific duty
was being avoided by making the substitute fabric a little lighter
in weight than cotton bagging. To plug up this loophole, Gratz
suggested that fabric should be called cotton bagging and taxed
as such in terms of its use and not its weight. In the third letter, a
manufacturing chemist, G. D. Rosengarten,[144] protested against
paying duty on the raw ingredient for the making of bicarbonate
of soda at the rate of the finished product. In all these cases, it is
clear that the business operations were carried on with a small
profit margin; an additional tariff of even a few cents could so re-
duce the profit as to make the business unrewarding.

77. JOSEPH GRATZ TO RICHARD RUSH, 1828 [145]

Philadelphia March 7, 1828

To the Honble Richard Rush   Secretary of the Treasury
Sir

In all next month I expect to receive by the Ship Pacific to arrive at this port from Madras—a large quantity of Madras and Veutapollence (?) Hndkfs, which have been manufactured at that place for me. These valuable goods, upon which there is assessed a high duty, are nearly all intended to be reshipped to the various markets in the West Indias where they are used. The manufacturors in Madras generally put into the same package Colours, and Patterns which should be kept seperate, if they are shipped as assorted in Madras to any one market their value will be greatly diminished, for the colours & patterns which are much esteemed at one place, and bring a high price, would be entirely rejected at another, but if separated so as to accord with the fancy of those who consume them—generally bring a profit to the shipper—which in the other would have a contrary result—and so abstract from the profits of our commerce.

My object in thus addressing you, is to obtain permission under the inspection of an Officer of the Customs, to arrange the Colours and patterns, and repack them in the same Trunks, of the "same quantity, quality, package and value as at the time of importation." The change would then be, to take Hndkfs of the same cost from one Trunk, and replace them with others of the same cost—All being of the same importation—and thus enable me to have the benefit of the Drawback,[146] and greatly encrease the value of the article in the Foreign markets. If this permission can be granted, it will greatly advance the Commerce in an article—where Capital and Tonnage would be profitably employed—the returns being generally in Coffee and specie

I am with great respect   Your Most Obent   Jo Gratz

78. BENJAMIN GRATZ TO
SAMUEL D. INGHAM, 1831 [147]

Philadia April 1. 1831

Samuel D Ingham Esqr
Washington City
Sir Being extensively engaged in manufacturing Cotton Bagging
in Lexington Kentucky, I was induced to ascertain at the Custom
Houses here, and at New York the quantity of that article imported,
and the rate of Duty at which it was admitted. I was informed
that none had been entered here, for some time as Cotton-bagging,
but that an article was imported corresponding to it in appearance,
invoiced as Burlaps, Ticklenburgs, or Osnaburgs, which in consequence of instruction received from the Comptroller of the Treasury [148] had been admitted at the ad valorem Duty of Twenty five
per cent, on account of its not weighing 16 ounces averdupois per
square yard, that weight constituting it Cotton-bagging, which
alone subjects it to the specific Duty of 5 cents per square yard.
By this construction of the Tariff of 1828 the American manufacturers of Cotton bagging are completely cut off from the protection intended, whilst the Scotch & other foreign manufacturers,
by reducing the weight of their bagging a shade below 16 ounces,
per square yard, introduce it under fictitious names, by the payment of the ad valorem instead of the specific duty; The most
extensive Importers admit that the article invoiced Burlaps &c. of
Forty and Forty two inches in width, is used exclusively for baling
Cotton and is in fact Cotton bagging. The result of my inquiries
in New York [?] was nearly the same, except that a small portion
of Cotton bagging was entered to the specific Duty.
I appeal to you as the head of the Department, to investigate
this subject, of such vital importance to the manufacturers of
Cotton-bagging, feeling confident that after a careful perusal of
the Act of Congress of 1828, you will decide that Cotton-bagging,
shall not be determined by weight, but the use to which it is applied
of Baling cotton, & similar to Cotton bagging made in our country,
which was designed to be protected by the present tariff

I shall leave Philada. next week for Kentucky, you will confer a favour by addressing me on this subject, at as early a period, as your convenience will admit

I am very respectfully your   Obdt Svt   Benj. Gratz

79. GEORGE D. ROSENGARTEN TO JAMES N. BARKER,[149] 1839 [150]

Philadelphia May 29 1839

James N. Barker Esq
Washington
Respected Sir

On calling to day at the Custom house, I am informed by Mr. Stewart,[151] that he has reported to you on the Subject of Some Bi-Carb Sode imported by me. That he has tried to get the best information on the differing of the two Articles (the Carb. or Bi Carb.) referring to some English chemical Works and to Some of our Druggists. With respect to the English Works, allow me to State, that they are very deficient on this Article, that the American Dispens: of Bache & Wood [152] is much more valuable, and much more to be relied on. Respecting the Druggists, allow me to say, that they argue from the principle, that is [sic] was the intention of Government to protect the manufact: Article which is the Bi Carb and Should therefore bear the duty. It happened that Mr Algernon S. Roberts [153] called at the Custom house at the Same time I was there. He on being questioned, imediately Stated to the officers that Carbonate of Soda is the Sal Sode. The Bi Carbonate is as I mentioned in my last only used for Medicinal purpose. As I know your desire to do in these cases justice to all parties, allow me to Send you this Opinion of Some disinterested practical As well as theoretical Chemists, before you finally decide on this Subject. Mr E Durand,[154] well known as an intelligent & respectable Pharmaceutist has promised to Send me his written Opinion on the two Articles. Whatever this may be, I shall take the liberty to enclose it in a letter to you, until than please postpone your decision.

100 lb of Carbon. Sode, when manufactured into Bi-Carbonate, will yield about 45 lb.

With great respect Your obed. Serv   G. D. Rosengarten [155]

XXXIII

Moses Myers and the Port of Norfolk, 1827-1829

After the failure of Moses Myers's business in 1819, one of the expedients to which Myers was led in the attempt to recoup his fortunes [156] was to apply to the federal government for the patronage position as Collector of the Port at Norfolk. When his application was submitted to the President of the United States, a petition supporting him was signed by 49 merchants of the town. Another petition, with 85 signatures, none of Jews, was presented by Frederick Myers to his father on May 1, 1827. All of the signatures had been gathered in one day.[157] Myers received the appointment and proved to be a meticulously honest and efficient government servant.[158] When an attempt was made to oust him from his position and replace him with someone else (probably as an incident in the general reshuffling of patronage jobs after the election of Andrew Jackson to the presidency), a petition urging that Myers be continued in the Norfolk Collectorship was signed by 227 Norfolk merchants.[159] Only one of the signators to this petition, P. I. Cohen,[160] can be identified as Jewish. Myers's integrity and his cooperative understanding of the problems of the merchants led to his being respected and trusted by his fellow citizens without regard to creed. With this support, Myers was reappointed and continued his excellent administration of the Customs office. His tenure was marred only by a long controversy with the Naval Officer for the port, one Thomas Gatewood,[161] who tried to extend the range of responsibility of the naval office and to exercise control over the collector's activities.[162]

80. MOSES MYERS TO
JOSEPH ANDERSON, 1828 [163]

Collector's Office Norfolk
January 15th 1828

Sir

The 18th section of the act of May 7th 1822 provides that "no Collector, Surveyor, or Naval officer, shall ever receive more than four hundred dollars annually, exclusive of *his compensation* as Collector, Surveyor, or Naval officer, and the fines and forfeitures allowed by law, for any services he may perform for the United States, in any other office or capacity." [164]

The practice under this law at this office has been to pay into the treasury, the surplus over four hundred dollars, this being retained for the services, clerk hire, stationary, &ca. incident to the duties of Superintendent of Light houses and Light Vessels; and as Agent for the Marine Hospital; whilst the fees & emoluments of the Collector, have always fallen very far short of the maximum, which by the same act, is fixed at three thousand dollars.

The gradual diminution of the foreign trade of this port, has so reduced the emoluments of the Collector, that the expences of Clerk-hire, stationary and fuel, have of late absorbed the whole receipts; and if no relief is afforded, it is estimated that the support of this office for the current year, will draw from the private funds of the Collector, about three hundred dollars, leaving to himself less than no compensation. It is an obvious fact, that while this reduction of receipts has been gradually increased, that the clerk hire and other expences have rather augmented; because the repeated changes, which by the acts of each successive Congress, subdivide and continually augment the number of Abstracts and Returns, and statistical statements; so that the Clerk-hire, stationary, and expences incident to a faithful discharge of the duties of Collector, have increased in an inverse ratio to the emoluments allowed. I may also add, that the local position of this office imposes on it a large proportion of the foreign and coasting trade, the fees from which are taken at interior offices, such as Richmond, Petersburg, Baltimore, Alexandria &ca.

The number of Light Houses, and Light Vessels under this Superintendency, are ten—imposing heavy and constant duties & responsibilities. The amount of commissions actually earned upon expenditures is, at a rough estimate, about six hundred dollars per annum. It appears to have been an oversight in framing the law, that such a state of things might exist, as to leave a Collector, whose grade is fixed at a maximum of three thousand dollars per annum, in a situation to pay into the Treasury a surplus of commissions for extra service; while he is compelled to contribute from his private means, if he has any, an equal sum, to support the expence of conducting the public business of the Custom-house—leaving him without any compensation whatever for his own services & responsibilities. While on the other hand some Collectors, whose fees & emoluments, after paying all Clerk-hire & expences, give a full maximum compensation of three to four thousand dollars, and leave a large fund to go into the treasury, amounting to about thirty five thousand dollars per annum; and yet receive the compensation as Superintendents of Light houses of four hundred dollars, for a less duty than is performed here.

Under these circumstances, I hope to be excused for asking your interpretation of that law; as I am not apprised that my construction has been hitherto given to it, as calls for the practice here, which becomes now so onerous. I have the honor to be

Very respectfully, Sir   Your mo Obedt.   Moses Myers [165]

Collr.

Joseph Anderson Esqr.   Comptroller of the Treasury
Washington

XXXIV

Benjamin Etting in the China-Trade, 1831

The Ettings, particularly Benjamin Etting,[166] were well established in the China-trade by the time of the shipment with which the document below is concerned. [167] As far back as 1825, Etting was already in this business, importing tea and silk and other valuable Oriental products.[168] Etting could scarcely have known, when he shipped the goods listed on this invoice to Joshua Moses [169] of New York, that he was helping to make history in the China-trade. Yet, it is a matter of record that the Philadelphia-built and Phila-delphia-bound *Atlantic,* under Captain McCall, made one of the fastest passages of that era, 98 days from Macao to Cape Henlopen, Delaware.[170]

81. INVOICE, 1831 [171]

Invoice of Merchandise shipped by Benjm Etting on board the American ship Atlantic. McCall, Master, bound for Philadelphia, for account and risk of Joshua Moses Esqr. N. Y. and consigned to order

—viz—

JM No 1 Ten Cases ea 50 Crape shawls, Damask flowers throughout, Borders & corners richly embroidered in variegated colours of Floss silk, 63 Inches sq. exclusive of
fringe   7 Tale is   500 @ 4.30—   2150   00

" 2 Two Cases ea 50 Crape shawls, Damask flowers throughout, corners & borders richly embroidered with one colour
62 10   100 @ 4.30—   430   00

No 3 Ten Cases ea 50 Satin figured and Damask,
crape shawls, 63 Inches square exclusive
of fringe   5 Tale   500 @ 1.98—   890   00
" 4 Ten Cases ea 50 Satin figured and Damask
crape shawls, 54 Inches square exclusive
of fringe   500 @ 1.28—   640   00
" 5 Three Cases ea 100 Damask crape shawls
assorted cols. 45 Inches square
exclusive of fringe   300 @ 94¢—   282   00
" 6 One Case 25 ps True Dye Scarlet 18 Tale
crapes, in half ps long folded   @ 6.25—   156   25
" 7 Two Cases ea 13 ps high col[ore]d Satins
18 yds 29 In. 32 Tale
26 pc $15 390—
4 ps True dye scarlet
2 ps ea case   c 2.75 11   401   00
" 8 Seventeen Boxes high col[ore]d
sewings 25 lbs ea Box, in ¼ lb.
bundles, colours Scarlet, crimson,
orange, yellow, Royal blue, sky blue,
pink, dark Green and White
425 lbs @ 3.07½— 1306   87
" 9 Ten Boxes sewings, Navy Blue ea 25 lbs
in ¼ lb bundles   250 lbs @ 3.07½—   768   75
carried ford   Dollars   7024   87

Amount brot. forward   7024   87
No 10 Ten Boxes jet black sewings ea 25 lbs
in ¼ bundles   250 lbs @ 2.76⅛—   691   87
" 11 Two thousand boxes fire crackers
ea box conts 40 packs   per box 924 1840   00
Dollars   9556   74

December 9 1821

Benj Etting

XXXV

The House of Rothschild Becomes
Fiscal Agent for
the United States, 1834-1836

The large group of letters printed below tell the story of how the House of Rothschild,[172] distinguished European Jewish international bankers, gained appointment as fiscal agents of the United States. Jewish banking firms in the United States, like R. and I. Phillips of Philadelphia [173] and J. I. Cohen, Jr., and Brothers of Baltimore,[174] were American agents of the Rothschilds, and they had, as these letters show, a part in securing the Rothschild appointment. It is also noteworthy that the commission charged to the United States by the Rothschilds for their services was very low; it is, indeed, conceivable that the agency was sought more for the sake of prestige than for that of profit. Besides the usual business transactions, the Rothschild agency included the special responsibility of collecting sums due to the United States Government and to individual American citizens under the terms of the agreement for the settlement of indemnity claims against France, for interference with American shipping during the Napoleonic era.[175] This delicate matter was carried out by the Rothschilds with success after the death of N. M. Rothschild, the head of the London branch.

82. R. & I. PHILLIPS TO
ROGER B. TANEY,[176] 1834 [177]

Philadelphia April 19th 1834

To the Honbl Roger B Tawney,
Secretary of the Treasy of the United States
Dear Sir,

Being the Authorised Agents of Mr. N M Rothschild [178] of London, who is at the head of his various Houses of London, Paris, Vienna, Naples, Frankfort &c &c we wait upon you now with a tender of his Service for the General Agency of the Govt. of the U. S. for Such Transactions as you may deem proper to entrust to him or them

Learning that the French Claim is about to be closed and the Money to be paid Shortly, we beg leave to State that Messrs De Rothschild, freres of Paris,[179] in Conjunction with Mr. N. M. Rothschild of London, will undertake to receive & remit, the amount either in Five Franc Pieces, Spanish or Mexican dollars, as they may judge most advantageous to our Govt. either from London or Paris; for which they will Charge, only the *Quarter of one per cent Commission and the Actual expenses.*

We make this tender on the part of our Friends Messrs Rothschild, so exceedingly low; trusting that you will give to them the Agency for the General Business of the United States; they having Branches in every Empire in Europe.

We beg leave at foot to furnish the address of their Respective Firms, and Should be happy to receive your early reply,

Remaining,　Dear Sir　Your, most, Obt. Sts.　　R & I Phillips
N. M. Rothschild at London.
De Rothschild, freres at Paris.
M. A De Rothschild [180] at Frankfort.
Baron Charles de Rothschild [181] at Naples.[182]

83. DE ROTHSCHILD FRERES TO
R. & I. PHILLIPS, 1834 [183]

Paris 17th May 1834.

Messrs R & I Phillips   (Private)
Gentn.

Mr. N M Rothschild of London, will probably have informed you, of his having addressed the Secretary of the Treasury of the United States (Mr. Taney) to make a tender of his & our Services, for whatever business the Gov't of the US. may feel inclined to confide to our Care. We have also addressed Mr Taney in the Same Sense & hope it will lead to a favourable result.

Our principal object being much less the profit to be derived than the honour of enjoying the confidence of your Government. We have been induced by that consideration to offer in those letters our Agency on terms extremely low & certainly much inferior to those on which any other House on this Side would undertake those operations, and if not only those overtures on our part but especially the above-mentioned terms Should become known among the Men of Business, at this time principally, when the head of one of the Paris Banking Firms is at New York with views perhaps Similar to ours, we fear it would Subject us, on the part of the Bankers, to a Jealousy, and ill will, which we wish by all means to avoid; and we Should feel extremely obliged to you, if you will without loss of time, Speak or write Confidentially to Mr. Taney on the Subject and explain to him that our Communication was & is intended of a Strictly Private Nature, & that we beg the utmost Secrecy being preserved in regard to this business, whatever may be the disposition or determination of the Competent Authority in this affair.

Please also to express to Mr Tany [sic] our perfect willingness to do at all times whatever the Govt may require. Entirely trusting on your Kindness we remain   Your Most Obedient Sts,

(Signed)   De Rothschild freres

84. R. & I. PHILLIPS TO
ROGER B. TANEY, 1834 [184]

Philadelphia June 20th 1834

Dear Sir,

We took the liberty of addressing you a few days Since with a letter from our Friend Mr. N. M. Rothschild of London [185] & now repeat the pleasure, with the further Tender of Messieurs De Rothschild freres of Paris,[186] to which we beg your attention, Soliciting that the Same may meet with your Sanction & ultimate Success. We beg to ask your noticing particularly the annexed Copy of letter rec'd this day from Messrs. De Rothschild, freres, expressing their anxiety that the *low* terms of negotiating & operating for our Government may be kept Secret & perfectly confidential, for the reason they Set forth.

We further incroach upon your time by remarking that we Should wish those communications only to be known to yourself & Such of the Honble Cabinet as feel interested therein. Likewise Should there be any Change in the Cabinet, we have to ask the favour of your reporting these Communications & invoking your influence for their ultimately receiving the Agency; Expecting Soon to hear from you,

We beg to remain   Most respectfully.   Yr Obt Sts

R & I Phillips

To the Honbl R B. Tawny [187]
Secy. of the Treasy. &c &c

85. JOHN FORSYTH [188] TO LEVI WOODBURY, [189] 1834 [190]

Department of State
Washington 6 August 1834

Hon Levi Woodbury,
Secretary of the Treasury,
Sir,

I have the honor to acquaint you that, under the President's Sanction, I have appointed N. M. Rothschild Esquire at London, to be the Banker of the United States, in Europe after the close of the present year. Messrs. Barings of London,[191] and Mr. Willink of Amsterdam [192] have been advised of this arrangement, and informed that their services in that character will then terminate: and have been requested to pay over to Mr. Rothschild any balances that may remain in their hands to the credit of the United States on the 1st. of January next.

The arrangement made with Mr. Rothschild is founded on his letter of the 14th of May last to you and the letter of his agents Messrs. R & I. Phillips of Philadelphia, of the 17th Ultimo in answer to yours of the 16th. and it is understood that the business to be transacted by Mr. Rothschild is to be done on the same terms as it is now transacted by Messrs. Baring brothers

I have the honor to be Sir   Your Obedient servant,

John Forsyth
[Sec'y of State]

86. N. M. ROTHSCHILD TO JOHN FORSYTH, 1834 [193]

London 29, September 1834.

To the Honorable John Forsyth
Secretary of State, Washington.
Sir,

I have had the honor to receive your much esteemed letter of 6. August last and feel highly gratified at the appointment of

Banker of the United States in Europe, which you have conferred on me with the President's approbation and observe that my functions are to begin on the 1. Jany 1835.

In offering you my most sincere thanks for this distinguished mark of Favor, which I cannot too much appreciate, I beg to add the assurance, that my most anxious cares will be directed towards the strictest and most punctual fulfilment of all the duties connected with my office and every transaction confided to my house, will, I flatter myself, not fail to obtain the entire satisfaction of the Government of the United States.

I fully adhere to your proposal; that the business transacted by me is to be done on the same terms, as it is now transacted by the present Bankers, Messrs. Baring Brothers & Co. of this place, and assure you, that every possible aid will be afforded by my houses in different parts of Europe, whenever occasion may require.

It is perfectly agreeable to me, that no interest is to be charged from either Side, in case of being in advance, and it is understood, that in no case a commission is to be charged to the United States by me, for collecting, receiving, or paying monies on their account.

You enclose a note of the Fifth Auditor of the Treasury, who is the Officer charged with the Settlement of the Accounts of the Bankers of the United States in Europe, which contains the necessary information as to the manner of stating my accounts, which are to be rendered quarter yearly and transmitted in Duplicate by different vessels to the 5th. Auditor of the Treasury [194] under cover to the Secretary of State, which I assure you will be done in the most punctual manner.

You accompany a list, shewing the Diplomatic and other Agents of the United States, whom you instructed to draw on me from the 1. Jany 1835, and should any of their authorized drafts on Messrs. Baring Brothers and Co: not reach London until after the business has been transferred to my house, I shall treat them as if they had been drawn on me. I take due note, that, until otherwise determined, all the agents will be directed to draw on my house here, also that Messrs. Baring Brothers & Co. and Mr. William Willink Jr. of Amsterdam will be immediately informed that their agency ceases on the 31 Decr. next, and that you have requested them to pay over to me the Balances which may then be in their hands, to the credit of the U. States, and to refer to me any drafts which may be presented to them after that time, to which purpose I present them the Triplicates of the letters you enclose.

I beg to assure you, that in case occasions arise, in which the interposition of my house, though not required by any Specific contract, would seem to be called for by the very nature of my relations with the Government of the U. States with a view to the protection of its interest, it will give me the highest pleasure to afford such interposition most promptly and effectually whenever required.

I have the honor to be Sir Your most obedient Servant,

N. M. Rothschild

I beg you will have the goodness to inform me, whether you wish me to address you by each Packet, or only when some business has been transacted.

87. J. I. COHEN, JR., & BROTHERS TO LEVI WOODBURY, 1835 [195]

Banking House of J. I. Cohen, Jr. & Brothers,
Baltimore, May 27th 1835.

Honbl. Levi Woodbury
Sec. Treasury U. States
Sir,

Accounts having been pr. this evening's mail received of the passage of the French Indemnity Bill,[196] we do not delay in availing ourselves of your permission, and the suggestion made to our Mr. D. I. C.[197] in the interview had with you a week or two since, to submit to you in writing our wishes to serve the Department in the Collection of the Government's claim against France.

Having recently extended our Business operations with Europe, we are desirous to receive the confidence of our Government in the Agency, which we presume would necessarily be created in fulfilling the stipulations of the Treaty, and which from our connexions with the House of Rothschild, we should be enabled to execute with every possible facility, and with the promptness which would be agreeable to the Government, and to our own wishes as Agents.

With these views, we propose to forego any pecuniary consideration, and offer to collect the claim free of any charge, other than the actual travelling expences of one of our Firm in the Agency, adding thereto such other costs as might be necessarily incurred in fulfilling the instructions of the Department. We are not aware of what is customary in proposals, or in the offer of services, to Government, in similar cases; on these points we have only to remark, that whatever requirements may be deemed proper or usual, there will be no difficulty on our part, in meeting.

We shall do ourselves the pleasure of a personal communication with the Department in a day or two. In the interim, we have the honor to remain,

With the Highest respect   Yr: Mo: Obt. Servts.

J I Cohen Jr Brothers

88. JAMES HOWARD [198] TO LEVI WOODBURY, 1835 [199]

Baltimore 28 May 1835

Sir

Messrs J I Cohen jr & Brothers having intimated their desire to be selected as the Agents to effect the necessary arrangements for the transmission to this Country, of the funds payable under the French treaty, it affords me pleasure to bear testimony to the high character & Standing of their house. Their foreign associations offer every facility that may be required, and should other measures not have been decided on, and should this important agency be entrusted to the charge of the Messrs Cohen, every duty it involves will, I doubt not, be discharged to the full & entire satisfaction of the Department

With the highest respect   I have the honor to be   Your Obt Sert

Jas Howard

Hon Levi Woodbury
Secy of the Treasury.

89. WILLIAM FRICK [200] TO
LEVI WOODBURY, 1835 [201]

Baltimore May 29th 1835.

To the Honble Levi Woodbury
Secretary of the Treasury
Sir

From Mr Benjn I. Cohen [202] I understand that he hath proposi-tions to offer before the Department of the government over which you preside, and at his request I take the liberty to introduce him to you as a member of the highly respectable banking house of Cohen & brothers so favorably known and deservedly esteemed in our City—The partners of this firm have long maintained a high credit both here and abroad, and I believe I speak the universal sentiment here, in saying that they are fully competent for any engagements and responsibilities, besides trustworthy to any extent that they may deem it judicious to pledge the credit and character of their firm. If the department should find it convenient to respond to the views of the Messrs Cohens, I am persuaded I do not mislead you in my estimate of their standing in our Community.

With sentiments of Respect & Esteem   Your obedient Servant
Wm Frick

XXXVI

Leadership in
"Booster" Organizations, 1837

The Jews in commerce in various cities were active to a degree in "booster" organizations whose purpose was to promote the interests of business in their cities. By the 1830s some Jewish business men had gained sufficient prominence and respect to become elected officials in these organizations. In 1834, for example, J. I. Cohen, Jr.,[203] the Baltimore banker, was elected president of the Convention to promote the Trade and Commercial Interests of the City of Baltimore.[204] Again in 1837, J. W. Zacharie[205] was active in the Chamber of Commerce of the city of New Orleans. In the capacity of committee chairman of one of the committees of this organization, he wrote the letter printed below, suggesting to Levi Woodbury,[206] Secretary of the Treasury, a way in which the commerce of New Orleans with the Mexican province of Chihuahua might be improved by reinterpretation of the tariff laws.[207]

90. J. W. ZACHARIE TO LEVI WOODBURY, 1837 [208]

New Orleans   September 10th 1837.

The Honorable Levi Woo[d]bury
Secty of the TreaSury of the U.S.
Sir.

The Chamber of Commerce of this City have had under consideration the advantages which would result to the trade & Revenue of the United States by such modification of the Revenue Laws, as would admit of allowance of Debenture on Merchandise exported by land to Countries west of Louisiana with the view of bringing this subject under the consideration of the Government, they appointed a Committee to draft a memorial to Congress praying that the Revenue Laws in relation to Drawback & Debentures should be so modified, (with such restrictions as may appear proper & necessary[,] as to allow the export by land the same debenture now granted on exports by Sea, The Committee being under an impression that, it was probably within the power of the Secretary of the Treasury under the Laws of 1805 to permit the export of Mdse for benefit of Drawback by Steam Boats to Countries lying West of Louisiana respectfully submit the subject to your consideration, previous to resorting to a memorial on the Subject which might create more publicity than they deem Judicious as the Mexican Government with their Jealousys towards our Citizens, which has already prohibited the importation of nearly every article of Domestic Manufature of the U. States might take more effective steps to prevent their introduction through this the only Channel left. On reference we find the Law of 1799 Sec. 75. prohibits the allowance of Drawback on goods exported to any foreign State immediately adjoining the U. States & article 92 same Law prohibits the allowance of Drawback on goods exported otherwise than by Sea. The law of 1805 Sect. 2nd amends or alters the Law of 1799. & allows the Drawback on goods exported to Ports Westward & Southward of Louisiana, but says exported from the U. States or Dist. of Mississippi in the manner prescribed by Law, now whether it requires that the goods Should positively go by Sea beyond the limits of the U. States is to be decided, & as many think, that as the Law says Westward of Louisiana it clearly admits of a consideration that would grant the Drawback as on reference to the Map a Westward direction will not reach the Sea before Striking the Pacific, thereby rendering the present construction a nulity.

The subject has been more immediately brought to the notice of the Chamber of Commerce of N.O. by the fact of the arrival recently of a large Caravan from the Province of Chihuahua at a point on Red River above the Raft & thence by Steam conveyance to this City bringing a large amount in Bullion for investment in Merchandise. Chihuahua being one of the Richest districts of Mexico in valuable mineral productions its Mines producing a large proportion of the precious Metals exported from Mexico & isolated as it is from Direct communication with the Ports on the Pacific & on the Bay of Mexico. You Sir will readily perceive the importance to the U.S. of Securing a direct trade in Bullion with that & other adjoining Provinces. The Benefit of inland drawback would measurably if not entirely direct that Trade by the Red River Route instead of the circuitous one through the Mexican Ports on the Bay.

This will more readily appear by a comparison of the distances from Chihuahua to the following places & the cost of transportation from them respectively & also a view of the heavy Charges & Duty payable on Bullion before exportation. The distance from Chihuahua to Matamoros is 1200 Miles Cost of Transportation 17. per 100lbs

"	to Tampico	" 1400	"	"	"	20 23.
"	to Vera Cruz	" 1600	"	"	"	25.
"	to City of Mexico	" 1200	"	"	"	16.
"	to Shreveport on Red River	800				
"	to Santafee	600				
"	to Quaymas Pacific	500	This Route is considered impractible [sic] for Transportation			

From Santafee to
Saint Louis Mo.
the Distance is
computed to be   1400

The Law of Mexico prohibits the exportation of Bullion it is subject

	to 5% for Essaying	
Coinage at Government Mint	5% and	
Export Duty on Dollars	3½%	

Making Thirteen and One Half per cent to which Bullion is subject before it can be legally exported through the Mexican Ports

Requesting the the [sic] favour of an early reply, I am respectfully Your Obedient Sert   J.W.Zacharie
                              Chairman Committee   of N Orleans
                              Chamber of Commerce

XXXVII

Jewish Participation
in an Expanding Economy,
1789-1840

No selected group of documents such as has been presented here can possibly tell the whole story of the participation of Jews in the expanding economy of the young American nation during the half century of its early national period. To tell this story in its fullest extent would require a complete enumeration of all the Jews in the country and the occupations to which they turned their hands at all stages of their lives. Even a partial enumeration, for a single community, would reveal contributions in many phases of economic endeavor that have not been hinted at in these pages.[209] In public records, and in family papers held by individuals throughout the land, there are surely many more clues that might be welded together to make up the complete tale.

Here, to climax this section on how the Jews made a living in America between 1789 and 1840, are two letters showing Jewish activity in railroading and land speculation—the economic activities most closely connected with and revealing of the physical growth and expansion of the American nation. With respect to both of these activities, it should be made clear that the story of Jewish participation is limited. In the early days of railroading, Jews appear as financiers, not as engineers or construction workers. As for land speculation, except in the South, where some Jewish plantation owners are recorded, the Jews made but few ventures in agriculture;[210] here again, their concern with land was for its exchange value, not directly for its productivity.[211]

91. MOSES E. LEVY'S [212] LAND CLAIM
IN FLORIDA, 1840 [213]

Washington 19 June 1840

Sir,

I have enclosed a copy of the Survey of a Tract of land lying on Black Creek, East Florida. Through the neglect of my agent & the inattention of the Surveyor in not notifying the claimants no notice was taken of my tract & it was surveyed as public land. In consequence of this; the land surveyed and confirmed to me, is offered for sale at the St. Augustine Land Office. & a part has already been sold by the Receiver. His reasons are also herewith enclosed.

I wish the sale of the land embraced in the Survey and confirmation stopped. & the Reseipts for each portion as have been sold called in as the purchasers are daily committing waste on my lands under a pretended title from the United States land office.

As this place is impossible for me to fix the precise boundary of the Tract confirmed to me, according to the U.S. Survey the creek called Governor's Creek in the old Survey is the same as Peters' Creek of the late surveys.

[Detailed inventory of the land claim is omitted.]

The above is believed to embrace nearly all lying on Black Creek which is the part likely to be sold now. By giving the above your attention as soon as your convenience will permit, you will very much oblige

Very Respectfully   your most obt. Servt.   M. E. Levy [214]

Hon'l James Whitcomb.[215]
Commission of the Lnd Office.

92. HELPING TO BUILD THE RAILROADS, 1838 [216]

Petersburg October 8. 1838

SIR: We send you inclosed the documents required to cancel Bonds given by us for Rail Road Iron imported in Ship Manchester

—on 22d Febry 1837
Barque Globe—— 18 May "
Ship Washington— 15 June "

You will be pleased to send *to us* an acknowlegment of these documents and an order to the Collector to cancel the Bonds. Our reason for requiring this is, that the present Collector [217] cannot find our bonds among the papers left by his predecessor,[218] who has gone to Europe and we wish to retain some document, in case they shall hereafter appear.

We are respectfully   Your Ob serv   Mordecai & Osborne [220]
To the Comptroller of the Treasury [219]
Washington.

I the undersigned Engineer of the Raleigh & Gaston Rail Road Company,[221] do hereby Certify that Mordecai & Osborne imported into the Port of Petersburg, for the said Rail Road Company on board the Barque Globe, Sillsbee master, from Bristol, on the 18 May 1837, 22632 bars of Rail Road Iron weighing 579 tons, in length 15 feet or thereabout, 2 inches broad, $\frac{1}{2}$ inch thick, with mitred ends and round holes, drilled and Countersunk, all which have been laid on the track of the Said Rail Road.[222]   Chas. F. M. Garnett

I George W. Mordecai President of the Raleigh & Gaston Rail Road Company, do hereby Certify that Charles F M Garnett is the Principal Engineer of said Road and that full faith should be given to his Certificate. Witness my hand this 6 day October 1838

Geo. W. Mordecai
Prest R & G R R Co

Collector's Office Petersburg
I J. W. Campbell Coll of the District of Petersburg do hereby certify that the Rail Road Iron Imported by Mordecai & Osborn for the Raleigh & Gaston Rail Road Company as Stated in the above Certificate of Ch. F. M. Garnett, Chief Engineer of the said R. & G. Rail Road, as imported in the Ship Washington June 15th 1837 corresponds to the Entries in this office. Given from under my hand this 7th day of Oct. 1838   J W Campbell Coll

Part Three
The Family and Social Life

The outstanding and most noteworthy feature of the social life of the Jews of the United States between 1789 and 1840 is that it follows so closely the pattern of social life in the American milieu. The small group of American Jews lived chiefly in the major seaport cities of the young country, although as time went on their business enterprises spread more widely into some of the smaller, often frontier, communities. The older established families inbred to a considerable degree. The young people of the Gratz family married into the Simon family, the Etting family, or the Phillips family. There was, too, a moderate amount of intermarriage. It is also worth noting that a significant group, especially in the older families, remained single, living in brother-and-sister households. In effect, the major families became one big family, and the extent of this sprawling group provided for a considerable part of the social life of its members. Visits to the sick or the well, correspondence, parties, and celebrations occupied the time of the members of these large groups.

It may be argued that the degree of cohesiveness and family sentiment displayed by the members of these groups should be regarded as characteristically Jewish. Certainly, there is evidence in the family correspondence collected below that both cohesiveness and sentiment were present in superlative measure. Joys and sorrows were not at all private affairs; each man lived his life in the clear light of family concern. Nevertheless, this cannot be shown to have been distinctive of the Jewish groups; the comparably well-established non-Jewish families, like the Adams family of Massachusetts or the Madisons of Virginia, held together in similar fashion. Again, although the evident and surface quality of these clans was unity, there were occasions when sharp breaks took place beneath a placid surface. The Gratz family had such a lasting feud, and, in its ramifications, it involved even the matriarchal Rebecca. On the balance, however, the force of familial affection and unity was far stronger than its opposite.

In general, because at this period the United States was a nation of relatively little social sophistication, and because marked distinctions of birth, breeding, and wealth had not yet had time to break down the egalitarian sentiments of the era of the Revolution which were still strongly rooted in the popular mind, larger, non-familial social affairs tended to be relatively simple and community-wide. Especially in smaller towns, ceremonial balls on patriotic occasions were attended by both Jewish and non-Jewish residents. Parades were popular with the old as well as the young. Faint heralds of an American theater were beginning to appear in Charleston, Philadelphia, and New York, and "first nights" were already important social occasions, especially when the play to be produced had been written by a member of the local community or when a distinguished actor or actress was to appear. Social clubs did not flourish until a later period, though in the few years before 1840 a number of them were founded. But each of the major communities had its "literary" society, attended by both Jews and non-Jews, and many a reputation for ability was originally founded at these clubs. The Masonic order was, of course, strong, and many Jews were to be found in its membership. Jewish fraternal orders, however, were still a thing of the future. It was in these simple ways that a larger social life than the family afforded was made available to the Jews of the time.

In the schools that most of the Jewish children attended as well as in many of the social affairs that occupied their leisure at a somewhat later period of life, Jews and non-Jews were brought together in a nonsectarian environment. Some of the friendships thus formed held together through life and the diversity of interests that the chances of life brought about. In this way, too, a breath of air from a larger world was drawn into the relatively constricted atmosphere of the clan-family. Travel was not easy, and yet, with the aid of a chain of relatives and friends in various cities, many of the young people had the opportunity to go on a sort of American version of the "grand tour" before settling down to a career. Often, this period of wandering was tied to the training of young men for business careers and to their introduction, through business associates, to a wider social group. Whatever the immediate occasion, the tour did serve to orient the young people to the lives and the society in which they were to live. We must not forget that adolescent perplexity and lack of direction is not a new thing in the world, but that each generation must find its own technique for easing the transition into adult responsibility.

Again, the American world of this age was one in which violence was very near the surface and likely to explode at any moment, not only in frontier communities but also in the more settled towns and cities. In addition, the Southerners maintained the old European code of honor, requiring a duel to avenge any insult. The Jews, too, reveal this occasional eruption of violence; while they are by no means everyday affairs, there were duels in which American Jews participated; there were fist fights; there was at least one case of homicide. We see again how the Jewish Americans blended into the American background by the occasional occurrence of these antisocial acts.

On the frontier, too, violence was to be found, both in its antisocial forms and in the socially accepted form of military activity, chiefly directed against the American Indians. Although in many cases, this type of activity was more mercantile than military, there were members of the Jewish group who participated in the necessary but unpleasant task of pacifying the frontier. There is no indication that the Jews felt any special sympathy for the Indians whom the expansion and pacification displaced. Again, the Jewish American thought as his fellow Americans thought, and he lived as his fellow Americans lived.

XXXVIII
A Son to His Father, 1790

Young Dr. Moses Sheftall [1] of Savannah went to Philadelphia late in 1790 to conclude his arrangements for marrying his sweetheart, Eleanor or Elkalah, a sister of Dr. Solomon Bush.[2] Since he had not heard from her for some time, Moses Sheftall was concerned lest his hopes be disappointed. The young lady assured him that she had written, and that her letters must have miscarried. This letter to his father tells of his happiness and asks for a parental gift "to begin the world with" so that the soon-to-be-married young couple may establish themselves. It is pleasant to be able to record that either this provision or some similar satisfactory arrangement was made, for, on February 14, 1791 (Moses Sheftall probably did not realize that this was Valentine's Day), he wrote to his mother: "Permit me to Inform you that the Wednesday after Purim is the day alotted to make your son happy by his being united to the Dear object of his affections and in behalf of that Dear girl receive the grateful acknowledgement of both our Hearts for your kind wishes towards us and with truest & most sincere duty do we acknowledge thy proferred Service of becoming a mother to the Intended partner of your sons Heart, whose constant study will ever be to merit a Continuance of your Kindness towards her, happy shall We be on the day which makes us one Thrice Happy should we have been could it been possible for my proud mama to have been present." [3]

93. MOSES SHEFTALL TO
MORDECAI SHEFTALL,[4] 1790 [5]

Philadelphia Novr 16th 1790

Honored Father/

after a passage of 8 days I arrived here in health, Immediately after landing I waited on Delany & gave him the Sum alloted for him, I also Settled with Mr. L. Philips [6] to his Satisfaction I am now boarding with him No 17 South third Street,

I have Seen Doctor Bush and on my meeting with him he gave me every Satisfaction that I as a man of honor could wish or expect, his Sister being in Town I waited on her who Express'd great Satisfaction at seeing me as you may readily suppose as her attachment appears unalterable toward me, I mentioned too her my not having received a Single line from her during my absence, she then declared to me upon her word She had wrote me four different Letters, this may I readily Conceive be the Case as Mr. Leaming [7] and Mr Hays [8] likewise Mr Phillips mentioned that they had wrote me none of which ever Came to hand. At this Period do I anxiously wait for my honored Father's opinion respecting my bringing out my Lovely little Girl as she has declared she is willing to go with me whenever I please or wait untill I think it will best suit me, now Sir Should my Honor'd Parent feel disposed to bring me forward into life by giving me Something to begin the world with that and the Prospect of Good share of Practice will make me happy with her I so sincerely love; many would be the reasons that I could give for my wishing to bring this Lady with me this Spring, one alone I am well convinced will Induce my Father to think me weight[y] that is In point of religion.

I trust you will write me on this subject fully & early, that I may better Judge how to act.[9]

I have seen Major Butler [10] of South Caroli[na] and he has pledged himself to Serve me all that he possibly can, & Doctor Rush [11] & Col. Gunn [12] are still my friends.

I am Endeavouring to get the sour crout [13] to send by Burrows.[14] My Duty to my mama I remain   honored Sir your ever dutiful Son

Moses Sheftall

XXXIX

A Daughter to Her Father, 1791

The "axis" between the Jews of Pennsylvania and those of Maryland is well-illustrated by this brief letter from Rachel Etting to her father. The names of elder Baltimorean ladies who have paid courtesy visits to the newcomer are familiar to her father; they are old acquaintances. Though her marriage has taken her to a new home, Rachel is not forced to make her way among strangers. The letter also exemplifies the close and devoted relationship between father and daughter that is so often to be found in American Jewish families.

94. RACHEL ETTING [15] TO BARNARD GRATZ, [16] 1791 [17]

Baltimore November 13th 1791

My ever Hond Parent

I was made very happy on Fryday last on the receipt of your welcome Letter, as an assurance of the welfare of my dearest father, is the first wish of my heart, continue to favour me frequent, thereby affording much satisfaction to me, and flatter myself with the pleasure of soon embracing you, and convincing you verbally, how very happy I am situated, and with the wish of entertaining my dear father, is the most earnest of my solicitations, do not disappoint my best of parents that of your not accompanying me, was painful, therefore entreat you will not prolong your stay, But hasten to make perfectly happy your grateful Daughter, I this morning was favoured with a visit from Mrs Levy [18] who was very pressing in her invitations to me, amidst the many I have received from the people who have called on me, one of the number was an old acquaintance of yours, a Mrs Hunter(?) who was very particular in her enquiries about you and wishes much to see you, from what little I have seen of this place, think I shall like it very much, as it far exceeds my expectations. My dear Sally [19] is well and intends writing to you, Mrs, Etting [20] and family beg their best respects to you, as does Mrs Solomons,[21] it is now late and am fearful of missing the opportunity, must conclude, with my most ardent wish for your health, and Contentment, remain your most affectionate and Dutiful Daughter

Rachel Etting

Please to present my best regards to Mrs and Mr Josephson, Mrs and Mr Cohen, with all other friends.

XL
A Brother to His Sister, 1793

The business-like tone of the opening of this letter of congratulation from Simon Gratz [22] to his sister Richea [23] on her engagement sets off with a delightful charm the pious and moral injunctions that follow. The ideal of the "mother in Israel" was clearly present to Simon Gratz's mind as he wrote; and it seemed to him that the ideal had been realized in his mother.[24] Thus this letter not only reveals the strong ties of affection that bound this sister and brother but also suggests that maternal example had much to do with setting the pattern for the members of a devoted family.

95. SIMON GRATZ TO RICHEA GRATZ, 1793 [25]

Lancaster August 5th 1793

The letter of the 1st Instant from my dear Sister I now seat myself to Acknowledge, its Contents I duly note, The Subject it treats on, is of the most interesting nature and I hope my dear Sister gave it the Consideration due; you are now about to enter into a state wherein I hope and pray you may experience nothing to give you pain, but on the Contrary, enjoy perfect happiness and tranquility, but my dear, you must remember that to ensure to yourself, and to the man you love a lasting Continuance of happiness, you must ever make it your Constant duty and Study to please; in short, Copy our Amiable and Virtuous mother, act as she does; and you will ensure to yourself and to all about you Contentment, but as a preliminary to all happiness, lett a due sence of Religion, and a proper Attention to the precepts and Commands of the great God always actuate you, and place your Sole Confidence & trust in him.

Be pleased to remember me Affectionately to Mr Hays.[26] I shall be down at Philadelphia immediately after the hollowdays [holidays], and shall then spend some time with you. Grandpa [27] desires his love to you & begs you would write and inform him how Aunt Leah [28] is, as his Greatful Son-in-Law Mr Phillips [29] has not thought proper to write him a line this 5 months. I shall write to you again Shortly but in the intrem, believe me to be with Constant prayers of your happiness your ever affectionate Brother and well wisher

Simon Gratz

XLI

An Aunt to Her Niece, 1795

Two themes appear contrapuntally in this letter from Aunt Shinah
(Simon) Schuyler [30] to her niece Richea (Gratz) Hays. The major
theme expresses joy and congratulations on both the birth of Richea's baby daughter and a marriage in the family. The minor
theme, constantly recurring in the letters of the aging or aged, expresses sadness because of waning health. Mrs. Schuyler, wife of
a doctor, was isolated and lonely in Lansingburgh. Her health was
poor, her sight was failing. She missed the attentions of her family.
The eighteenth century was certainly not kind to some of the old.

96. SHINAH SCHUYLER TO RICHEA HAYS, 1795 [31]

Lansingburgh April 6 1795

My dearest Richea's agreeable Epistle has too, long, remained un-
answered, tho not forgotten by your afflicted aunt. I have been
almost deprived of sight the violent disorder of the winter before
last had weakened my Eyes since I have had frequent inflammations
and they are exceedingly dim at present but I can no longer continue a silence—which deprives me of hearing from my Dearest
friends. I sincerly congratulate you and your worthy husband on
the birth of your lovely Fanny its beauties have been discribed by
my dear Simon [32] and Hyman [33] and I immediatly conceived the
idea of my Richea, at her age I wish I could clasp her in my fond
arms—which happiness god grant I may experience this summer.
I tremble With the apprehensions of not accomplishing my darling
wish—its ever nearest my heart, the embraceing my dear aged
parents and family should I not encompass my desire. I fear the
dreadfull consequence of another disappointment as I shall certainly
fret myself to *Death*—which will at once end all earthly anxiety—
we enjoy so scanty a portion of happiness in this sublunary abode

without health and distant from all my immediate connections that I feel a discontent prevade me which I would willingly shake off as not inherient to my naturel dispos[it]ion-your dear enliv[en]ing society will I hope disapate all gloom. I have still another cause to congratulate you on the marriage of my dear Fanny [34]—as soon as the intelligence arrived I intended immediately writing to my dearest sister [35] to convince her I sincerly participated in all her happiness that was denied me for I could scarsely peruse they letters that conveyed the pleasing information. Present her my dearest Richea my mo[st] tender gratulations on my Fannys felicity and on your own account in presenting her a grand Child as she has ever been the most tender affectionate parent. She must be infinitely happy in her Childrenns offspring. I confess my astonishment on hearing of the Marriage of Fanny to R. Etting [36] as you never mentioned his attentions to her—when last in Lancaster I heard him well spoken of by the girls. I have never seen him since a boy—from that to the period of manhood it frequently happens, favorable changes in poi[se?] & understanding—from Education or other effects with a good Company—or a laudable ambition will make a man shine that was depressed in youth. R. Etting was I very well recollect good disposition'd. Simon mention'd him as an exceeding worthy Character which gives me infinite satisfection, as I feel myself interested in whatever concerns my Dear Family. Is he in Business or in Sheriff's Office? When you write to Baltimore please to present them my most affectionate Salutations. I sincerly pray every good may attend them. I have anxiously expected your dear father all this winter I went to Albany once my dear Doctor inquired particular for him—we could gain no information. Tell him lands are now at immense Value which may not last long. He had best view them at an advantagious season. *May* would be most propitious to good fortune.[37] My tenderst Love awai[ts?] my dearest Sister's. How does your kind Husband [38]—mine often talks of our Richea and Joins me in wishing to emb[race] her lovely Daughter impress on its sweet lips ten thousand kisses for both. Write soon my dear girl and all the news. So Hetty is with you I hope her conduct may be such as to render [you] all happy my Love to her tell her my happiness will depend on her good conduct! oh let her be virtious— and she must make us all happy poor girl I think she has been cruelly neglected—let her sisters and you my Richea watch over her she deserves our compassion. Do you ever hear of poor Relahs Children—how are they [   ] was a lovely boy I hope they are all well when I sat down I thought to write a few lines to my dear girl—I now find it impossible to break off—true it is I love to Converse with my Richea tho my dim Eyes will scarce admit of [my concluding?] in praying for your health and happiness may you continue long a Blessing—and Blessed—is the ardent wish of

Shinah Schuyler

after looking over my letter I find I can scarcely read it pray endeavour to peruse, and excuse it I dare not attempt another untill my Eyes gain Strength.

XLII

Letters to a Christian Friend, 1805-1809

These letters document the continuing friendship of Rebecca Gratz [39] and Maria Elizabeth Fenno,[40] who, by the time of the second of these letters had married Judge J. Ogden Hoffman [41] of New York. Maria Fenno Hoffman was not only a leader in New York society but also a member of the literary circle that included Washington Irving.[42] Irving was, in fact, engaged to Matilda Hoffman, daughter of Judge Hoffman by his first wife. It was in this way that Irving came to know Rebecca Gratz and, if the legend be true, to suggest her to Sir Walter Scott as the living model for the character of Rebecca in *Ivanhoe*.

There is a sense in which it can be said that Miss Gratz drew all the "outsiders" with whom she corresponded, both Jewish and non-Jewish, into a large family circle. She passed news of them from one to another so that even if they were never personally acquainted her comments made them feel so. She was, of course, unusual in this respect, and the amount of her correspondence that has survived is also remarkable.[43] Yet her exceptional talent for friendship has a representative character and her letters preserve for us much of the flavor of social relations in this period.

97. REBECCA GRATZ TO MARIA E. FENNO, 1805 [44]

Philadelphia Feby. 22nd 1805

I was just going to begin in my ordinary way to answer your letter, circumstantially, when the date the 22nd of February caught my attention and turned the whole current of my thoughts. For some minutes I have been reflecting on the former honors that were paid to it and the illustrious Hero to whom those honors were so justly due. But a few Years have passed since the birthday of Washington was hailed with enthusiasm by every american: now it passes unobserved, but by a scanty number whose languid patriotism is content with giving a dinner to get drunk in celebration of the anniversary.[45] This however is the general doom. All things of this world shall pass away and be forgotten.

But your letter, my dear Eliza, your letter requires an answer and you will forgive my not attending to it before. If I could participate in all the pleasure, all the rapture you communicate, I should not have delayed one moment to tell you so, but experience has proved to me that the source from which it is derived, will not continue to produce the gratification you expect.

It is three years, since, as great an admirer of Cooper [46] as yourself, B. H. was introduced to him and thought nothing would afford her greater pleasure than to hear him converse, to be acquainted with a man, who so emminently possessed the power of delineating the passions & characters of human nature she thought too his mind must be stored with a large portion of the excellencies he could so well represent, and with all the enthusiasm of her character expressed her admiration feeling herself perfectly secure, that a Player & a married man would be sufficient apology for all she might say, and that no one would think she harboured a thought that it would be improper to express. Indeed I believe she expressed much more than she seriously thought or felt, but not so much as was repeated to him, he is a man of great vanity and thus encouraged, sought every opportunity of being with her, joined her in the street when ever he saw her, and walked past the house a dozen times a day. Until his wife heard it, grew jealous and became unhappy. B. too was equally a sufferer, nay a much greater sufferer—for her home was continually abused, every kind of calumny was invented that could stigmatize her character and not only Phila. but perhaps where her name was never heard before resounded with the scandal, which she very little meritted.

I do not attach any kind of disgrace to C.s conduct with her. He is a gay, dissipated young man married to an old woman whom he cares nothing about and consequently neglects to seek for pleasures abroad. This to be sure is violating his duty in the most material point and if women were as pure moralists as an author of

a novel delight to make his heroine, would be sufficient to exclude
him from female society, but in the present state of manners 'tis
a venal fault and too frequently has occurred to be punished, and
in him perhaps, is more excusable than many others. I do believe
his conversations with B. were such as she might have listened to
from any other married man, of her acquaintance, but she so frequently expressed admiration, and perhaps felt that kind of par-
tiality which Girls are apt to call by the most passionate name, that
every one condemned her imprudence. Her friends might excuse,
but the rest of the world most severely censured.

it is for this reason My Eliza, that I do not partake in the pleasure
you express. I have no fear of you falling in Love with him, or into
the errors from which she has suffered, but that from the recent
noise their intimacy made, he will be more particularly observed
and as he is not generally admitted in female society, those Ladies
with whom he is seen, will be considered less tenacious of their
company or more indifferent to the general opinion which has always excluded players (except in a few instances, where merit has
triumphed over prejudice) from the higher rank in society. Be not
affected at what I have said, if I did not love you! I should not
have thought so seriously on the subject. If I had loved you but
a little, I should not have hazarded your displeasure, but as I love
you with the sincerest affection and proudly aspire to be called your
Friend, I must try to deserve that title by prefering your future
welfare even to your present gratification.

Mr Ewing [47] returned yesterday from Washington I asked him
concerning your Friend Mr Dunscomb, he says he saw him, but
for a few minutes and had but little conversation with him, which
sufficiently exhonorates D from the charge of making any boast to
him and I strongly suspect it was on some recollection of an *old*
report that Mr. E mentioned to Rachel what has so much surprised
him.

I thank you for James Pauldings [48] verses they are very pretty
and deserve to be preserved, but I shall not expose you to his censure by shewing them, when you see him, give my respects, or compliments or regards to him, we frequently talk of him, and are
high[ly amused with] parts of his letters which he sometimes in-
dulges u[s with the sight] of. In one of them honorable mention

was made of —— and two whole pages filled with the ebbulitions of wit & pleasantry inspired by her *Venus & Minerva-like* qualities.

My Mother & the girls send you their affectionate love, in which Sim & Jo unite; we expect Hyman home in about a fortnight, my sisters Hays & Etting with Miriam & the Girls send theirs. Matilda has a bad cold but is not sick with it. She was at a Ball at Nicklins (?) on Monday and will come here as usual to morrow.[49] My best love to my dear Maria, I will write to her very soon. Sally had a letter from Muriel(?) a few days ago, which mentions that Rodman would be in New York in a few days, remember me to him if he is with you. To my dear Anne, present my affectionate love and tell her "when summer comes again" I hope she will have time to think of her Phila friends. I have been confined for a whole week with a swelled face, which as the Mumps are fashionable, has been supposed to proceed from that disorder tho' I have had no pain, however it has kept me out of the way of hearing news and therefore must be my apology for telling you none and that is the reason I have told you of them. God Bless you, my dear Eliza write to me soon, & tell me I have not forfeited your affection which is so valuable to your friend　　　　　　　　　　R[ebecca] G[ratz]

98. REBECCA GRATZ EXPRESSES HER CONCERN, 1809 [50]

March 7th 1809

My Dear Maria

We are greatly distressed at the accounts of our dear Matildas [51] illness. I have thought of nothing but her, since I learned of it, your letter alarmed me, but I was quite indisposed myself and not able to write yesterday. Mr Hoffman's letter has however put all my pains & weakness to flight, in the consideration of the greater evils which impend over my Beloved Friends. God in his mercy will I trust spare the dear Girl to you, for a Blessing—she has ever been deservedly your darling, and my heart is cheered with the hope that her existance will be preserved to fulfil, the promise which her early virtues hold out to her affectionate parent, The mail arrived so late to day that I had not time to tell you how sincerely I partake your sorrow or how earnestly I hope & pray for her recovery. I sent immediately to inform Charles N.[52] and expect he will be the bearer of this, his presence may be consoling to Mr Hoffman, tho' I trust he will be relieved before he arrives. her youth, and patient disposition are greatly in her favor, and the affectionate attendance she receives will keep her mind from despondency. Who are her physicians?

I know my Dear, you cannot avoid a large share of fatigue, your feelings & inclination will keep you at her bedside but I beg for your infant's sake that you will endeavour to keep up an appetite, and a tolerable share of composure, which you know are indispensable as a nurse.[53]

Wednesday

Mr Hoffman's letter My beloved Maria, has brightened my hopes. God is merciful! and will listen to the prayers of the afflicted. May our Dear Matilda soon be restored to reward the anxious sufferings of her tender Parent. I am quite grieved at her Fathers misery, but hope tomorrows letter will be written in greater confidence Charles I find does not leave town until Tomorrow. I will not trouble you with a longer letter. My heart is with you, and my prayers meet yours at the mercy seat of God for the boon of health to our mutually Beloved Matilda Adieu My Dearest Friend, ever yours

RGratz

XLIII
The Code of Honor, 1832

There were not many Jewish plantation owners in the South before 1840. But Jewish merchants and their families, living in the South, readily adopted the aristocratic patterns of behavior that were prevalent in that region. The *code duello* which guided southern gentlemen in avenging slights, whether real or fancied, to their honor was a part of the romantic and chivalric atmosphere of upper class society before the Civil War. Southern Jews, no less than their non-Jewish contemporaries, became involved in this pattern of permissible, and even socially approved, violence. Mordecai M. Noah, during his Charleston years, several times narrowly escaped becoming a principal in duels.

The Myers shooting is typical of one phase of violence in avenging insult, though not by duel. Here, the insult to be avenged was the beating of a father. The son, a hot-headed young man, cut through fine points of the code of honor to take direct revenge by shooting his father's assailant. That a court adjudged this homicide to be manslaughter rather than murder is evidence than young Myers' action was approved by the society around him. One might speculate on the reasons for the avoidance of a duel in this instance; was it merely Samuel Myers's hot temper that led to direct action? Or, since a duel had to be between social equals, was there perhaps implicit in the choice a reflection on the social standing of the victim? [54]

The requisite of social equality was met in the case of the Stark-Minis duel. Early in the spring of 1832, James J. Stark, a member of the Georgia legislature, made derogatory remarks about the religion of Dr. Philip Minis, who was of a prominent Jewish family of Savannah. The insult having been given, the affair festered. Apologies were tendered, and then withdrawn; further provocations occurred. Both participants were caught in the web of the code of honor, and withdrawal without loss of face was impossible.

The tragic climax was reached with the death of Stark. Local passions were deeply aroused by the duel, yet a jury sitting in judgment several months later found Minis not guilty. Indeed, even though several states had laws prohibiting dueling, it was rare for juries to find duelists guilty of murder.

99. THE STARK-MINIS DUEL, 1832 [55]

August 9th

10 p.m. This has been an eventful day. At a little past 12, Stark [56] and Minis [57] met at the City Hotel when M. pronounced S. a coward. S. advanced and, Spalding says, put his hand in his pocket and drew something. He could not ascertain precisely what, when Minis drew and shot Stark through the upper part of the left part of the thorax, [the bullet] passed behind the top part of the scapula, and through it into the side of the door which leads back from the bar room of the hotel.

This difficulty took its origin from abuse uttered by Stark last spring at Luddington's bar room. Stark, when Minis was not present, one night without any provocation, cursed Minis for a "damned Jew", a "damned Israelite", "he ought to be pissed upon", "he was not worth the powder and lead it would take to kill him", and abuse of a similar character. Some person had gone to Minis and told him that he was very much abused by Stark round at Luddington's, and he had better go there. After the first words uttered by Stark, he had wished to kick up a difficulty with me; but it had been adjusted, and I had gone off. While the company were still at the bar taking the drink to which they had been invited by him, on our difficulty being settled, Minis entered the room, and John informs me that on seeing him enter, he exclaimed, "Minis, I am damned glad that you have come here." Minis stayed a long time in company, but Stark said not one word about him. When Minis asked me what S. had said about him, I refused to tell him, observing that he, Stark, had had an opportunity of saying it that night before his face; and, as he had not done it, I thought that what he had said ought to be a matter of indifference. Bryan, that morning, I believe, went to Stark as Minis' friend, and on his return, told Minis that he was perfectly satisfied with Stark's explanation, that it was satisfactory in every point of view.

Last 4th of July, at the Mansion House, the affair was spoken off, and it was observed that Stark had made an apology. This Sturges [58] denied, saying that Stark had told him that what he had said was in justice to himself, but not as an apology to Minis. Bryan then wrote Stark who was in Glynn County, requesting him to contradict the reports in circulation about Minis. Now, the reports alluded to were that Stark had made no apology; and, of course, that Minis, after demanding one and not receiving one, had backed out in not following it up. Stark replied that whatever reports were in circulation, he had nothing to do with their origin or circulation. Bryan replied that he was glad to hear this, recalled to Stark's mind the expressions used by him when he apologized, and asked for them in writing. Stark replied, and the body of his letter acknowledged that he had done an unnecessary injustice to Dr. Minis, but still did not mean it as an apology to him.

M. then wrote to Stark, saying that as he, S., had confessed doing an unnecessary injustice to him, M., he demanded an apology, or that satisfaction which one gentleman should afford another. This letter was written July

August 9th at 12m.

Stark sent M. an answer that he should have satisfaction, and Mr. Wayne [59] would make the necessary arrangement. Mr. Wayne handed in his articles, to fight with rifles at 5 that afternoon. Spalding objected to them. He objected to the rifle as unusual, but if his friend could obtain satisfaction no other way, he accepted the rifle as the weapon, with certain provisos, which he submitted as articles to be agreed on between him and Wayne. The time fixed on was instantly rejected as being too soon, and before Spalding left, I observed that were I in Minis' place, I would not fight with so unusual a weapon, and such short notice.

When Spalding was about leaving M's office at 12 o'clock, Minis observed that, as regarded arrangements for time, any time the next day would suit. Minis' rifle was then at the gunsmith's. Wayne, on Spalding's delivering his objections, said they were of no weight; no preliminaries were discussed. Wayne said he must insist on his articles, and according to one of them, he and Stark would be together at Scriven's Ferry at 5 that afternoon. Spalding said (verbally) that it would be of no use, for that neither he nor his principal could possibly be there. Wayne and Stark accordingly proceeded there, made a flourish, shot rifles, etc., and returned to town flushed with a victory over the [aff]air.

Immediately upon their return, it was rumored all about that Minis and Stark were to have fought, and that Minis forgot the hour. Now, unless they went over the river to create that impression, for what purpose could they have gone over, for Spalding repeatedly assured Wayne that neither he nor his principal could be on the ground. Or, was it because the courage was screwed up to the sticking point for the day and was in danger of getting loose or breaking if kept too long on the stretch? What! Give a man but five hours' notice! I was to have been Minis' surgeon, and I never dreamt, when I was told an answer was to be given at 12, that I would have to go that afternoon. . . .

I have heard it said that Minis was openly laughed at, as a coward, by Stark's bodyguards. In the course of the morning, as it had been suggested that Minis ought to show himself in public and not keep out of sight, as if the atrocious calumnies circulated about him had any foundation, Spalding and he walked to the City Hotel, and went into the public bar room. Wayne and Stark were not in the room, when Marm went upstairs to them and said Minis and Sp'g were below and wished to take a drink with them. They went downstairs, and when M. saw Stark, he said, "I pronounce James Jones Stark a coward." As M. said this, Spalding, who was reading the papers at the desk, turned and saw Stark put his hand in his pocket, as if to draw something, and advance upon Minis; and it was drawn and pointed when M. fired. Wayne, in his affidavit, said he believed Stark was in the act of drawing a pistol when M. fired. The question then will hinge on this point: which attempted to draw first? No difficult one it will be to decide. Wayne told Dr. Waring [60] that he attempted the pistol out of Minis' hand, and in so doing, momentarily lost sight of Stark and cannot say whether S.'s pistol was presented or not. Spalding's testimony fills up this interval, for he saw something presented before M. fired. . . .

14th. Judge Law (the first person who had called upon with

regard to the unfortunate circumstance between Minis and Stark) called upon with the following which he wished me to insert as editorial

"On Friday last a melancholy occurrence transpired in this city. Mr. James Jones Stark lately of Glynn County (formerly of Savannah) and member of the legislature from that county, was fired at with a pistol by Dr. Philip Minis, also of Savannah, within the bar room of the City Hotel. The ball struck Mr. Stark in the breast, and penetrating thro' the body, came out through the spine. He died instantaneously. A coroner's inquest was held who returned a verdict against Dr. Minis of deliberate murder. Dr. Minis has been arrested and committed to the jail of this county, to be tried in January next. We forbear entering into further particulars as we do not desire to excite the public mind, already sufficiently inflamed. Mr. Stark was interred on Saturday with military honours by the Sav'h Vol'r Gds. of which company he was a member, and his body followed to the grave by a large and respectable assemblage of the citizens of Savannah".

Upon reading the above, I objected to allowing any notice of the extra judicial verdict of the jury with regard to "murder" to be taken in the columns of the Georgian while I had any control over them. I asked him, as a lawyer, whether it was not stepping beyond their right thus to pronounce a verdict of deliberate murder against a fellow citizen who had not been tried. He reminded me of his being the judge upon which I apologized. But in the course of conversation he allowed that a verdict of a jury of inquest was not evidence before court. I then said, why publish such a verdict as the one in question for many people beleive that a jury of inquest has the same power as a Grand Jury. I told him I would give him an answer at 9 o'clock tomorrow morning. It must be recollected that the above was written by a judge of the Superior Court, a relation by marriage it is true, but the very judge before whom in course of time the guilt or innocence of Minis is to be tried. I explained to Judge Law that it had been my intention to have noticed it in this morning's paper but that my absence from the city nearly all day yesterday had prevented me. Tomorrow I shall return Judge Law his communication and tell him that this affair shall be noticed by me under the editorial head in that manner which my own judgement dictates as follows:

"A most melancholy occurrence transpired in this city on Friday last. James Jones Stark, Esq'r, of Glynn County, formerly of Savannah, was shot at the City Hotel by Dr. Philip Minis, through the breast and almost instantaneously expired. This is indeed a most unfortunate circumstance which has cast a gloom over the whole community as both parties are extensively connected in this city. We forbear any details connected with this melancholy occurrence, or expressing any opinion with regard to the merits of the case as Dr. Minis is in the custody of the law, and at the proper time and before a competent tribunal, the whole affair will undergo a judicial investigation."

XLIV

A Friendly Letter, 1812

Mary Elizabeth Fenno,[61] who became the wife of Giulian C. Verplanck,[62] was one of the non-Jewish friends of Rebecca Gratz. She was the sister of Maria Fenno, who married Judge Ogden Hoffman. Their father was a prominent journalist and member of the literary coterie in New York City. The Hoffmans and the Verplancks were socially as well as intellectually in the forefront of New York society. They belonged to the old Dutch elite; yet they seem to have taken Rebecca Gratz to their hearts—and whoever took Rebecca took her whole family and all her friends as well. The letter below is charming and gossipy; it may be surmised that it was this quality of bringing people together into a larger human circle that endeared Rebecca Gratz to her friends.

Yet, she could be serious, too, about her charitable and educational activities and about events in the national and international scene. Two months after the date of this letter, writing from Philadelphia to Mrs. Verplanck, Rebecca spoke of the first impact of the War of 1812. "I do not suppose you crave the gossiping news of our city—amidst such beautiful woodland scenery as you are encompassed in. I wish you my dear friend, a continuation of that tranquil happiness which is above all price, and in such turbulent times may be doubly dear from the power of contrast. Our friend Sedley is here, escaped from Balt. with some wounds and the entire discomforture [sic] of his establishment there." [63] Even in this more serious moment, however, her approach was, as always, in terms of the individual rather than of the larger group.

100. REBECCA GRATZ TO MRS. VERPLANCK, 1812 [64]

I thank you, My dear Eliza for your letter which arrived in good time to prevent our anxiety for your welfare Gertrude had been a day earlier in her communications of the unpleasantness of your journey and I fear'd you might suffer some inconvenience from its effects. we were lamenting all day that you should be exposed to such excessive heat, but fancied before the sun [set(?)] you were safely lodged at Brunswick. However, badly off as you were, you might have pitied the state of solitariness you left us in, our house scarcely seemed like home and we are hastily tired of so small a family. I hope your husband did not think us *quite* so dull as we really are. Novelty, and your presence might a little have blinded his perception of this truth, and when you next bring him to see us, I hope we shall have more Brothers to introduce him to, and those he already knows will be more at leisure to pay him due attention. This weather will certainly soon drive you from the city if it reaches you. And if I were as generous as I ought to be, I should, spite of selfish regret, be glad our having escap'd it here as we are fully convinced within the last week, that this house is many degrees warmer than any we ever inhabited before and if we could at all reconcile ourselves to the idea of leaving our Brothers to plod on through the toil they are doomed to abroad without having now & then some comfort at home, we should be tempted to retire into the country immediately. Brother Simon wishes us to do so, but we will not consent at present.

Ann has been in expectation of a visit from her father, which will probably delay their leaving the city for a day or two, but they are moving some of their furniture to day, every thing looks so languid & wearisome in town, and so animated & joyful in the country that it seems impossible for any one who has sense or feeling to hesitate between them. We have had a most splendid marrying here of Miss Scott & Mr. Pedersen,[65] the attendants came from afar and shine magnificently, the ceremony was performed on Wednesday evening and the rejoicing kept at the bridal house for three succeeding days—punch drinking & visiting in the morning, large dinner parties and riding in the afternoon in such style as has not been seen on any similar occasion within my recollection, if they are not happy, what a deal of labour is here lost; if they are, this is not the way I should like to enjoy it.

We have just heard of Mrs Fonsards arrival from New Orleans, her health is the plea, for leaving her husband, who is stationed there during the summer season. And Mad[.]Moreau [66] quits hers on the same account, perhaps for ever. It is evident Cupid is not always fettered in the chains of ———— particularly in france, or by frenchmen in any country. Our country-woman Mad Fonsard is still beautiful, sensible, agreeable and apparently very amiable, yet she is here, and her husband, an aged man bound by his duty to continue in a sickly climate. She has left him to the care of his daughter, but I should consider it very reproachful to admit any affection superior to my own if I were so situated. She brought us a letter from Jo who will not be home until next month, he is well and says the place is healthy, he thinks he shall not lose much by his adventure, besides what it has already cost him in the long & hazardous journey he has had by land & water already and the dangers of the sea, which is still to be encountered. I hope the time he has employed, will be redeemed by the experience he obtains, all of which must be taken into the account, and then he must determine whether the balance is in his favour or against him. It will be unkind to tell him how much pleasure he lost by not being at home during your visit, but I follow the plan of the Old Quaker, who kept telling his servant, all the time he was whipping him, that it was for [his good].

[R]emember me affectionately to your Husban[d] and tell My dear Maria to write & let me know when you [leave] town, and something about her own affairs.

Sally & Rachel send you their best love, Simon & the *young gentlemen* beg leave to kiss your hand. By the bye, I received a serious reprimand for not sending for Simon before you left us on Monday morning, he came up to bid you Adieu after we left home and was much disappointed—tell your husband so and present his friendly salutations.

Adieu My Dear Eliza, believe me, I rejoice in your happiness and am ever with sincere affection   Your attached   RGratz

June 10th 1812

XLV

A Travel Letter to a Friend, 1812

The passage of centuries makes little change in the major interest of young men. True, young Mordecai Myers [67] observed the differences between the well-made roads of the northern states and the "mud ponds" of Virginia, and commented to his friend Ben Gratz [68] on these matters. True, too, he visited the shipyards in Washington and saw the frigates that were being built there for action in the War of 1812. There is, indeed, no direct reference in this letter to the War then in progress; except that, for those who lived in that exciting year, its high point was the victory of the American frigate, *Constitution,* over the supposedly "invincible" British warship, the *Guerriere,* on August 19, 1812. But for all this, the most fascinating subject, to which young Myers recurs several times, is that of pretty girls.

101. MORDECAI MYERS TO BENJAMIN GRATZ, 1812 [69]

Octr 27th 1812 Richmond

Dear Ben,
After a most tedious journy of three days from Washington I arrived at this place; The scene which presented itself to my view was strange indeed; & the contrast striking between the well made roads; the neat cottages & rosy faced girls of those No. States thro which I have passed & the perfect mud ponds, for they do not merit the nam[e] of roads, the filthy hovels & pale, pu[ny] whining fair ones of those southern states.[70] I have become a comple[te] Northern man; There are some pretty girls here; Young Marx has a handsome sister & if I had not something else to think about I would fall in love with her. I came very nigh being in love with Miss R Etting but I did not like to come in contact with my friend Jack;

I have been here four days & have received much attention from the persons to whom I had letters, Richmond is a little different in appearance from Pha; the inhabitants appear very gay & fashionable however; & I have now but a partial view of the gayety of the place as the weather is extremely bad & has prevented my going about; I have still a dreary journey before me; the young man who promised to stay at Washington had left there in the mail about four hours before I arrived; I visited when in Washington the frigates that were there (?) building; they appear as if they could play the same game with an equal force as the Constitution did with the invincible Gueriere; I promised Gratz to write him will you be so good as to tell him I will accomplish my promise immediately as I arrive home. Remember me affectionately to yr sisters and brothers & to Miss Ettings Mr E & H & G's families, tell Jo I will write him, I will be a great letter writer or I ought [to] be [with] so many correspondents. P S excuse my paper.

Your friend

M Myers

Richmond Va
Mr Ben Gratz

XLVI

A Family
Round Robin Letter, 1814

Two of Benjamin Gratz's sisters, Rebecca and Sarah,[71] joined his
brother Joseph (Jo)[72] in writing this letter to young Lieutenant
Benjamin Gratz, who had volunteered for service in the War of
1812. There are several topics discussed in this multiple letter:
Benjamin's failure to be elected by his fellow soldiers as an officer
of the Washington Guards,[73] Sally's (Sarah) health, and other
family matters; but the most interesting sentences are Rebecca's
reminder to her brother that the Feast of Tabernacles (Sukkoth)
is about to begin, and her apparent sureness that Benjamin will
not have remembered the occasion, so that his prayers will be, as
she said, "silent orisons."[74]

102. FAMILY LETTER TO BENJAMIN GRATZ, 1814[75]

Philadelphia September 28-1814

My dear Ben
I have just seen Edward Ingersoll[76] who tells me the second
Washington Guards have disgraced themselves by not giving you
rank. Let this not disturb you. Go on in the respectable manner
that you have since you have been in camp and you will retain
the respect and esteem of all your officers and that of the men
whose respect and esteem you would value. There will be some
vacancies in the Staff of your Brigade or some other which, possibly if you wish, you can get. However I expect to be in camp in
a few days when we can talk the matter over.

Dr Phisic[77] has been to see our Sister Sally. She is more composed since you left home and I think better. Simon is so well as
to be out. The remainder of the family are well I will get Captain

himself to tell you about his company, God Bless you my dear
fellow.

Yours   Jo Gratz

My dear Ben

We have had no more such scenes as distrest you so much on
the morning of your departure Drs P. & K [78] have changed Sallys
medicine they now give her some powders that will confine her to
her room (not ever easy) and I have some prospect of getting a
very good nurse. Sally slept well last night, and has been better
than usual to day. Simon is quite well again and all things much
more comfortable than you left them. I hope you are not discouraged from visiting us again we are every where liable to cares
& disappointments and vexations, and when they overtake us early
in the course of life they are salutory lessons, if late we are provided
with experience enough to know how to bear them. from our
cradles we are taught that they are to be encountered, and tho'
unacquainted with the kind that will fall to our lot. we have the
same remedies to apply to every evil. *fortitude and patience* and
these will suit almost every case. poor Becky Rawle [79] was interred
this morning. her bereaved family will long very long deplore this
heavy affliction. all who knew, or heard of her must sympathize
with them—must grieve for her loss. This evening My dear B.
commences the Tabernacle, May you pass it in health and cheerfulness we shall remember you in our prayers. and petition our
Almighty Father to accept your silent orisons and include you
among those visited with happiness long life and success. let us
hear from you soon and believe me ever most truly   Your Affectionate   Sister R G

My dear Ben   I have almost written myself out of breath in two
very long letters to NYork, which has occupied all the morning
since my *formidable* visit of Physicians. I sit alone, and of *course*
quarrel with no one I told Dr Physic of my nervous irritability
which he assures me he will subdue. I was bled yesterday, was
ill all this evening with sick headache, but am more tranquil to day,
and very sad at the loss of poor Becky Rawle The family are in
the deepest shades of woe. Cate Ogden [80] has I believe gone to

NYork as Captain is to write I will only say God Bless you with every laudable wish of your heart for good May he prosper you now & ever more Prays my beloved Brother your fond sister

Sarah Gratz

XLVII
Sisterly Advice, 1815

The ties of deep concern and affection that bind the Jewish family are clearly revealed in this document of advice from an older sister to her younger brother. There is a simple, almost naive, confusion here of religious, moral and prudential precepts. For Judith Cohen, who wrote these words for her brother Levi [81] as he was about to cross the Atlantic Ocean to Liverpool, and ultimately to seek out an older half-brother, possibly in England, man's duties to God and man's duties to his fellow man flowed into one another.

103. RULES FOR LEVI COHEN, 1815 [82]

Rules for Levi Cohen's Perusal When He
Has Leisure   Rule the 1st.

Fear God and keep his Commandments and he will ever protect and guard you from evil, Honor your superiors and they will Love you, be particular in keeping the law you were brought up to, keep truth in all your doings and you will never be brought to shame. Let your actions be such that you will allways deserve praise without price, keep no vicious company if you can not keep company with your superiors or equals keep none at all, and be sure when, Please God you arrive at Liverpool to inquire for one of your own persuasion and go to them or him tell without falsehood your story, ask the Captain's permission as soon as you arrive to let you go ashore and be care-ful of your cloathes, and do not be too communicative to inquisitive people, the first house you get to be sure to write to your Brother and wait for an answer to know how you are to come to him, be grateful to your Benefactors and treat them with that respect that due to their Reverence, do not forget the aged parent you have left behind, but keep in your memory the many troubles he has undergone for

you, the anxiety he will be in untill he hears of your arrival, Do
not forget to write to us by the first opportunity, make yourself
as agreeable to your shipmates as you can be and do anything
in your power to oblige them. Let Virtue be your guide and remember these are the sentiments of your affectionate sister

Judith Cohen

April 20th, 1815

XLVIII
Husband and Wife, 1816-1817

This group of letters was written by Solomon Jacobs [83] to his wife Hetty [84] during two successive summers when she was visiting her family in Philadelphia. Solomon makes much of the loneliness of his enforced (if temporary) bachelor state. In spite of this rather literary insistence on the way in which the absence of his wife and child affects him, the letters indicate that his life is tolerably full, not only with business activity but also with social occasions. The couple was apparently quite prosperous, and the several friends to whom reference is made were at a similar stage.

By 1817, however, a minor recession had set in, heralding the depression of 1819. Many businesses were failing. Another letter from Jacobs to his wife, September 7, 1817, reflects the sudden change in economic conditions and their effect on the social situation in Richmond. "Richmond is as dull as ever I saw it, there are a great many from Town. Still the number of inhabitants seem not decreased, but there is no stir, no bustle—either in business or any thing else—no Horse racing, Bull baiting or cock-fighting, no runaway matches, no phenomena, Sea *monsters*, mermaids or Unicorns. . . . But really the number of persons about to remove hence to the western country will make quite a chasm in the place and will greatly thin the ranks of the Congregation." [85]

104. SOLOMON TO HETTY JACOBS, 1816 [86]

Richmond/ Sunday/ August 11th 1816

My Dear Wife

I am this moment gratified with your affectionate letter of the 7th. I have also to acknowledge the rec[eip]t of your esteemed letter of the 4th on Thursday last—a day or two after I wrote to you, I will reply to both generally—without distinguishing their dates.

I am thankful to God for all his mercies and kindness to me, but *most fervently so,* for the high health in which my dear Wife and Infant are sustained by his omnipotent bounty, and which I pray may be continued (as I hope it will be deserved) to you both many, many years.

I sent the message you required—in writing to Mrs. Burrows—immediately on rect of yr letter, she thanks you and desired her respects.

I have told Fanny what you desired respecting the Beds &c. She will do all you wish when I get off, she has been somewhat engaged for me but more so with her children, who have both been afflicted with bowel complaints, but are getting better: poor Liz has been in low spirits ever since you left home. She rarely raises her head, and I have never seen her smile, since. Edgar still grows, prodigiously, will be fit to drive you out in your carriage next summer (but we must have one first, bad prospects, Tobacco down in Europe and every where else. Cant you introduce the fashion of sneezing smoking & chewing among the ladies, it would help out?) Susan as you left her, I dont think her mended, and know she can *not* be *spoiled.* Austin wishes you home again, Julias boards out as usual, and Mr Wilkinson is placed at a decent boarding house, and myself poor *solitary self,* never take any thing at home but breakfast, solus per solo, my standing custome I give to Fitzuhs tavern, say every other day, and when I do take dinner any where else, he abuses me for it.[87] I really think my health improved by the salt-water air of Norfolk, bathing in brine and the volatile guacum (?) the last is potent and makes me atopic, morning and evening I take it with wine. I think however it affects my head & ear unpleasantly. I might have gotten away today, but am quite early enough, and the weather here extremely pleasant. I have slept every night with a blanket on my bed. I shall however start tomorrow afternoon or next day if no unforeseen event turns up. I have horse and sulkey all prepared, have determined not to take a servant along, shall be able to make out very well without one, and shall be compelled to spend money enough without being obliged to purchase another horse &c &c. I will give you accounts of the progress I make when at the springs, together with the effects, and manage to write to you often as you may wish, and shall place my *greatest enjoyment* upon the *frequency* of *your* letters, and accounts of the health and happiness of yourself and child—together with your friends. Never add another word of apology, you know my dislike that way. Even offenses are aggravated by apologies. Why then make them where praises are due. your two last letters were the *more inestimable* to me because they were longer than the first. *Write* me *every thing*, the huge city of philadelphia, the Athens of America will assuredly afford subject matter at any time to fill a sheet, if with nothing else, at least with folly which you know I deal in largely.

I like your description of the Char--t--on nabobs, "great houses, splendid furniture, brilliant Jewels, and plenty of *cash* to figure with abroad." Pray my dear, why did not you, simply ask the very prudent Lady, if her husband also gave her *a purse* to put it in? I should marvel *it* to have been a *"Redicule".* Folly thou art apparent, and innocent too when the possessor acts only upon himself, but most *foul* when the world is made to pay for thy antic freaks, gaudy as the Pea Cock is, he, even he, disdains to wear any but his *own ligitimate plumage:* much as I love you my dear, and our sweet babe, sooner than impose on confiding friends or strangers by *fraud,* sooner than wrong the poor widow—or helpless orphan—of their bread, to *pamper pride,* or feed ourselves, I would wander with you in unknown Forests, live on shrubs or herd grass, or, if no other alternative offered would starve. People argue falsely that "they must live ["] not so—if they can-not live honestly, there is neither use nor necessity for them to live at all. I write not at random, have been as poor (as that in tender youth, without protection or friend) as any body, and defy the Tongue of Slander to say, I acted otherwise, than up to my present maxim. Thank God, *we* are now blessed, if not with *wealth* and high *sounding eclat,* at least with a *competency,* honorably obtained by industry and economy. Persevered in for a number of years, I think too, that we both have the prudence to keep it, and with *it* and a tolerable share of luck (or rather no ill fortune) we shall remain *independent* during our lives and leave our children wherewithall to start them in the world. A fig for splendor, I would not yield my feelings, honest contentment (even with a dry loaf) and independence of mind, for a palace. I am betrayed by indignant feeling into too great length, yet it may not be unprofitable, we are all subject to go wrong. We may check this by jogging each other, a great prince once kept in pay a man to remind him every morning thus—"Prince you must die," and Profited by the admonition.

You have above a draft on Mr Cope [88] for a balance due me, *indorse* your name on the back and send it to him. He will pay it forth-with. You did not understand me before, I am glad you did not send to him without, it would have been improper. I presume this will be as much as you may want. *Yet observe,* you are by no means to abridge yourself in any thing you want. If more can be applied to your use, or comfort, advise me, and you shall have it forth-with. I have no more due me in philada but can send on by mail. We shall not want any Bed linen from Phila. I bought an excellent ps of Irish sheeting (59 yds) yesterday.

Your Father and Mother will both read this and consider it as far as applicable in answer to their valued letters, they may see how it is. You have occupied (as you are wont to do in the affections of your friends) all the space. Your Mother will credit me a short time, and not discontinue writing, I will pay with interest in the mean time if she stands much in need of a letter, or my daughter will *"lend her one":* any inability there, I draw on a *well known stock,* my amiable friend Miss Rachel. As to Moss' [89] family, you mistake my feelings, I am mortified, that they should omit in what is a duty both to me and themselves, be it so, yield not an inch to them, if a retort can not reach them. It must be because *they* are o[bdur]ate & want feeling. As to Mr Moss whose affections are pretty much "wrapped" up in [the s]ale of Goods, he is con-nected by no tie of blood and I know (*now*) the basis of his friendship. but there are those and of the softer sex too whose kindred affections *ought to have a deep stake,* and vibrate this way. I will not indulge in what I might, but a Mother tottering to the grave, and *Grand Mother* too, present strong natural claims: if you had an aged Ice plant for a long time, watched, nourished and watered, you would feel gratitude for the attendant, were he even a stranger, from my youth *&* in *poverty,* my old mothers care devolved on me, how I have acquitted myself others may say. It was a duty I con-fess I owed, yet it was not less a duty of other children and *Grand children,* do away consanguinity between them and myself, and

I should still be the last person on earth treated by them with neglect, if correct feelings held empire over the soul. Even Clary, who has from childhood nursed, watched and waited on the parent stock, from which they are each of them a shoot, is entitled to attention and gratitude from them. And what I write upon this subject I could wish them to know, if my wife and child have no claims on their gratitude, still, *nature* and good policy should prompt them to good offices, that upon their return they might be influenced to additional kindness, to the *superannuated mother, who gave* being to *them all.* . . .

Your Affectionate Husband   S. Jacobs

Direct your letters to me, "White Sulphur Springs, Greenbrier County Virginia," put every word or your letters will go wrong. It may be well for your papa to mention to the post office that they will go quickest by the way of Staunton in *Virginia.* . . . I have just read Carvalhos sermon,[90] vapid, stale & flat as spoiled beer. Yet froth and sentiment without body. . . .

105. SOLOMON TO HETTY JACOBS, 1817[91]

Richmond, 15th July 1817

My Dear Hetty,

Your affectionate letter of the 10th from Harrowgate was handed me by yesterdays mail. I am happy to find that you have gotten such excellent quarters, and more so at your being so well pleased with them; our darling child I hope will derive benefit from the country air, indeed from your Fathers letter of the 11th just received, she has already mended considerably. I understand that the whooping cough reaches its climax in about 30 days to 6 weeks and, that after 40 days, it is no more contagious. if this be the case, you will soon have considerable relief, both, from the improvement of our dear Miriam and the opportunity it will afford you of being more frequently with your Sister and her little paragon of beauty: but there may still be danger of her taking something worse from Miriam than the cough, to wit, the *uglies,* or, if beauty prevails transcendently Miriam will I hope catch a spark of it from Anna. I wish it may light upon her nose, she may perhaps need it there.

The passage is nearly finished and looks very well. The paper is perfectly neat without being tawdry there will be enough to reach clear up to your chamber and the pantry: the whole house and establishment is now as handsome as it can be made to appear, the grass plat, and grass walk in front look green and beautiful, and the whole now wants no other embellishment than the mistress to smile upon them. believe me my dear I miss you more than I expected, make much of your present visit for I very much doubt whether I shall as readily consent to your leaving me again. I lay last night nearly the whole of it thinking of you and Miriam. Still I am unwilling that you should return, until toward the fall; Bowel complaints are very prevalent here—with both Adult and Infant. Edgar is quite ill with it. Mordecai Lyons,[92] his wife and one of his children have it. Would you believe it, he has the name of keeping a cheap store, has a considerable run, both Town and Country, and quite a resort for Ladies, his *immaculate* Brother in Law might *grin* applause, if he could see the *poor* fellow likely to gain a good livelihood for his young, helpless family.

I have nothing new to write about, ——— nothing in the way of business. Still my presence at home is indispensible you know the inefficiency of Archer, not more then my great grand sire would be cut out of a Log of wood. Could I pursue only my inclination, I should not be long from my wife and child, but, my love, this world (*you* do *not* half *know it*) is governed by sordid means, *interest, money* is the Lever, that can raise or depress the world. Nay, actually does so, and it behoves every head of a Family to guard those whom he holds most dear from a depression. I am determined therefore not to neglect my affairs and thereby produce inconvenience or misfortune, trust in God we shall never be over-taken by it, and in any event not to subject myself to my own censure if it should *come*. Every thing considered then, you can-not seriously persuade me to go on and remain from home any length of time, without some person of *capacity* and who has the *motive* to guard my interest here. If I do go on for you, I shall be com-pelled to return forth-with. . . .

I thank your father mother very much for their kind attention and letters, I must take the beginning of a sheet to write to them, I generally intend to subjoin a letter, or note to each of them, in the letters I write to you, But I get astray and never stop until the whole of my paper and time for mail is exhausted. make my affectionate regards to them and to Bell(?), Rachel, and all the Family. Yourself, be assured of the unalterable love of your affectionate Husband   S. Jacobs

Kiss my dear Child for me.

Mrs Raphael Mother & Henrietta desire much love. Write as often as you possibly can.

XLIX
Letter to a Sister-in-Law, 1820

Benjamin Gratz and his wife Maria [93] carried the Gratz name and its wide business enterprises into Kentucky, making their home in Lexington—although this letter caught up with Mrs. Gratz while she was staying in Frankfort. Since Kentucky at this time was an outpost of civilization and since communication with the more settled parts of the country was not yet an easy matter, Rebecca Gratz felt that her news from brother Ben was inadequate. In this letter, she reported to Maria on the passing of a recent yellow fever epidemic, a plague that hit Philadelphia about once in every decade. She consoled herself, however, by reminding Maria that the ravages of yellow fever were much more severe in the southern cities than in Philadelphia. An interesting feature of this letter is Rebecca's reference to a small box of handmade clothing that the Philadelphia "girls" of the Gratz family had prepared for their Kentucky relatives, each piece marked with the names of those who worked on it. This was a delightful way of keeping the family ties green in the minds of both the givers and the receivers of this handiwork.

106. REBECCA GRATZ TO MARIA GIST GRATZ, 1820 [94]

My Dear Maria,

Last week Mrs Boswell [95] took charge of a little box containing a few little articles of which I beg your acceptance they have given me a great deal of pleasure to prepare, and the girls were delighted to be employed for you. The pieces are labeled with the names of the workers you will perceive you are not endebted to me for any fancy work and you must charge to the account of distance, the smallness of the offering. I should have been much pleased to have completed the wardrobe had not the bulk of larger articles detained me. It is a long time indeed since I have heard from you, or my dear Ben, and you can scarcely conceive how much I was disappointed at our Brother Hyman[s] detention. We had supposed he was on his journey and I was beginning to calculate the days until his return, when the account arrived that he had changed his plans. I sincerely hope he will be able to come home before the winter sets in, his absence has already been more than twice the length I expected.

Our city begins to resume its usual appearance, the citizens are returning to their habitations and strangers begin to pass thro' undismayed by the alarm of Yellow-fever, indeed when we compare our situation to the southern cities we can not be sufficiently grateful for escaping the dreadful calamity with which we were threatened, and they are suffering under. Poor Savannah has been visited in wrath. Fire & pestilence have brought down her glory and filled her streets with mourning & lamentations New Orleans too is the scene of disease & death. Ellen & I have really grieved for poor Mr. Larned, his short brilliant career is too soon arrested. Frequently his name reached us accompanied with praise on recounting some circumstance in the routine of duty, which seemed to indicate that he was rising in honors & usefulness. On Saturday we were shocked to see an obituary notice of his falling a victim to the Yellow fever, pray did you know his wife? I find she is mentioned with great sympathy as being bereaved in the course of one year of almost every tender tie of Nature—her Mother, brother, child & husband! What my dear Maria, can that poor woman have left in this world, to render her weary pilgrimage supportable? If she has not a heart stedfast in the love of God, and submissive to his will, she must fall into despondency and so die. But as Stern[e] sings, "God tempers the wind to the shorne lamb," and he is not less tender of his other creatures, poor Mrs Larned will not be forsaken. His aged Mother will be sadly shaken, she gloried in her son.

Our sister Rachel is preparing to come to town, her son Horace [96] is really a noble boy. I shall be quite rich in company when her numerous little folks get back. We have been so small all summer and since Jo's absence have hardly been able to keep house at all, when the gentlemen do not come in town to dinner, we emigrate up street and take up our quarters at Mr Hays's.

Tell My dear Ben, his friend the Major accompanied by his wife paid me a visit yesterday and appears very anxious to see him. Mrs Biddle [97] also enquired if you were not to be here in the spring, they are desirous to meet old friends in new conditions. H. Williams & his fair Julia too court your favor, they anticipate great pleasure in comparing the happy present with the gay past and say to have you located in the neighbourhood would be completing the compact our sisters send affectionate greetings to you all, and so do their sons & daughters, Ellen [98] means to write you a letter. She has long desired to so, but from putting it off too long, finds it difficult to begin, as she feels an apology necessary unless she can produce a letter worthy of itself to attract your favor and you know how apt over anxiety to do a thing well, is to produce a difficulty where none exists, give my best love to My dear Brothers. I shall write to Hyman soon. I beg My dear Maria for a letter from you. I have been expecting one these two weeks and every time the postman rings have a disappointment not at all favorable to my other correspondents. Make my affectionate respect to Col. Morrison [99] and my regards to Mrs. M. remember me also at Canewood to your excellent Mother.

and believe me My dear sister, with [ve]ry sincere affection and best wishes for [your] health & happiness your attached   [RG]

Oct. 3rd 1820

L

An Aunt to Her Nephew, 1825

Besides showing another aspect of family relationships, this letter from Sally Etting [100] of Baltimore, to her nephew, Benjamin,[101] of Philadelphia throws further light on the activities of Jewish business-men in the China trade.[102] Mrs. Etting inquired about three items, china, tea, and Cantonese silk damask, all of which were regular imports in this important branch of American foreign trade. The Ettings of Baltimore were a well-established family and lived, as appears from Mrs. Etting's description of her rose garden, in com-fort. They were a well respected family in the community and among the first to benefit, shortly after the time of this letter, from the removal of some of the legal restrictions on the Jews of Maryland. Yet, Mrs. Etting saw nothing demeaning in offering to act as an agent for her nephew in the sale of tea, and passed on to him re-quests for commercial information in the same tone as she passed on gossip of family and friends.

107. SALLY ETTING TO BENJAMIN ETTING, 1825 [103]

Balt May the 19 1825

My dear Ben

with pleasure I heard from the Girls you are about to make us a visit my dear Son and me shall expect you every day untill we see you I wrote a few lines Monday by Miss Alexander to your dear Parents I hope they recd it Mr. Cohen was *kind* enough when he was on his way to the Boat to call & say he was just going too late for any one to write a line by him. Have you sold all your Goods & have you done well by them I want to know all your Concerns for I beleive no one takes a more sincere interest for your than your Poor Old Aunt Sal. Have you many Chests of Tea such as my Brother got from you & what is the price he tells me he dont know as the Chest was a present from you to Rachel, if they are not too high I think it likely I could dispose of them. You have not yet let us know what we owe you on the China[;] tis very beautifull & every time I look at it I see something new to admire by dear Ben bring down a little Black Tea for we cannot get such as you have been drinking & I wish you to be fed as well here as at home tis a high joke to invite company & request them to find their own provisions. Do you think it possible to find out the person that makes Mint Lozenges I should be very glad if you can get me two pound please pay for them & forward them by first opportunity the Crape & them I will settle with you for. Our little Garden looks beautifull tell your dear Father it is worth while to come down & see it I am writing at a Window surronded by Roses how often do we wish to have him & your dear Mother with us your Uncle talks of moving next week I have no news to tell you for in the literal translation of the word I am a very homely Girl. To all friends give my love the Girls all send theirs to our dear Brother Sister & the Children God Bless & protect you all prays your affectionate   friend   Sally Etting

Mrs Caton [104] requested me to ask you the price of the first quality silk damask in Canton.[105]

LI

A Brotherly Letter, 1826

The younger members of a large family like the Ettings or the Gratz's often found it desirable, at the beginning of their careers, to establish themselves in small towns. Here, they handled business commissions for their relatives and friends in the city, taking advantage of every opportunity of communication by letter. It must have been especially trying for a young lawyer like Gratz Etting,[106] accustomed to the full social life of Philadelphia, to tie himself down to an office in the country town of Bellefonte. He seems to have little patience with his rustic clients, and still less with the other residents of the "stupid country" who had not the wit to become his clients.

In Bellefonte, it is quite possible that Gratz Etting was the only Jewish resident. Had there been others, this letter would surely have contained some reference to them. Away from his own family, and without any natural social groups into which to fit, his life must have been very dull, and his impatience is quite understandable. The misfortune to which he referred in the beginning of his letter gives us a valuable bit of information. Eleven years after the Battle of New Orleans, a significant American victory of the War of 1812, unfortunately fought after the British had already agreed to the terms of the Treaty of Ghent, celebrations of the victory kept Andrew Jackson, the victorious commander, in the public eye.[107]

108. GRATZ ETTING TO BENJAMIN ETTING, 1826 [108]

Bellefonte [Pa.] January 15th 1826

Dear Ben

Man sometimes suffers severely for his pleasures, not always in proportion to the excess of them. We celebrated the anniversary of the Battle of New Orleans by a Ball on Monday Evening when I had the misfortune to sprain my instep. I have suffered from it more than I supposed such an accident could occasion—the foot swelled immediately and became inflamed. I was confined to bed for two days and was bled and dieted. I cannot yet walk except upon my heel, and am unable to go to my office. It is better today. I trust by remaining quiet for a day or two to have the use of my foot again, which is certainly very essential for our purposes.

When you received the amount of the draft on Smith & Co,[109] I will thank you to pay Mess Rianhard, Senat & Co.[110] One hundred & eighty dollars on account of their Judgment against Alexander Mahon. The Balance of twenty dollars you will please pay to Mr. Folwell the Tailor on acct of My Bill.

You say the times are hard with you: the usual cry of Merchants! But we here have reason to complain; as respect myself I have not had a new client for two months and am heartily sick of this stupid Country.

As soon as I can go out the taxes of B. Philips [111] shall be paid and the Recipt [receipt] sent to him. He is a very troublesome fellow I know well, and suppose he pesters you with this trifling matter, which he told me to do at any time, and that he did not wish the receipt except by a private opportunity

In my letter to our dear Mother I requested inquiry made for my lost dog. I am happy to say he has been brought home by Mr. Reed who accompanied the Judge. Receive my thanks for your good intentions. There will be a waggon with Iron from Mess. Valentines & Thomas for Jacob Lea in the City about the end of this week, which is to be imme[di]ately loaded with plaister. You may send if you please the —— by it.

I hope our Brother Henry [112] will be successful, his perseverance has certainly been great, he has already sacrificed too much time, which would have been more advantageously spent in acquiring a knowledge of his profession.

Thank my dear Isabella [113] for her few lines and tell her it will always give me much pleasure to hear from her. To our dear Parents Sisters & Brothers remember me affectionatly and to the family individually tender my sincere love.

Very truly ys.   Gratz Etting

LII
A Jewish Will, 1827

There is no evidence to indicate that Jewish slaveowners treated their slaves any better or any worse than did their fellow-Americans. It is clear, however, on the basis of a number of cases, that Jewish slaveowners followed the example of such leading Southern Americans as Washington and Jefferson in making provision, wherever possible, for the freeing of their slaves.[114] In many cases, slaveholding Jews granted freedom to their slaves in their wills; a typical instance is to be found in the will of Isaac H. Judah,[115] a Virginia Jew of the late eighteenth and early nineteenth century. Generally, the rate of slave manumission was high in Virginia until about 1830, and Judah fell into the pattern of his time and place by making specific grants of freedom to some of his slaves in his will. Foreseeing the possibility that some of his heirs might attempt to interfere with the enforcement of his wishes in this matter, Judah declared very forcefully that should "any of my heirs or legatees . . . in any way whatever obstruct my wishes or intentions . . . I direct that any and every provision and legacy herein contained shall be considered as revoked and utterly null and void."

109. WILL OF ISAAC JUDAH, 1827 [116]

In the Name of God, Creator of Heaven and Earth Amen.

I Isaac H. Judah of the City of Richmond and State of Virginia seriously considering the uncertainty of human life and my mind being impressed as to the great necessity of making provisions of my worldly matters in the event of a termination of my terrestial existance do make and ordain my last Will and Testament in manner and form following which I enjoin and require to be fulfilled and executed in every respect according to my intentions and wishes in manner and form following that is to say: . . .

2nd. I give and bequeath my slave Maria to David Judah [117] one of my Executors hereinafter named to be held by him in Trust for the following uses and purposes viz: That said David Judah shall hire out the said slave Maria for fifteen years ever considering the happiness and comfort of said slave in selecting the persons to whom she is to be hired and using his own discretion and good feelings on the subject; that all sums of money received by him for the hire of said slave shall be carefully deposited in Bank or placed out on interest from time to time with indisputable security and at the expiration of said fifteen years or so soon thereafter as the same shall be required by her the said Maria in writing attested by two or more respectable witnesses, it is my will & desire and I do hereby direct my executors hereinafter named to manumit and set free the said slave Maria and such *children* as she may have at the time by Deed or Deeds duly executed and recorded according to law and that the money which may have arisen from the hiring of said slave with whatever interest may have accumulated thereon shall be paid to the said Maria if alive and if not to her children then living as soon as she or they may be made free as aforesaid.

3rd. I give and bequeath my slave Betsy to David Judah one of my executors hereinafter named to be held by him in Trust for the following uses and purposes viz: That the said David Judah shall hire out said slave Betsy for fifteen years ever considering the comfort and happiness of said slave in selecting the persons to whom she is to be hired and using his own discretion & good feelings on the subject; that all sums of money received by him for hire of said slave shall be carefully deposited by said David Judah in Bank or placed out on interest from time to time with indisputable security and at the expiration of said fifteen years or so soon thereafter as the same shall be required by her the said Betsy in writing attested by two or more respectable witnesses it is my will and desire and I do hereby direct my Executors hereinafter named to manumit and set free the said slave Betsy and such children as she may have at the time by Deed or Deeds duly executed and recorded according to Law and that the money which may have arisen from the hiring of said slave with whatever interest may have accumulated thereon shall be paid to said Betsy if alive and if not to her children then living as soon as she or they may be made free as aforesaid. . . .

5th. I give and bequeath to Philip Norbone Wythe and Benjamin Wythe free mulatto boys and brothers whom I brought up, in consideration of their attachment and fidelity and my natural regard [118] for them the following property viz: To Philip Norbone twenty five feet of ground on the Brook road fronting on the road and running back one hundred and twenty seven feet to a fifteen *feet* alley adjoining Simon Blocks Lot on the South and bound on the North by the Lot hereinafter devised to his brother Benjamin Wythe and I also bequeath to him said Philip Norbone the sum of Three hundred Dollars to be paid to him by my Executors within five years according to the discretion of my Executors and the situation of my Estate to him his heirs and assigns forever. To the said Benjamin Wythe I give and bequeath twenty five feet of ground at the intersection of M Street and the Brook road in the City of Richmond fronting twenty five feet on the Brook Road running back one hundred and twenty seven feet to a fifteen foot alley and bounded on the south by the Lot herein devised to his brother Philip Norbone and on the north by M Street and also the sum of Five Hundred Dollars to be paid him by my Executors within five years according to their discretion and the situation of my Estate to him said Benjamin his heirs and assigns forever. . . .

14th. It is my will and desire that my faithful old slave Toby shall be maintained & clothed during his life by my executors at the expense of my Estate. . . .

17th. I give and bequeath all the remainder and residue of my Estate that has not already been devised and bequeathed or that shall not be hereinafter devised and bequeathed to the following named persons their heirs and assigns forever, viz to my sister Sarah De Paz [119] one share or portion; to my Sister Grace Marks for her tender regard and love from a child Two shares or portions; to my sister Rebecca Seixas [120] one share or portion; to my brother Manuel Judah [121] one share or portion; to my brother Baruch H. Judah [122] and Manuel Judah his son and Ryne Judah his daughter one share or portion to be equally divided between them; to my brother Gershom Judah [123] and to my sister Rachel Rehine [124] one share or portion to be equally divided between them and the eighth and last portion of the same I give and bequeath to my nephew and namesake Isaac Marks the son of *my* sister Grace Marks to him his heirs and assigns forever.

LIII

A Distraught Mother to Her Son,

1828

Poor Mrs. Etting [125] was torn, when she wrote this letter, between joy and sorrow, and she scarcely knew which to express first. Her son Benjamin [126] had written to her to tell her of his engagement,[127] and, with maternal love, she wanted to let him know her pleasure. But she had heard, too, that another of her sons, Henry,[128] who was also in Baltimore with Benjamin, was ill. She wanted to express her concern and to impress on Benjamin the need for keeping her informed of Henry's progress. Torn between these two emotions and desires, she comes alive in this brief letter as a real mother with the gift of faith.

110. FRANCES ETTING TO BENJAMIN ETTING, 1828 [129]

Philadelphia March 26th 1828

In the fulness of my heart I clasp you to my fond embrace with joy supreme and congratulate you my dearest, most excellent Son in realizing your wishes. Yes my belov'd your happiness is far more dear to me than my existence, may your felicity equal all I ask for you then you will enjoy what you so deservedly merit, language cannot express half I feel and the sensations that inhabit my breast. I am happy very happy for you my Dearest Ben, but a cloud of sorrow and apprehension hangs hevy over my imagination for our lovd Henry whose indisposition makes me miserable, where [were] it not for the circumstances of his illness, I should be too happy for mortal existence. You are at present with him your kindness, prudence and affectionate attention will alliviate his sufferings and appease my trouble. A few lines from Mr Cohen informs that he is better, To this good gentlemen I am truly grateful, am in ignorance of his disorder although sensible of his sufferings, which God in his infinite mercy mitigate and restore my dearest Henry to perfect health. Allow me my son to abstract my ideas a little from you, Henrys situation alone can absorb me at this important moment when my thoughts love to dwell on objects dear to my soul. Harriet I judge is every way calculated to render you blest, my opinion on this subject you are acquainted with and I have long thought she possess'd your heart, amid your struggles to conceal it her acquiessence and Mr Marx's conduct is grateful to my feelings and when I have the happiness of seeing you shall indulge in conversation when my Pen cannot do justice, tis when we feel most our faculties refuse their functions the agitation of my feeling, and perturbation of my mind is almost insuportable. Restoration of health to my dear Henry and your action can alone, bring peace to my troubled breast, did I possess all the tongues in the world they could not tell what I feel and all the joy and blessings I invoke. Yesterday I addressed a letter to the Object of your affections a variety of feelings surround'd me, but I hope she will believe that I will recieve (?) her to my heart, as one who possesses your affections and mine. I very much regret that you did not hear from home since you left and deeply distressed at your reproach. Unconscious of ever neglecting you *one moment of my existence,* did you not say "There is no occasion to write to me unless something transpired" & all with you was joy and gladness but melancholy sat heavy at my heart on parting with my lov'd Henry and in a few days succeeding oppressed by sorrow I parted with our Gratz [130] such sensations have already too often occurd. Your Father and Sister's are most joyful at your prospect of happiness in attaining the object of your choice and, congratulate you with all their hearts on this most pleasing event. excuse their not telling you so by this conveyance they have to ——— and so have I, your Father who you know is fa[s]tidious on some occasions did not deem it proper to proclaim our joy—his ideas do not agree with mine. I conveyd the news, to Aunt H[etty Etting] yesterday and feel ——— to communicate it further since your letter of this morning, think not on Objections, you have the entire approbation of those most truly interested, and I aver with candor I never was more happy, no selfish feeling has one moment obscured the sunshine of my anticipated joy, the Union of her you love, will complete my felicity. More to me than Son you are worthy of Gods best gifts and may heaven shower on you   everlasting blessings most sincerely   and ardantly prays your devoted Mother   F E

in charity to my fealings do tell me of my Dearest Henry as soon as possible.

LIV
A Marriage Proposal, 1830

In the social code of the early nineteenth century, a young man needed the consent of a girl's parents before he began a serious courtship—object, matrimony. Without this consent, there were, of course, flirtations; but when matters took a serious turn, the suitor had to open his pleading before a stern judge of his suitability. There was, in this case, a good reason beside youthful nervousness for the trepidation that Moses Nathans's [131] errors in composition attest. He was of German descent, and Daniel Solis [132] was of Sephardic ancestry; many Sephardic Jews regarded marriage with Ashkenazim as a step down on the social ladder. This, in itself, might have been a sufficient reason for the older man to reject his daughter's suitor. It is pleasant to be able to record that after a period of hesitation,[133] Daniel Solis consented to the marriage of his daughter, Benvenida Valentina Solis, to young Moses Nathans.

111. MOSES NATHANS TO DANIEL SOLIS, 1830 [134]

Philadelphia November 14th 1830

Dear Sir

I can no longer do so great violence to my own inclinations as to retain in my own breast—a passion which has pray'd on my Spirits for a long time—and I flatter myself that the Integrity of my Intentions will excuse the fredom of these few lines whereby I am to acquaint you of the great value and affection I have for your amiable daughter whome I have had the hononour [sic] of being acquainted with for Some time.

I would not Sir attempt any Indirect address that should have the least appearance of Inconsistency with her duty to you and my honourable views to her Choosing by your Influence. If I may approve myself to your worthy of that honour to commend myself to her approbation.

If I might have the honour of your Countenance, Sir, on this occasion I would open myself and Circumstances to you in that Frank and Honest Manner which should convince you of the Sincerity of my affections for your daughter and at the same time of the honourableness of my Intentions

Sir of my Reputation or Capability I will say nothing But am ready to make appear to your Satisfaction

this Sir I thought But Fair and honest to acquaint you with that you might Know Something of a person who sues you for your Countenance in an affair that I hope may one day prove the greatest happiness of my life, as it must be, if I can be bless'd with that of your daughters approbation. And the Favour of a line, I take the Liberty to subscribe myself   Your Obt & Humble St

Moses Nathans

LV

Pursuing Indians in Florida, 1836

Myer M. Cohen was a lawyer and resident of Charleston who was among the representatives of his home city in the South Carolina State Legislature.[135] When the citizens of Charleston, and the South generally, became enthusiastic about participation in the Seminole campaign in Florida, Cohen joined a company of volunteers.[136] The lengthy, hastily written book that he made of his experiences is thoroughly journalistic and marred by occasional sallies of rather poor wit. It is, however, interesting for its revelation of the bungling and fumbling that went on, though Cohen rejected the easy temptation to blame all this on the generals.

The passage reprinted below details a peculiarly inept pursuit of a band of Indians who were spreading destruction and depredation through the area.[137] The small annoyances of camp life as well as the larger are presented here. The events described may be taken as typical of the conditions met by those Jewish Americans on all frontiers who took part in Indian wars and skirmishes.

112. MYER M. COHEN'S JOURNAL, 1836 [138]

Camp Bulow, February 25th. Two day's rations having been prepared, Col. B.[139] orders a move. The line of march is taken up at 9 A.M. by the companies of Jones, Henry, Quattlebaum, Hibler and Doucin,[140] for Bulow's plantation, on which the Indians were reported to be in considerable force, having a stockade, swivel, &c. After a fatiguing march of twelve miles, rendered more so by the delays of the wagons, we arrived here, found no foe, took quiet possession of the fort and a four-pounder, and encamped for the night.

We gazed, not without regret, on a scene over which ruin brooded, or stalked with no stealthy pace. The noble mill and mansion are utterly destroyed, and an extensive Library of splendid works is scattered over the field, torn, or fired, as if the Seminole will not that we should sip of the pleasant waters of the Pierian spring, "the pure well of English undefiled," to the savage, but a sealed fount. Here we rescued a Milton and Shakspeare, and mean to make them the companions of our otherwise weary way, the solaces of our heart-heavy hours. Think of one of these insensate sons of the forest, with a "Paradise Lost," or a "Hamlet," holding it up, looking at it, and trampling or burning it. What to *him* is the mighty English lion? What to him the sweet swan of Avon? In *his* hands they are but "as a jewel of gold in a swine's snout," as Solomon saith. But I check my wanderings. Let paradoxical Rousseaus go write essays to prove the superiority of savage over civilized life, and let learned Academies crown them therefor.

Camp Henry, February 26th. Leaving Capt. Doucin's company to garrison the fort at Bulow's, we take up the line of march with what provisions and baggage we can carry on our backs. The tents, &c. are sent round by boats, which we found at our last encampment. Our road is through heavy sands and occasional swamps; wet pine barrens on either hand, succeeded by thick scrub. The bridge on the road having been destroyed, we go round about two miles, come to a watering place, at the base of a steep hill, shaded by foliage almost impervious. Here we find a miserable ox, nearly starved to death, having been tied to a tree by the Indians, who have never returned either to save or slay. We gladly cut him loose, and quickly let him roam where he will.

We passed onward, traversing in our course the plantations of Ormond, Darley and Dummett, which were in ruins.

Having stopt several miles behind the regiment with a sick soldier, as I carelessly hurried up, the men winked, nodded, beckoned; but 'twas all dumb show to me, till coming nearer, I heard the whisper, distinctly audible amid silent hundreds in the quiet woods—Indians, Indians, Indians. And I found that as the companies were proceeding on a causeway leading from Dummett's to M'Crea's, the report of three rifles were heard, and immediately after, several Indians were descried watching our movements. We are now certain of a brush. Every precaution is taken to prevent an ambush, or the escape of the savages. Capt. Quattlebaum's corps is ordered to advance, so as to outflank the foe on the right, and Capt. Jones' company, on the left, the Irish Volunteers and Capt Hibler's command forming the centre. Never did officers or men behave with more coolness or firmness; yet all are, not only ready, but anxious for the conflict. I am placed in command of a party, and directed to despatch an express on the earlier intelligence of Indian approaches. To effectuate this, one of the men is made to climb the tallest tree, reconnoitre and report. Notwithstanding my stern orders for silence, some of my troop continually interrogate the scout as to the prospect from the tree top. These questions, with his answers, remind me of Fatima in Blue Beard, and her oft enquiries of sister Ann; "Sister Ann, do you see any body coming?" His replies were almost in the words of "sister Ann." "Oh yes! I see a great dust, a great way off. Now I see something moving, now I see a large body, but I cannot tell which side they are moving, they may be cattle; no, they are men, and they are approaching, but I don't know if they are white, black, or red men. Yes I do, they are, yes, now I see them plainer, they are *Indians,* and a heap of 'em, and coming right towards us." I post a mounted express to the Colonel, and by the time he returns, the scout aloft discovers that they are our own troops. Capt Quattlebaum's riflemen, who I stated were sent out in advance. As they returned from a fruitless search, the sun shining on their tin canteens, shewed who they were. To complete this account, I add, that while some of my command were constantly interrogating the scout, others were with great difficulty kept from sleeping. Such are the differences between individuals,. Such is man! the strangest sex in the world. (except woman.)

Having scoured the hammocks in every direction, and stationed troops at every point where the Indians were likely to escape, we find that they have nevertheless given us the slip. After reconnoitering M'Crea's where a corn house is seen yet burning, we are ordered to fall back upon Dummett's, so as to have the causeway between us and the Indians, should they be in force. As we are retiring upon Dummett's, a fine fat bullock is discovered, which the savages had shot and partly skinned. I need not add, we carried the prize with us.

At Dummett's stationed with Capt. Hibler's company, in the ruins of the sugar mill, I very politely invite Dr. Strobel [141] to partake my couch; the which accepting, he and I creep into a bake house of the burnt building. Overcome by excessive fatigue, we fall, or rather rush into a deep sweet sleep, from which we are aroused by a discharge from the guns of the two sentinels of the broken wall, just over our heads. Endeavoring to get out, by getting my feet out, (for from want of width in our bed chamber, we only proceed feet foremost) I find I am impeded. I conclude that I am pinned to the wall by one of the mosquitoes which are here perfect Anaks, regular Titans. But I discover that my spur (which from fatigue I had not pulled off) had caught in the Doctor's sword guard. In extricating the rowel, I happen to run it rather deeper than is pleasant through his epidermis: whereupon the Doctor exclaims, "the Lord deliver us! what gallinippers! Cohen, did you ever feel such?" No, said I, (divining what spurs him "up to such a sudden flood of mutiny") I never did feel any *exactly* like that, but it's not as biting as a rifle-ball, so let's bolt out. 'Tis a tough job, what with the spur and the little space, but I have ever found that man *creates* a way of doing what *must* be done, so out we got.

The officer of the guard orders a detail to beat the bushes for Indians. While they are looking at each other, doubtful which side to go, the Doctor steps up, cocking his double-barrelled gun, and heads the party to the woods, exclaiming "forward, men! I'll lead you on, cock Y'r guns, for in partridge shooting, we must be prepared to take them on the wing." Whereupon, we scour the scrub, observing a moving light as we enter it, and pursuing it, see and shoot, no Indians, and return. The light proves to be only an inoffensive fire-fly. . . .

Camp M'Crea, February 27th. We leave Camp Henry, as I name our last camp, in compliment to the Captain of the Irish Volunteers, and his gallant corps, who so well represent Ireland in generosity and bravery. Our boats arriving last night, we go down early this morning to the landing, on the Tomoka, where we cook our *spoil*, to prevent its *spoiling*. After eating one hearty breakfast of *fresh* beef, we proceed to this place, distant from Augustine about fifty miles, and but a few miles from Anderson's, (the scene of the Dunlawton battle, . . .).

A company being left in charge, a party is sent out to scour the adjacent country, which is already *clean* of Indians. We, however, discover traces of their recent visits and a yet smouldering fire. We return after a wet and laborious expedition, the fatigue of which prevents this day's journal from being so tiresome to readers, by inducing me to abridge it. So I only add, that we send down to the boats which had come round, thence procure and pitch our tents, and establish ourselves. And now for bed, that is, for palmetto-leaf couches, and pine-stump pillows.

February 28. To-day we are out in the scrub and hammock land, up to our heads in briars, and our knees in mud. I start on horseback, but finding it impossible (as the guide foretold) to progress with my horse, I have him returned to camp, and proceed afoot. I enter the hammock just after Col B., who is seen toiling laboriously, and heard hacking at round rate, but coming to the spot, I can find no trace of his work, on which the lithe woods have completely closed. My valued friend, Adjutant M.,[142] who is close behind me, tells me that he heard me making a terrible to-do, but that, on his arrival at the same point, he can't ascertain what it's all about. The fact is, that he who follows, "takes nothing by motion" of his predecessor, as we lawyers phrase it, each having to carve a path for himself with his own sword. The vines woo us most lovingly, and clasp us with so tenacious an embrace, as to render parting scarce practicable, Major W.[143] informs me that he could not keep his fileleader in sight, so dense was the shrubbery.

Camp M'Crea, March 6. Events are so few and unimportant, that I have not journalized since the 28th.

On the 29th, Col.B. and staff, with Jones' and Henry's companies, went down to Major Herio's, on the Halifax, 12 miles south of our present position, and found it exhibiting the usual evidence of visits from the Indians, who come but to blast. At Williams', a neighboring plantation, the mill was standing. Our troops remained at this place, 'till two companies U.S. arrived under the command of Major Kirby,[144] who will take post there and establish a depot, if advisable.

We have thrown up an extensive breast-work, (with deep trenches around it) constructed a commissary store-house and mounted a small cannon a-top of it. This piece we named M'Duffie,[145] to do honor to one who honors Carolina and the country at large, uniting the incorruptibility of Aristides, with the eloquence of him who

"Shook the Arsenal,
And fulmin'd over Greece,
To Macedon and Artaxerxes' throne."

We have also levelled the embankments, burned the grass, cut the palmetto and scrub, and removed all objects that were within rifle shot of our camp, behind which the enemy could conceal himself.

Having nothing else to do, let's grumble a little. We have a great deal of sickness in camp, but thanks to luck and the Doctor, no deaths. It has been raining and blowing from N.E. for three days, without intermission.

The men are in fine spirits, and nothing mars the pleasure, which, in every expedition, is derived from unanimity of feeling, except the difficulties of intercourse with other places, and the deficiencies in our list of comforts. Officers, who were forced to leave Augustine without any thing but the single suit on their backs, find it impossible to procure a change of clothing from their ample stores at that place. Capt. H.[146] had to leave his trunk there, and borrow a pair of socks here, and is almost barefooted. It is near a month since the regiment sailed from Charleston, and yet we have only been empowered to proceed fifty miles.

Now that the stockade and other labours are completed, we are absolutely idle, (except at drill) and frittering away that precious time which might be employed in serving or in saving the country. They say we are waiting on the Carolina horse. Why were they not furnished with the means of transportation, and all things needed to bring them here two weeks ago, as was expected?

March 7th. Col. B. and Adjutant M. left us early yesterday morn for Augustine, and returned this evening, alone, 100 miles in two days. The very necessity which could induce this perilous ride, speaks trumpet-tongued as to the state of things. We felt solicitous for their safety, and thank heaven they have returned unscalped to their friends in camp, as they are dear to our affections, and invaluable to our future operations. They went to tender communications to Gen. Eustis,[147] and receive commands from him.

Our regiment is strung along the entire line from Augustine to Camp M'Crea, where there are but five companies out of ten.

Here we remain, awaiting orders, and never more than two or three rations at a time in store. We should have been in the field and at our solemn work. God send us a quick departure, and a forward march upon the foe. . . .

March 10th. The scene shifts, we are no longer still, the curtain of the campaign is lifted, and the bloody drama of war has commenced. Nay, the first act of the tragedy has just been performed. The Indians are upon us. At day-light this morning, I am aroused by the horrid whooping of about fifty savages, and the clear, sharp, ringing report of their rifles, so easily distinguishable from a Harper's Ferry manufacture.

It is but the work of a second to draw the girded sword, cock the belted pistol, and rush towards the quarter whence the yells issued. I see the animating sight of the companies of Doucin, Quattlebaum, Henry, Jones, Hibler, repairing rapidly their posts. I hear the awful cry, "they are shooting down our unarmed men like dogs." shrieked in a tone of agony from the lips of (I think) Col. B., who had hastened to the battle field with a windlike velocity.

What a scene presents itself! A half hundred hideous, copper-coloured savages, some dressed most fantastically and frightfully; others but half-clad with hunting shirts; the rest naked; all with glaring eyes, black hair, and red-painted faces; jumping and screaming like insensate brutes, looking like gaunt and famished wolves thirsting for blood and springing their prey. Our unarmed men hurrying towards camp, bleeding, falling, groaning, dying! All this within 150 yards of the fort, the cannon of which we dare not use, lest we slaughter our own soldiers, who are between it and the foe.

The ruins of sugar-mill are about two hundred yards from our tents, with extensive hammocks in the rear, and towards them our men are in the habit of going daily, to procure wood and sugar cane. This morning an unusual number had gone thither without arms. The Indian wretches must have previously noted their wont, and stealing down before day, secreted themselves in the ruins, allowing twenty or thirty of the soldiers to pass beyond them from a campward direction, without show of fight. But no sooner do they retrace their steps, cumbered with their heavy loads, than the Seminoles emerge from their concealment and scatter themselves, so as to cut off as many as possible. The manoeuvre succeeded but too fortunately for them, but too fatally for three of our regiment.

The line of battle is instantly formed, and leaving a few men to guard our fort, (which is struck by the Indian balls) and protect the sick and the stores, we give hot pursuit. Need I add, we strain every nerve to o'ertake the enemy? We had been greater brutes than they else!

Their spy, stationed on the wall of the sugar mill, watches our movements, and gives the whoop, which is their signal for retreat, and like affrighted kites, they abandon their prey. Powers of rapid locomotion, and superior knowledge of the *locale*, enable them to escape our clutches.

Having chased the Indians as far as practicable, we return to ascertain our loss, We discover two of our regiment, Winser and Barefield, of Cpt. Doucin's company lying dead, a few yards from the mill. They are both shot through the heart, and butcherly scalped, to the very corners of their heads. Continuing our search we discover poor old Kennedy [148] (the only aged man in Capt. Henry's Irish Volunteers) dead, but unscalped. After being shot down, he is fired at, and rushed upon by a dozen Indians as he lay on the ground weltering in his blood. We bring in the dead, and bury them with military honors. No volunteer this morn eats a welcome meal; it sticks in our throats, almost choked by horror at the sight of butchery upon defenceless men, but a few moments before full of life and hope. Or our food rests heavily upon our hearts, swollen by regret, that our fellow-soldiers have fallen low, in a foreign grave, and their murderers unpunished by us. But the day of retribution, we trust, is not distant. No man returns from the field the same being that he was yesterday; we are changed, we are roused. Our blood is up, and can only be appeased by blood. Our brethren's shades shall not "complain that we are slow," or their "ghosts walk unrevenged amongst us." These sentiments may have a savage sound, but they only evince that it is the curse of savagery, by its deeds to extend its dominion, even over the civilized mind. Yet our sternest retaliation will only be the strictest justice upon a fiendish foe.

LVI

Maintaining Family Ties, 1838

This letter starts as one of condolence to Maria Gist Gratz, wife of Benjamin Gratz, on the death of a sister. The tone is remarkably sentimental; Rebecca even uses as consolation the fact that the children of the deceased Mrs. Boswell were undutiful. On the whole, it must be admitted this part of the letter is rather perfunctory, and that Rebecca's real concern is not shown until she comes to talk of the members of the Gratz family and their close connections in the Jewish community. There are several interesting references in the letter to the problems of domestic service, whether in the slave states or the free; the particularly charming euphemism, "your sable household," is used by Rebecca in reference to her sister-in-law's slaves. The subject of Maria's bereavement, lost sight of after the first paragraph, comes into view again in the eminently practical question raised in the postscript.

113. REBECCA GRATZ TO MARIA GIST GRATZ, 1838 [149]

Phila Jany 14th 1838

By a letter just received from Washington, My dear sister we were informed of your loss, and most sincerely do I sympathize with you, for I know your heart will be grieved, at the severed tie which nature & affection bound, and yet I hope you were prepared for your sisters removal. Tho' I felt greatly shocked to hear of her death, she was extremely interesting to me, from the peculiar misfortunes that made her widowhood more desolate, and perhaps if we could think wisely & kindly, without the particles of selfishness, of which is mixed in all human affections, the removal of those most dear to us, under similar circumstances should not be lamented. Long life would not have been a blessing to Mrs Boswell, for the dearest wishes of a Mothers heart were disappointed, and she seemed to love her children as much as if they had repaid her with duty and respect. What then had this world to offer her? God has been merciful to call her to "where the wicked cease from troubling, & the weary are at rest." Let me hear from you soon my dear Sister, that you acquiesce in this trial, and that your own precious health has not suffered. I hope Mrs. Bledsoe too is well, present her my love, and say that I continually think of her sweet kind treatment, and am grateful.

I am happy to tell you our dear Joe [150] is quite well, he is beginning to look better, and is more cheerful. He wrote to our dear Ben [151] a few days ago and I suppose told him so himself, he often talks of you, all, and brings your domestic scene to my minds-eye as I left it, except that he says you contemplated some changes in your sable household so that I find even among your own, you are no better off than we are, for I too have been changing. Old John is the only personage you would know in my establishment but I hope you will not find much difficulty where I know you have not much taste for occupation. And speaking from experience, find it erksome [sic] & unsatisfactory.

Our friends here are well. Sister Hays [152] *hopes* to spend the winter at home, tho' every now & then, a letter arrives from Baltimore directed by Sam Etting [153] which threatens to invade that privilege, if Ellen can but keep herself quiet this season she may be well hereafter. but if her husband has a dinner or wine party, I would not give much for her chance

Harriet [154] took her departure this morning for Richmond on a visit to her parents. The weather is so fine & mild as to tempt her. she took the children & her husband will follow next month & bring them home. Mr Marxs [155] health is so precarious that she could not bear to let the winter set in (if we are to have any this year) without going to obtain his blessing, and Ben [156] thought so too. Gratz Moses [157] has gone to Carolina to be married. He received your affectionate message before he started and stopped long enough at Washington to see the Blairs.[158] Lizzie wrote that he thought of returning by the same route, and then she should see "Sister Mary" first. I hope indeed he is providing for his happiness. every one speaks well of Miss Ash, and she knows into what a limited sphere she must for a long time expect to move as a poor physicians wife. She has been a great belle, and had better offers they say, but none that touched her heart before. Gratz expected to be home again next week, but I doubt whether he can dispatch such an important affair so rapidly, particularly as he has never before seen her family, and I think it will not be respectful to her Mother rushing back without making himself acquainted with her. Every week brings us accounts of Miriam,[159] always agreeable & from herself. Henry Etting [160] is settled at Pensacola & sends home for a house keepe[r] not being able to procure a trustworthy slave.

Joe tells me, we may hope to see your dear Boys in the spring, and I trust you & dear Ben will bring them that your own minds may be satisfied and all our hearts gladdened by a visit. If I were not particularly stupid this morning I would make an apology for such a letter but as it speaks for itself the best I can do, is to make it short. Tell my dear brother, my love does not depend upon my humour, and I always brighten when I think of him. May God bless you all, My beloved Maria, and keep you a happy united family, may your children fulfil the promises of their boyhood, and become men worthy of such parents. Believe me your affectionate Sister   RG

I purchased a dress for you. Shall I send it unmade or exchange it for one that will be of present use? [161]

LVII

Letter to a Niece, 1839

Miriam Cohen (Mrs. Solomon Cohen) [162] was one of the Philadelphia group in the Gratz family. When she accompanied her
husband, first to Georgetown, South Carolina, and then to Savannah, Georgia, it became Rebecca's obligation to keep the old ties
alive and, in some cases, to serve as unofficial purchasing agent for
Mrs. Cohen's domestic needs. Thus, in December, 1838, Rebecca
described to Miriam her efforts to shop for furnishings to be shipped
to Savannah: "tomorrow I shall send a bill of lading to Octavus
[Cohen] as you direct and I hope the articles sent will be approved
of. I assure you we did the best our circumstances allowed, and
did not exceed your limits in our *purchases* one dollar but the box-
ing & insurance could not be paid for with the money sent as you
seemed to anticipate, you will find only one doz cordial glasses,
they are all I could purchase to match the set." [163]

At other times, Rebecca tried to keep Miriam *au courant* with
the intellectual and cultural trends in Philadelphia. It is to this attempt that we owe the excellent account of Dr. Combe's lectures on
phrenology in the letter printed below with its interesting notes on
Lucretia Mott, the great lady of the abolitionist movement. Nor, as
the reader will see, was family gossip and social chit-chat neglected.

114. REBECCA GRATZ TO MIRIAM COHEN, 1839 [164]

Phila Feby 10th 1839

After the exercises of Sunday Morning, My Dear Miriam, I am
not very fresh to come to you but also habit has so long appropriated this day to the pleasure of communicating with absent friends
that I do not like to relinquish it while any of those I best love
are absent and it seems by some necessary arrangement in this best
of all possible worlds—that separation of Family and friends be-

long to the currency[?] of human society—and therefore must have
its uses. It is certainly a great trial of the affections perhaps a test,
and may further be the means of sending our sympathy abroad over
the earth into countries we should have no interest in, which
are yet inhabited by fellow beings to whom the interchange may
be of use. We thus receive & communicate the knowledge of different spheres and our benevolence is encreased the further we experience the benevolence of others. The account you give of Savannah is truly gratifying, and tho' you were happy in Georgetown,
because the home of your Beloved, you will certainly have many
advantages in the City which you could not have commanded
there. And as intellectual society is one of the most fertile sources
of improvement, your capability of enjoyment will advance, as
you have opportunities of rising in its circles. I have often regretted
that your Husband should be confined to so small a community
as Georgetown and I have no doubt he will feel as if his spirit
was free to take a wider range among its peers and try its strength
among more equal competiters. I congratulate you on Mrs Myers'
encrease of family, and safely tho' I do not know whether so many
responsibilities are indeed a blessing, considering how little opportunity is afforded of giving each the instruction they need, and the
start in the world which even the rougher sex require.

I received a letter on Thursday Eveng from the Secretary of the
Navy,[165] not such as our young friend Julian [166] would wish, but
yet not entirely discouraging. He cannot at present give him a
warrant, but I will transcribe an extract which shows his disposition on the subject

"It is due to our ancient friendship and a thousand recollections
that now press upon my mind, to explain to you distinctly why
I cannot at this time gratify both you & myself by granting your
request. The number of midshipmen is limited to two hundred and
fifty, and by a custom, that has almost become a law, these have
been apportioned among the states in the ratio of their representatives in Congress. Georgia has now her full number and will not
be entitled to any more except a vacancy should occur in the
state. When that happens, I will not forget you, but I entreat
you to bear in mind, that the higher a man stands here, from the
President downwards, the less he can consult his private feelings,

or do as he pleases. If Mr Myers from his connexions in Georgia could procure the recommendations of some members of Congress from that quarter, it would aid me in doing what is my wish to do, although your request is enough for me."

I shall reserve the whole of this letter to shew you my dear Miriam when we meet, it is so characteristic of the warm hearted James Paulding, so worthy of the friendship that years of absence and changes of condition & station has failed to interrupt. The girls try to persuade me that it has helped to raise my "self esteem" for they are altogether *phrenological*,[167] but I insist that my own "adhesiveness" and the confidence I have ever maintained in the character of my old friends, will keep that organ perfectly easy. Mr Combe [168] finished his Course of lectures on friday night and has been requested to repeat them, what he accordingly means to do. His old Class are going to present him with a service of Plate and he had one of the most flattering audiences our city could furnish. I believe the whole medical faculty [169] attended & Ladies of all classes, from the life of Fashion down quakers & all, even Mrs Lucretia Mott,[170] was one of his auditors. One morning he invited his pupils to a private lesson on the temperaments, when he wished them to take his place and let the audience in turn tell the temperament of the person standing at his desk. After about a dozen gentlemen had occupied his place, a thin female voice was heard saying it would be pleased to have a Lady stand forth. Mr Combe observed that it was by no means unusual, but after a pause, no one appearing it was suggested that the proposer should set an example. Accordingly a small emaciated grave looking person descended and stood before us. Mrs Eckard [171] whispered to me, I would make a bet, that this person is an abolitionist, and so it turned out, for next day I heard she was Mrs Lucretia Mott.

We had callers from Kentucky telling that your Uncle Ben [172] met with an accident in the Rail road car on the 28th Ult. and was severely bruised on his shoulder & ankle. Happily no bones broke as was the case with several of the passengers. I hope the next account will tell of his recovery. The passengers all jumped out of the car which descended the inclined plane without a break and was taken to pieces & upset [?]. Marias [173] health much improved & the boys well. Your Uncle Simon,[174] is better, but I have not seen him again. Louisa [175] told yr Uncle Reuben,[176] he did not desire it. She said much that I need not repeat and whether it be her own opinions or others that she gave, I shall not enquire, as her father is recovering, were it otherwise I might be induced to seek for the truth. Sister Hays [177] expects to leave home on tuesday or wednesday. She had a letter from Sara urging her on and she reluctantly complys. Ellen is better and Rosa quite well. Julia will be here, about the 16th she is waiting to see Mary Rhinelander married, and her friends Jane & Kate due to embark with their father in the Great Western on a short visit to England. Phil Rhinelander has gone to Egypt and so his Sister will not wait for his benediction on her marriage. Did you read Steven[s]'s book? [178] I think it would send me to Egypt too or to Petrea if I were across the Atlantic. Our Reading morning class takes in Sally Hays & Miriam Etting. And as soon as the work in hand is finished we will accompany or follow you to the court of Ferdinand & Isabella.[179] The Ettings are all well. Frank [180] & Marx you would call perfection, the latter reasoned thus with his Mother the other day. She said Marx I wish you would be good, I hate to whip you. Well Mother, does it hurt you to whip me; it pains me very much then why do you do it? Maria Minis [181] can tell you of Sallys darling her daughter begins to creep about and is very sweet. Your father & the girls are quite well. They heard from Gratz yesterday, he had taken Mary and the boy to Trenton. They are all well. Sister Hays has just come in & desires her best love your uncles also send their's God Bless you My dearest Miriam, remember me affectionately to your husband and to all my friends. Kiss my little namesake for me, and believe me devotedly yours   RG

LVIII

Family Differences
and Difficulties, 1839

After some moralizing on New Year's resolutions, Rebecca Gratz reported the poor health of many members of the family. Particularly interesting is her comment on the desperate illness of her brother Simon, from whom she had been estranged for a good many years. Although she was ready to reexamine her own actions to see whether the estrangement could justly be laid to her charge, her prejudgment was that her sister-in-law's interpretation of these acts and remarks was responsible for this break in family unity.

115. REBECCA GRATZ TO MARIA GIST GRATZ, 1839 [182]

Jany 9th 1839.

A thousands thanks sweet sister, for the happiness your two last letters have bestowed. I did not mean to have been your debtor on the New Year, but old Time on his silent march overtook me before my duties were fulfill'd and will I fear have many registers against me, when my great account is called for—of omissions— not only through ignorance but delays. It is well to have a point in every year to sum up our accounts as well for our moral improvement as for the affairs of business with our fellow beings. And truly I have had a charge this morning that will carry me back through many years of my life, to examine my conscience, for actions and motives of action, for feelings indulged, without the sanction of judgment, and to trace consequences through a long train of causes, up to the present unsatisfactory result.

Our Brother Simon is ill, and has for some time been labouring under a disease, for which as yet he has found no remedy, tho' he has successively tried the skill of various Physicians. You know our long estrangement has not destroyed my affection for him or my interest in his family and about ten days ago, or more, I determined to go out to see him, our Sisters & Reuben accompanied me, we were admitted to his chamber, but very coldly received, particularly me. he looks very sick but does not seem conscious of the dangerous state, his Drs & family apprehend. I told Mr Etting [183] a day or two ago, that I was going again and this morning he came, to tell me of an interview he had with Louisa [184] in the Street, in which she said she thought our visit had been made with the intention of asking *forgiveness* and she summed up such a long string of injuries received from me, from the first hour that I saw her, & during all our intercourse that I do not wonder at the cold looks of my brother, supposing that she has influenced him to think of me through the same medium. Now I thought in times gone bye that I was doing a duty and making many sacrifices in favor of my brother's family, the first out of Love & gratitude to him, the second because I incurred the disapprobation of those I lived with and was bound to obey in all things not immediately against my conscience. And in my intercourse with these children, my affections were so much engaged that I confess all the embarrassments & disadvantages of their situation [185] I took to heart and when they cast me off in the family rupture [186] I grieved about them and pity them still. God knows what is to become of them, when their Father is no more.[187]

There is a part of your letter My Dear Sister, that gives me much concern. You speak of your health as seriously affected, but as your dear Husband is watchful, and Dudley your leech I hope soon to have better accounts. Your New Years gift I treasure, in "my heart of hearts." And give due credence to your husbands feelings, nor indeed is my confidence one jot the less. Nor has my love ever known abatement, it is agreeable sometimes, and why not on the New Year to examine our hearts and renew compacts when we can, of affection or trust, as we do leases, strengthening the old ones, by free and willing offerings, and sometimes raising our grateful estimation, by the memory of our first loves and hopes of future improvements. Every parent realizes such feelings, and in the various relations I have been placed in, both private and public, I have experienced it too. if I did not dislike to trouble you with the vexatious changes & chances of some of my affairs, I would tell you how quarrelsome I have become and what sharp notes have been uttered. But I would rather turn your attention to the family circle, where I know both you and Dear Ben take a deeper interest. Sister Hays has just left me, she spent the evening here and when she can be induced to take exercise, is pretty well. Her daughters write to her every week and she is kept at her desk very constantly. She said the other day she had got so familiar with her pen, that she thought she would write to you. It was so long since she had read one of your sweet letters. Ellen too accuses herself of being in your debt, poor soul, she is such a victim to nervous diseases, palpitations of the heart & depression, a terror of some undefined evil, that it is piteous to read the description of her sufferings. I hope her mothers society will do her some good, and if she enjoys it here, the benefit of medical aid may be had at the same time. Saras letters always speak of Lizzie, and your sister. the last was written on the 1st all the pagentry of the *Court* was displayed on that day. And your niece bore the palm of admiration among the fair & young. Our Sara has not yet returned from Bordentown the little baby was sick, or the servant away, and something or other has detained her until I fear she will not see her Uncle Joe, who returns to Harrisburg on Sunday. Jo has kept his health & spirits amazingly for the winter, except in the beginning he has not complained of cold, and is so much interested in the Gas works that he goes up to the N. Liberties once or twice a week in any weather. He & all the rest of the family reciprocate your good wishes, & pray for the restoration of your health, and the completion of your happiness, half of your boys are no longer children, and the others are fast outgrowing the title. I keep their gauge by some of their old companions, and since Horace has put on a long coat, fancy him & Bernard a couple of young gentlemen. Say the kindest words of affection to all your sons for me, and tell them they can never outgrow my love. I am glad you have dear Mrs. Bledso with you, it must be such a mutual comfort she so idolizes you, that every thing from your hand must be acceptable, and you have so long exercised kindness & sympathy to her that it will be a consolation to you to remember you did so to the last. Present her & Sara with my love. I wish you could see Fanny with her grandchildren, they are such fine little fellows, that one does not marvel at the dotage bestowed on them. The Drs. boys have improved too, and are coming in for their share of notice, Sally does not forget that Jo was his Uncle Bens favorite, and they all root & branches desire to be remembered as loving kinsfolk to you both. Do not forget my dear Maria, that you have exercised my anxiety about your health; and either write, or request my brother to do if it fatigues you. I hope Mr Cooper is mending. Dear Ben is always seeking to do good. May God reward him what a luxury he must enjoy in contributing to the comfort of a good man, and receiving the blessings of his family. Hyman has just come in and seems inclined to fill one of these *love* ends. So I shall only tell you Miriam sends hers to you from Savannah. Becky desires me to enclose you a kiss, and I repeat again & again my warmest assurance of being your & my dear Brothers most fond & devoted RG.

LIX

A Few Words of Parental Advice, 1840

Though not as eleborate as the Hebrew "ethical wills" that have survived from the middle ages, this charming and unpretentious fragment springs from the same impulse of the Jewish parent. It is the fruit of forethought and of the desire, as far as possible, to spare one's children the bitterness and embarrassment of doing the wrong thing. Some of the advice in documents of this sort is ethical; some is on the lower level of expediency and prudence. The writers seem to share with Thomas Hobbes the realization that manners are "little morals." If the grander ethical concepts furnish the fuel that powers human relations, these smaller yet not insignificant matters—kindness, courtesy, and considerateness—supply the lubrication without which unhealthy frictions might destroy the social machine.

Rachel Cohen,[188] the daughter of the writer of these words, was about to leave home on a visit to Burlington (probably New Jersey). It was her first absence from her home. Judging by the "exhibitions of temper" against which her father warned, she must have been in her early teens. By the standards of her time, sterner than our own, maturity of behavior was expected of her. Her father's advice pointed her toward that maturity. The tone of his words seem somewhat formal to our casual taste, but his pride, love, and concern break through the formal surface. His Rachel must have known this, for she treasured his words; and thus they have been preserved for our delight.

116. BENJAMIN I. COHEN [189] TO RACHEL COHEN, 1840 [190]

Make it your habit, no matter what may the habits of others to *rise early*. Enquire the hours of Breakfast, Dinner &c and be sure that *in this, and in all other respects* you *conform to the ways of the house*. Let the family of which you are an inmate be thereby not inconvenienced, else their time and yr own is rendered unpleasant and your absence will be desired.

Let me again inculcate as I could wish to do most urgently, *cleanliness* in *appearance* and *in fact*. Keep your body pure, the surface of your skin free of blemish, use during the summer season especially *water* freely, on rising and on *retiring*, besides the good which in all respects is the result of such habit, *health* is vastly promoted.

You are to recollect after yr arrival in Burlington that you are under Mrs Emory's guidance and responsible to her for all your actions, nothing must be done without her knowledge and *consent,* and let all your movements be dictated by a strict sense of propriety.

If at any time whether at home or abroad, you meet with *dissapointment,* bear it with patience & without murmur, *no pouting*. Reflect that tis for the best, and that exhibitions of temper (which I regret to say I have seen latterly rather too much of) do not mend the matter. Patience under good government, is evidence of a kindly disposition and of sound sense.

In your intercourse with society recollect your youth, with the youthful, be animated & gay as you please, in the presence of maturer age do not be prominent. *Converse* when yr conversation is sought, and when had, let it be in moderate tone, not so loud as to annoy those who may be near and do not desire to hear

Your host or hostess must not be put to expense on yr account without return, I refer of course now to the *direct* expenses, that is to say for instance for Postage, porterage &c. Make it yr business always in such cases to repay the amount expended for you *no matter how small the amount,* the greater yr attention to small matters the more do you evidence your conscience of propriety.

Notes

The following abbreviations have been used throughout the notes.

A.J.A.	American Jewish Archives, Cincinnati, Ohio
A.J.H.S.	American Jewish Historical Society, New York
DAB	*Dictionary of American Biography*
Elzas, *JSC*	Barnett A. Elzas, *The Jews of South Carolina*, Philadelphia, 1905
Ezekiel and Lichtenstein	H. T. Ezekiel and G. Lichtenstein, *The History of the Jews of Richmond, 1769–1917*, Richmond, Va., 1917
Grinstein	Hyman B. Grinstein, *The Rise of the Jewish Community of New York*, Philadelphia, 1945
JE	*Jewish Encyclopedia*
Osterweiss	R. G. Osterweiss, *Rebecca Gratz*, New York, 1935
PAJHS	*Publications of the American Jewish Historical Society*
Phillipson, *Letters*	David Phillipson, ed., *Letters of Rebecca Gratz*, Philadelphia, 1929
Pool, *Old Faith*	David and Tamar de Sola Pool, *An Old Faith in the New World*, New York, 1955
Reznikoff	Charles Reznikoff, with the collaboration of Uriah Engleman, *The Jews of Charleston*, Philadelphia, 1950.
Schappes	Morris U. Schappes, *Documentary History of the Jews in United States*, New York, 1952
Stern	Malcolm Stern, *Americans of Jewish Descent*, Cincinnati, 1960
Thorpe, *Federal and State Constitutions*	Francis Newton Thorpe, ed., *The Federal and State Constitutions, Colonial Charters and Other Organic Laws*, Washington, D.C., 1909
W. & W.	Edwin Wolf, 2d, and Maxwell Whiteman, *The History of the Jews of Philadelphia*, Philadelphia, 1956

Notes

Part One. The Place of the Jews in American Life

1. Constitution of the United States of America, Article VI, section 3.

2. Constitution of the United States of America, Article II, secton 1, paragraph 7. The New York *Times* (Jan. 21, 1957, p. 16, col. 3) reported that President Dwight D. Eisenhower "added 'so help me God' at the end of the oath," thus indicating that it is still regarded as basically a secular oath form to which each President as he is inaugurated may add his own sectarian phraseology.

3. Articles in addition to, and Amendment of, the Constitution of the United States of America . . . , Article I [December 15, 1791]. There is a large literature of commentary and discussion on the meaning and extension of the clauses of this article dealing with freedom of religion. See, in particular, Leo Pfeffer, *Church, State and Freedom* (Boston, 1952); Anson P. Stokes, *Church and State in the United States* (New York, 1950); Thomas I. Emerson and David Haber, *Political and Civil Rights in the United States. A Collection of Legal and Related Materials* (Buffalo, N.Y., 1952), chap. VIII; and Evarts B. Greene, *Religion and the State* (New York, 1941).

4. There were actually three ordinances, 1784, 1785, and 1787, enacted in connection with the development of a policy for the settlement of the territory northwest of the Ohio River. The third of these is usually referred to as the "Northwest Ordinance." It provided the form of the temporary administration of the territory. See *Dictionary of American History*, IV, 181.

5. "Treaty of Peace and Friendship between the United States of America and the Bey and Subjects of Tripoli of Barbary," signed at Tripoli, Nov. 4, 1796. Full text reproduced in *Naval Documents Related to the United States Wars with the Barbary Powers* (Washington, 1939), I, 177–79.

6. Although this is the text that appears in the official government publication of *Naval Documents* . . . , there has long been grave doubt whether it adequately represents the original Arabic of the treaty. Even Mordecai M. Noah realized that there was a discrepancy. More recently, since the annotated English translation of the Arabic text was made by Dr. C. S. Hurgronje of Leyden in 1930, it is clear the Arabic has nothing to say that parallels Article XI of the treaty as here presented. But, as Sherman D. Wakefield pointed out in "The Treaty with Tripoli of 1796–97," reprint from *Progressive World*, Dec., 1955, p. 4: "It should be remembered that it was the Barlow version which was read by

President Adams and the Senate and ratified by them. The *American* government, if not the Tripolitan, agreed that the government of the United States is not founded on the Christian religion." See also Max J. Kohler, "The Doctrine that Christianity is a Part of Common Law . . . ," *PAJHS*, XXXI (1928), 105–34.

7. According to the Rev. A. P. Mendes, "The Jewish Cemetery at Newport," *Rhode Island Historical Magazine*, VI (1885), 81–105, the Newport Congregation was organized in 1658. The earliest cemetery deed on record is dated February 28, 1677. See Max J. Kohler, "The Jews in Newport," *PAJHS*, VI (1897), 67–68.

8. From Lewis Abraham, "Correspondence between Washington and Jewish Citizens," *PAJHS*, III (1895), 90–91. Original manuscript in the Washington Papers, Library of Congress.

9. George Washington (1732–1799), first President of the United States, visited Newport on the date of this address, Aug. 17, 1790.

10. Moses Seixas (1744–1809). See N. Taylor Phillips, "The Levy and Seixas Families of Newport and New York," *PAJHS*, IV (1896), 189–214.

11. From Lewis Abraham, "Correspondence between Washington and Jewish Citizens," *PAJHS*, III (1895), 91–92. No date is given for this reply. Edward Frank Humphrey, *Nationalism and Religion in America, 1774–1789* (Boston, 1924), chap. XVII, pp. 503–16, collects many specimens of addresses to Washington from religious bodies of different denominations and excerpts from Washington's replies. These are interesting for purposes of comparison.

12. From Lewis Abraham, "Correspondence between Washington and Jewish Citizens," *PAJHS*, III (1895), 93–94. No date given.

13. For the history of Congregation Mikveh Israel, see W. & W., pp. 114–45.

14. The early history of Congregation Shearith Israel of New York is presented in Pool, *Old Faith*, pp. 3–48. See also Grinstein, *passim*.

15. For Congregation Beth Elohim of Charleston, see especially Elzas, *JSC*, pp. 30–35; see also Reznikoff, *passim*.

16. There is no satisfactory account of the beginnings of Congregation Beth Shalome of Richmond, Va., chiefly because of the loss of records. Ezekiel and Lichtenstein, chap. XLII.

17. From Lewis Abraham, "Correspondence . . . ," pp. 88–89. No date given.

18. "In 1790 they were incorporated as a body politic by the name of Parnass and Adjuntas of Mickva Israel at Savannah." Cf. *PAJHS*, I (1893), 10.

19. Under date of June 22, 1790, Ezra Stiles, president of Yale College, wrote: "An Address was lately presented to G. Wash. by the Synagogue or Heb. Congrega. at Savanna in Georgia." Stiles then quoted the last paragraph of Washington's reply to prove that the President was "a Revelationist." See Franklin Bowditch Dexter, ed., *The Literary Diary*

of Ezra Stiles . . . (New York, 1901), Vol. III: January 1, 1782–May 6, 1795, p. 397. Stiles was one of the more noted of the early Christian Hebraists in America and was ardently devoted to the teaching of Hebrew in the College. See *The Literary Diary* . . . , under date of June 30, 1790; and George Alexander Kohut, "Hebraic Learning in Puritan New England," *Menorah Journal*, II (1916), 206–19; and *Ezra Stiles and the Jews; Selected Passages from His Literary Diary Concerning Jews and Judaism* (New York, 1902).

20. Thomas Jefferson (1743–1826), third President of the United States, was the chief advocate in his time of religious freedom in America.

21. H. A. Washington, ed., *Writings of Thomas Jefferson,* (New York, 1854), VIII, 113.

22. See also Jefferson's memorandum of Jan. 1, 1802, to Attorney General Lincoln, referring to the opportunity given him by the Baptist address to condemn any alliance of church and state. Jefferson expressed unfavorable opinions of the Jews, however, in his letters to William Short, 1820; Charles Thompson, 1816; and Ezra Styles, 1819.

23. Mordecai Manuel Noah (1785–1851). See below, *passim,* and *DAB*, XIII, 534.

24. Simon Wolf, *The American Jew as Patriot, Soldier and Citizen* (Philadelphia and New York, 1895), p. 61.

25. This was Noah's discourse at the Consecration of Shearith Israel's reconstructed synagogue building on Mill Street. Noah also sent a copy of this speech to Thomas Jefferson; his covering letter, which must have been like that to John Adams, included the following comments: "Nothing I am persuaded can be more gratifying to you, than to see the Jews in this country in the full enjoyment of civil and religious rights, to know that they possess equal privileges, and above all to feel, that to your efforts in the establishment of our Independance [sic] and formation of our Government, they in great part, owe these inestimable privileges. There are few in the Civilized, or if you please in the Christian world, that can boast of having reached forth the hand of assistance towards these unfortunate and persicuted [sic] people. The example which our country has set, now operates favourably in Europe, and the Jews are attaining consequence and distinction abroad." A photostat copy of this letter, written May 7, 1818, and endorsed "recd May 17," is in the A.J.A. For Jefferson's reply of May 28, 1818, see Simon Wolf, *The American Jew* . . . , pp. 59–60.

26. John Adams (1735–1826), second President of the United States, though politically conservative, was liberal in matters of religion.

27. For Joseph Marx (1772–1840), see Ezekiel and Lichtenstein, *passim.* He was born in Bremen and lived in Richmond; he married Richea, daughter of Myer Myers of New York.

28. Printed from the MS. in the Library of Congress, Jefferson Papers, Series 2, Vol. 62, p. 40, by Max J. Kohler, "Unpublished Correspondence

Between Thomas Jefferson and Some American Jews," *PAJHS*, XX (1911), 11–12.

29. Thomas Mann Randolph (1768–1828), son-in-law of Thomas Jefferson, was Governor of Virginia, 1819–22. *DAB*, XV, 370.

30. The French Sanhedrin was a Jewish assembly convened by Napoleon I to give legal sanction to the principles expressed by the Assembly of Notables in answer to the twelve questions submitted to it by the government. See *JE*, XI, 46.

31. Max J. Kohler, in *PAJHS*, XX (1911), p. 12, from Library of Congress, Jefferson Papers, Series 2, Vol. 62, p. 45.

32. For Dr. Jacob de la Motta (1789–1845), physician and public servant, in frequent demand as an orator, see Schappes, p. 603, n.2 to Document 70.

33. Max J. Kohler, in *PAJHS*, XX (1911), 21, from Library of Congress, Jefferson Papers, Vol. 6, p. 119.

34. MS. in the Papers of James Madison, Library of Congress, Vol. 67.

35. Francis Newton Thorpe, ed., *Federal and State Constitutions*, III, 1679–80.

36. Thorpe, *Federal and State Constitutions*, V, 2793.

37. Thorpe, *Federal and State Constitutions*, V, 2647, 2648.

38. Thorpe, *Federal and State Constitutions*, III, 1889–90, 1908.

39. Thorpe, *Federal and State Constitutions*, VI, 3422, 3420.

40. A classification of clauses relating to religion in various state constitutions prior to 1840 is given at this point for comparison with the clauses cited in full in these documents. Information from Thorpe, *Federal and State Constitutions, passim.*

Complete Religious Freedom: Alabama, 1819, Art. I, secs. 3–8; Arkansas, 1836, Art. II, secs. 3–5; Florida, 1838, Art. I, secs. 1–3; Georgia, 1798, Art. IV, sec. 10; Illinois, 1818, Art. VIII, sec. 3; Indiana, 1816, Art. III; Kentucky, 1792, Art. XII, secs. 3–4; Maine, 1819, Art. I, sec. 3; Michigan, 1835, Art. I, sec. 4; Missouri, 1820, Art. XIII, sec. 4; Ohio, 1802, Art. VIII, sec. 3; Rhode Island, 1842, Art. I, sec. 3; South Carolina, 1790, Art. VIII, sec. 1; Texas (Constitution of the Republic of 1836), Declaration of Rights, no. 3; Vermont, 1793, Declaration of Rights, Art. III; Virginia, 1776 (also 1830), Art. I, sec. 16; Art. III, sec. 11.

Partial, or limited Establishment: Connecticut, 1818, Art. I, secs. 3–4; Art. VII (Christian); Pennsylvania, 1790 (also 1838), Art. IX, secs. 3–4 (Theistic); New Jersey, 1776, Arts. XVIII–XIX (Protestant); New Hampshire, 1792, Arts. IV–V (Protestant); Mississippi, 1817, Art. VI, sec. 6 (Theist), but see also Art. I, secs. 3–5 which conflict; 1832, Art. VII, sec. 5 (Theist), but see also Art. I, secs. 3–5 which conflict.

No Test Act: Delaware, 1792, Art. I, sec. 2; Illinois, 1818, Art. VIII, sec. 4; Indiana, 1816, Art. I, sec. 3; Maine, 1819, Art. I, sec. 3; Missouri, 1820, Art. XIII, sec. 5; Ohio, 1802, Art. VIII, sec. 3; Vermont, 1793,

Declaration of Rights, Art. VIII; Virginia, 1776 (also 1830), Art. III, sec. 11.

Ministers ineligible for Office: Delaware, 1792, Art. I, sec. 9; Kentucky, 1792, Art. I, sec. 24; Louisiana, 1812, Art. II, sec. 22; Mississippi, 1817, Art. VI, sec. 7; Texas (Constitution of the Republic of 1836), Art. V, sec. 1.

Conscientious Objection Allowed: Vermont, 1793, Declaration of Rights, Art. IX.

Oath of Office, Secular: New Jersey, 1776, Art. XXIII; Texas (Constitution of the Republic of 1836), Art. V, sec. 2.

Oath of Office, Alternatives Allowed: Indiana, 1816, Art. XI, secs. 1, 4; Kentucky, 1792, Art. VIII, sec. 5; Art. VII, sec. 1.

Oath of Office, Theistic: Maine, 1819, Art. IX, sec. 1.

41. The term "blue laws" originated in 1781. It "was taken up to refer specifically to the legislation of the New Haven Colony. . . . Rather rigid Sabbath, sex and sumptuary regulations prevailed generally in Puritan New England." *Dictionary of American History,* I, 204.

42. 2 Doll. 213; 1 L. Ed., 353.

43. Jonas Phillips was born in 1736. See Rosalie S. Phillips, "A Burial Place for the Jewish Nation Forever," *PAJHS,* XVIII (1909), 106. He died at Philadelphia, Jan. 29, 1803. See N. Taylor Phillips, "Family History of the Reverend David Mendez Machado," *PAJHS,* II (1894), 59. *Census,* 1790, Pennsylvania, p. 226, lists: "Philipps, Jonas (mercht)" and describes his property as extending on "Market Street South from River Delaware." His household consisted of one free white male of 16 years and upwards including heads of families; five free white males under 16 years; four free white females including heads of families; and one slave.

44. See John Samuel, "Some Cases in Pennsylvania wherein Rights Claimed by Jews Are Affected," *PAJHS,* V (1897), 35–37. The first census records two persons by the name of Abraham Wolf; *Census,* 1790, Pennsylvania, pp. 92, 129.

45. 3 Sergeant and Rawle, 47 ff.

46. Samuel Badger was commissioned as alderman of Philadelphia July 24, 1815, and is still listed as serving in that capacity in 1830 in *Picture of Philadelphia.* . . . (Philadelphia, 1835), p. iv. At this time the position of alderman was the lowest rank of judicial office, equivalent to justice of the peace or police magistrate.

47. Zalegman Phillips (1779–1839), graduate of the University of Pennsylvania in 1795, attorney-at-law, is reported in the *Philadelphia Directory for 1802,* p. 193, in offices at 41 N St; in the *Philadelphia Directory for 1814,* unpaged, at 190 Spruce; and in the *Philadelphia Directory for 1820,* unpaged, at 185 Chestnut. He was the son of Jonas Phillips, who was fined in the case reported in Document 17 and note 43. See also W. & W., *passim,* for his many other activities.

48. In legal parlance, this is an action to recover a penalty under a statute which awards part of the penalty collected to the party bringing the action and the remainder to the state. The plaintiff in such an action describes himself as suing "as well (*qui tam*) for the state as for himself."

49. Jasper Yeates (1745–1817) was appointed associate justice of the Pennsylvania supreme court in 1791 and held this position until his death. His *Reports*, in 4 vols., cover the years 1791 to 1808; other opinions by Yeates appear in the 4 vols. of *Binney's Reports* and in the first 2 vols. of *Sergeant and Rawle*. See *DAB*, XX, 606.

50. Town Council of Columbia South Carolina *vs.* C. O. Duke and Alexander Marks, 1833; 2 Strobhart, 530.

51. John Bannister Gibson (1780–1853); see *DAB*, VII, 254.

52. Philips *et al.* Ex'rs against Gratz *et al.*, Adm'r, Pennsylvania, 1831; 2 Pen. and W. 412. See *PAJHS*, V (1897), 36–37.

53. The cases referred to in these documents are typical instances in which the Jewish religious observances of one or more of the parties were an issue. There were many other cases to which Jews were parties but in which religious questions did not arise. It would be, of course, difficult, if not impossible, to trace every such case during the period of this history; yet, this seems to the editors a fruitful field for further research.

54. See Document 20.

55. Jacob Henry was the son of Joel and Amelia Henry; see Schappes, p. 597, n. 2, and not, as had been suggested, a member of the Gratz family who had changed his name. See also L. Huhner, "The Struggle for Religious Liberty in North Carolina. . . ," *PAJHS*, XVI (1907), 46–52.

56. See Huhner, "The Struggle for Religious Liberty in North Carolina . . . ," *PAJHS*, XVI (1907), 52.

57. *Proceedings and Debates of the Convention of North-Carolina, called to amend the Constitution of the State, which assembled at Raleigh, June 4, 1835.* . . . (Raleigh, N.C., 1836), pp. 214–19, for the speech of Weldon N. Edwards of Warren County, in support of full religious freedom; pp. 219–40 for the long supporting speech of James W. Bryan of Carteret County; pp. 254–64, wherein Kenneth Rayner of Hartford County in arguing for abolition of the provision introduced (p. 263) "the Catholic and the Jew" as those "placed under the ban of proscription"; the comment, pp. 306–19, of James S. Smith of Orange County, expressing a willingness to amend the test-act to allow political office holding by Catholics, "But he was not willing, by expunging this Article, to let in Turks, Hindoos and Jews. . . . If a Turk comes to our country, let him be a Mussulman and enjoy his Religion; but if he thrusts himself into our Civil Compact, he ought to worship as Christians worship" (p. 308); and many other comments on this one question which occupied a disproportionate amount of the Convention's time. Specific reference to Jacob Henry was made only once, by William Gaston (p.

281). See also *Journal of the Convention called by the Freemen of North-Carolina, to amend the Constitution of the State. . . .* (Raleigh, N.C., 1835), pp. 49, 67, 100–1, all dealing with the state test-act.

58. J. Agar, *The American Orator's Own Book* (New York, 1859), pp. 227–30, presents the text of the speech as given here. There are earlier appearances; Edwin Wolf, 2d, has kindly called the editors' attention to a publication in *The American Speaker* (Philadelphia, 1814), only a few years after the occasion that called it forth. The version from manuscript given by Schappes, pp. 122–25, may very well be a draft.

59. Solomon Etting (1764–1847), was born in York, Pa., the second son of Elijah Etting (1724–1780) and Shinah Solomon. After Elijah's death, the widow and family moved to Baltimore, although it was some time before Solomon Etting was definitely committed to living there rather than in Pennsylvania. *Census,* 1790, Pennsylvania, Lancaster Borough, p. 135, records "Etting, Solomon: free white males 16 years of age and upwards. . . . 1; free white males under 16 years of age. . . . 2; free white females. . . . 3." See Aaron Baroway, "Solomon Etting, 1764–1847," *Maryland Historical Magazine*, XV (1920), 1–20; Henry Necarsulmer, "The Early Jewish Settlement at Lancaster, Pennsylvania," *PAJHS*, IX (1900), 33.

60. Thomas Kennedy (1776–1832). See Clara Riley, "Thomas Kennedy, 1776–1832," in *Goucher Kalends* for 1916; T. J. C. Williams, "Washington County, Maryland," in *Maryland Historical Magazine*, II (1907), 350.

61. See E. Milton Altfeld, *The Jews' Struggle for Religious and Civil Liberty in Maryland* (Baltimore, 1924); Joseph L. Blau, "The Maryland 'Jew Bill,' a Footnote to Thomas Jefferson's Work for Freedom of Religion," *The Review of Religion*, VIII (1944), 227–39; and B. H. Hartogensis, "Unequal Religious Rights in Maryland since 1776," *PAJHS*, XXV (1917), 93–99.

62. Jacob I. Cohen (1789–1869), banker, oldest brother of Mendes I. Cohen, see Aaron Baroway, "The Cohens of Maryland," *Maryland Historical Magazine*, XVIII (1923), 366–69; and Schappes, *passim;* and Stern, p. 26.

63. Ebenezer S. Thomas (1775–1845), a nephew of Isaiah Thomas, the distinguished eighteenth-century American printer, was trained by his uncle as a printer and journalist. He worked in Massachusetts and South Carolina before taking up residence in Baltimore, which he served in the State legislature. Later he moved to Cincinnati. *National Cyclopedia of American Biography*, V, 393; see I. Blum, *Jews of Baltimore* (Baltimore, 1914), p. 7.

64. J. I. Cohen to E. S. Thomas, Baltimore, Dec. 16, 1818; MS. draft in the Mendes Cohen Collection, Maryland Historical Society, Folder II.

65. Henry Marie Brackenridge (1786–1871). See *DAB*, II, 543, for an account of the eventful life of this lawyer, author, and adventurer.

66. "Report of the Select Committee," 1818, as printed in *Sketch of Proceedings in the Legislature of Maryland, December Session, 1818, on what is commonly called the Jew Bill.* . . . (Baltimore, 1819), pp. 5–6, 7–8.

67. *Sketch of Proceedings.* . . . , pp. 12–13.

68. Thomas Kennedy to Jeremiah Sullivan, Annapolis, Jan. 12, 1819; MS., Mendes Cohen Collection, Maryland Historical Society, Folder II.

69. From a collection of undated clippings in the Mendes Cohen Collection, Maryland Historical Society, Folder II. In addition to the clippings reproduced here, the Collection includes others from the Natchez, Miss., *Independent Press;* the Danville, Va., *Republican;* the Winchester, Va., *Genius of Liberty;* the Shepherdstown, Va., *Eagle;* the Philadelphia, Pa., *Franklin Gazette;* the New York *National Advocate;* and the *National Intelligencer.*

70. From the *Maryland Censor.*

71. From the Philadelphia *Aurora.*

72. From the Philadelphia *Freeman's Journal.*

73. From the Charleston, S.C., *Southern Patriot.*

74. William G. D. Worthington was named Colonel from the City of Baltimore; he was holder of various positions in the government service. See Schappes, p. 168.

75. Charles Carroll of Carrolton (1737–1832), last survivor of the signers of the Declaration of Independence, Revolutionary leader, Senator from Maryland in the first Federal Congress, 1783, and brother of John Carroll, the first Roman Catholic bishop in the United States. *DAB*, III, 522.

76. J. I. Cohen, Jr., to M. M. Noah, Baltimore, Feb. 2, 1819; MS. draft (or copy) of the original letter in the Mendes Cohen Collection, Maryland Historical Society, Folder II.

77. For further information about the *National Advocate* and Noah's position in American political journalism of the age, see Part Four, *passim.*

78. Roger Brooke Taney (1777–1864), who had a distinguished political career as Attorney-General, Secretary of the Treasury, and Chief Justice of the United States Supreme Court, and who was a Roman Catholic, served in the Maryland State Senate from 1816 to 1821.

79. That is, the Federalist Party.

80. William Gwynn, editor of the *Federal Gazette,* whose office was at the corner of St. Paul's Lane and Roger's Alley. *Baltimore Directory for 1819,* unpaged.

81. For Jacob I. Cohen, Jr. (1789–1869), see this Part, note 62.

82. From a MS. copy inserted loosely between the pages of the printed copy of Worthington's speech in the Mendes Cohen Collection, Maryland Historical Society, Folder I.

83. In the printed copy of Worthington's speech in the Mendes Cohen

Collection, Maryland Historical Society, Folder I, a loose manuscript is inserted containing the following note (by Mendes Cohen?): "The following note in the handwriting of Col. Worthington and signed with his initials is transcribed from page 40 of his copy of his speech, which I have found in the hands of my friend Mr Francis Burns

" 'This speech was highly spoken of by Jared Sparks, Esq, Editor of the North American Review. As I was told by a Rabbi it was translated into Hebrew. The facts stated in it & its profuse circulation throughout the state, it was said, mainly aided in repealing that part of the Constitution of Maryland in a year or two afterward.

" 'The Jews always treat me with great politeness and friendly attention, which I attribute to this speech.

" 'W. G. D. W.' "

No Hebrew translation of Worthington's speech has been found.

84. See the comment of J. I. Cohen, Jr., this Part, Document 30.

85. Reproduced by Altfeld, *The Jews' Struggle* . . . , pp. 32–33, from the text originally published as an advertisement in the *Washington County Herald*, Aug. 18, 1823.

86. From the printed original in the Mendes Cohen Collection, Maryland Historical Society, Folder II.

87. Altfeld, *The Jews' Struggle* . . . , p. 204.

88. Benjamin Chew Howard (1791–1872), lawyer and politician, was elected in 1820 to the Baltimore City Council; in 1824, he was sent as a delegate from Baltimore to the Maryland House of Delegates. Elected as a member of Congress, he served 1829–33 and 1835–39. In 1843, he became Reporter of the United States Supreme Court, a position he held until 1861. See *DAB*, IX, 275.

89. Benjamin C. Howard to Solomon Etting, Annapolis, Jan. 5, 1826; MS., Etting Papers, 1826, The Historical Society of Pennsylvania.

90. John S. Tyson (died 1864). His speech during the debate was printed in pamphlet form 50 years later, *Speech of John S. Tyson, Esq., Delivered in the House of Delegates, of Maryland, 1825, on the Jew Bill* (Baltimore Press of O. D. Jenkins & Company, 104 W. Fayette Street, 1876).

91. *Niles Weekly Register*, XXXI (Oct. 14, 1826), 102.

92. Philadelphia, 1833.

93. G. F. Streckfuss, *Der Auswanderer nach Amerika* (Zeitz, 1836), p. 23; translation from Rudolph Glanz, "Source Materials on the History of Jewish Immigration to the United States, 1800–1880," *YIWO Annual of Jewish Social Science*, VI (1951), 131–32.

94. Henry Clay (1777–1852) of Kentucky, perennial candidate for the presidency and outstanding senatorial spokesman for the Unionist sentiment of the growing mid-west. *DAB*, IV, 173.

95. Solomon Etting to Henry Clay, Baltimore, July 15, 1832; MS. copy in the Mendes Cohen Collection, Maryland Historical Society, Folder I.

96. Henry Clay to Solomon Etting, Washington, July 16, 1832; MS. copy in the Mendes Cohen Collection, Maryland Historical Society, Folder I.

97. Robert Y. Hayne (1791–1839), see below, this Part, note 132.

98. Probably Moses Myers of Norfolk, Va.; see *The Norfolk Directory* (Norfolk, 1806), p. 23; Walter H. Liebmann, "The Correspondence between Solomon Etting and Henry Clay," *PAJHS*, XVII (1909), 81–88. It has been suggested that Etting's letter was not motivated by a sense of indignity at Clay's mildly antisemitic remark, but rather that Etting who was a friend of Clay thus gave his friend the opportunity to make a public proclamation of his unprejudiced attitude. See Nathan Ricardo, in *Universal Jewish Encyclopedia*, IV, 189, s.v. Solomon Etting. See also Part Two and Part Three, *passim.*

99. Benjamin Gratz, brother of Rebecca Gratz, settled in Lexington, Ky. See Part Three, for family correspondence between the Philadelphia members of the Gratz family and this brother.

100. [James Fenimore Cooper], *Notions of the Americans, Picked up by a Traveling Bachelor* (Philadelphia, 1828), II, 246. Noah was appointed Sheriff of the City of New York in 1822. See Isaac Goldberg, *Major Noah: American-Jewish Pioneer* (Philadelphia, 1936), pp. 156–60; Schappes, p. 604, n. 3.

101. Reuben Etting (1762–1848), brother of Solomon Etting, note 59 above. In the Mendes Cohen Collection, Maryland Historical Society, Folder I, there is a tax receipt signed by Etting as United States Marshal for Maryland bearing the date of 1791. There is no evidence beyond the signature on this receipt for Etting's appointment prior to 1801, as given in all previous discussions. It should be noted that, in reply to a questionaire from W. G. D. Worthington, Solomon Etting himself had referred to Reuben Etting as "Marshal of Maryland, appointed by Mr. Jefferson." *Speeches on the Jew Bill in the House of Delegates of Maryland . . .* (Philadelphia, 1829), p. 113. The duly appointed United States Marshals for Maryland before Etting were Nathaniel Ramsay, 1789–94; Jacob Graybell, 1794–1800; David Hopkins, 1800–1; *Senate Executive Journal*, I, *passim.* It is possible that Etting acted as an assistant or deputy marshal without formal appointment; see Part Three, Document 96, in which Shinah Schuyler inquires whether Reuben Etting is "in Business or in Sheriff's Office."

102. Original certificate of appointment, a printed form with hand written insertions, signed by Abraham Hammond, Secretary of State, in the name of the "president" of the State of Georgia, William Rabun, in the B. H. Levy Collection. Other Georgia appointments of Jews for which copies of documents are in the American Jewish Archives are Governor John Milledge's appointment of David Bush of Louisville, Va., as Major in the Burke County Militia, 1803, signed by Thomas (?) Marbury, Secretary of State, and a later appointment by Governor

William Rabun of David F. Bush as Colonel of the 7th Regiment of the Militia, dated 1819, and signed by Abraham Hammond, Secretary of State. This printed form has an appended oath, executed and signed by Bush. Characteristically, for this early period, the oath places support of the State Constitution prior to support of the Constitution of the United States: "that I will bear true faith and allegiance to the State of Georgia, and to the utmost of my power and ability observe, conform to, support and defend the Constitution thereof, without any reservation or equivocation whatsoever, and the Constitution of the United States. So help me God."

103. See Part Two, Documents 65–67, 73, 80, 82–89, and Part Four, Documents 125–37.

104. Paul Hamilton (1762–1848), Governor of South Carolina, 1804; Secretary of the Navy, 1809. *DAB*, VIII, 189.

105. Samuel Delucenna Ingham (1779–1860), Secretary of the Treasury, 1829–31. *DAB*, IX, 473.

106. Paul Hamilton to Lewis Levi, West Bank, Dec. 30, 1799; MS., Mendes Cohen Collection, Maryland Historical Society, Folder I.

107. Solomon Etting to Samuel D. Ingham, Baltimore, June 14, 1830; MS. RG 56, Miscellaneous Correspondence, Treasury Department, Port of Baltimore, National Archives.

108. "The site of the first hospital established in Baltimore was selected by Captain Yellott . . . as a temporary retreat for strangers and sea-faring people during the epidemic of yellow fever, which raged in the city in 1794." *History of Baltimore* (Baltimore, S. B. Nelson, Publisher, 1898), p. 486.

109. Francis B. Heitman, *Historical Register and Dictionary of the United States Army from . . . 1789, to . . . 1903* (Washington, 1903), I, 629, records Simon M. Levy, who was a sergeant in the 4th Infantry, 1793–1801; appointed as a Cadet to the Military Academy on Mar. 2, 1801; was commissioned as a 2d Lieutenant in the Engineers, Oct. 12, 1802; resigned his commission, Sept. 30, 1805; and died, March, 1807. See also *PAJHS*, XXV (1917), 96: "Simon M. Levy, the hero of Maumee Rapids, . . . was one of two in the first class sent by Maryland to the Military Academy at West Point."

110. Jacob Mordecai (1762–1838), founder (1809) and proprietor (1809–18) of the Warrenton, N.C., Female Seminary. See *PAJHS*, VI (1897), 39–48.

111. John Caldwell Calhoun (1782–1850), distinguished Southern statesman and patriot, was Secretary of War in the Cabinet of President James Monroe. *DAB*, III, 411.

112. Jacob Mordecai to John C. Calhoun, Warrenton, Jan. 13, 1818; MS., RG 94, Records of the War Department, Office of the Adjutant General, U.S. Military Academy, Application Papers of Cadets, National Archives. The reverse of the document carries the note: "No. Carolina /

Mordecai Alfred/ *1775*/ Gloster A B *1781*/ to be Cadets/ Recommended by/ Honble Nathl Macon/ Jacob Mordecai Esq/ / Appointed/ 24 Marh 1819/"

113. Alfred Mordecai (1804–87). RG 94, Records of the War Department, Office of the Adjutant General, U.S. Military Academy, Merit Rolls, 1820–23, National Archives, reveal Mordecai's successes at West Point. In his first and second years, Mordecai was the second ranking student in his class, behind Cadet William T. Washington, who had been appointed from the District of Columbia. In the third and fourth years, Washington having left the Military Academy, Mordecai became the "high stand" man in his class, although in his third year he stood no better than twentieth in drawing. In his fourth year, though still weak in drawing, his total score, in 8 subjects and conduct, was 1928; the second highest score was 1808. It is refreshing to note that four of his classmates outdid Mordecai in conduct. Extracts from an autobiographical memoir by Alfred Mordecai are to be found in Jacob R. Marcus, *Memoirs of American Jews, 1775–1865* (Philadelphia, 1955), I, 216–31. See *PAJHS*, VI (1897), 47.

114. Brigadier General Joseph G. Swift was Inspector of the United States Military Academy from Feb. 28, 1815, to Nov. 12, 1818. See Edward C. Boynton, *History of West Point . . .* (New York, 1863), p. 313.

115. Jacob Mordecai to the War Department, Warrenton, Oct. 27, 1818; MS., RG 94, Records of the War Department, Office of the Adjutant General, U.S. Military Academy, Application Papers of Cadets, National Archives. The reverse of the document carries the note: "Warrenton No Carolina/ 27. October 1818/ Jacob Mordecai/ applies for Cadets/ Warrant for his Son/ appd/"

116. Jacob Mordecai wrote another urgent letter on this matter to the War Department, Richmond, Dec. 4, 1818; MS., RG 94, Records of the War Department, Office of the Adjutant General, U.S. Military Academy, Application Papers of Cadets, National Archives. The reverse of this document bears the note: "Mordecai Alfred/ of North Carolina/ to be Cadet/ /recommended by/ I G Swift/ and his Father/ Honble N. Macon/ Jacob Mordecai/" and, at another place, "Alfred Mordecai/ Warrenton/ No Carolina/ 15 years of age/ / The within Character/ may be relied upon/ as true/ *I G. Swift*/"

117. Edwin Warren Moise (1811–68) was the second son of Hyam Moise (1785–1811) and Cecilia Woolf Moise (1789–1871), the daughter of Solomon Woolf of Charleston; see Stern, p. 139.

118. Edwin W. Moise to "Respected Sir" (John C. Calhoun), Charleston, Jan. 27, 1823, MS., RG 94, Records of the War Department, Office of the Adjutant General, U.S. Military Academy, Application Papers of Cadets, National Archives.

119. Charles J. Steedman was Naval Officer at the Port of Charleston in 1835.

120. Charles J. Steedman to John C. Calhoun, Washington, May 7, 1823; MS., RG 94, Records of the War Department, Office of the Adjutant General, U.S. Military Academy, Application Papers of Cadets, National Archives.

121. John A. Alston, a planter of rice, has proved unidentifiable except as the brother of Governor Joseph Alston (see note 126 below).

122. Abraham C. Myers was first Quartermaster General of the Confederate Army during the Civil War. See Elzas, *JSC*, p. 221.

123. John A. Alston to Richard Rush, Georgetown, S.C., Feb. 28, 1828; MS., RG 94, Records of the War Department, Office of the Adjutant General, U.S. Military Academy, Application Papers of Cadets, National Archives.

124. Abram Myers, reported in *Census*, 1790, South Carolina, p. 14, Camden District, Chester County. "Myers Abram. Free white males of 16 years and upward . . . 2; free white males under 16 years . . . 3; free white females . . . 2." Admitted to the bar, 1796; see Elzas, *JSC*, p. 128, and J. B. O'Neall, *Biographical Sketches of the Bench and Bar of South Carolina*, II, 602.

125. Thomas R. Mitchell (1783–1837), Representative from South Carolina, 1821–23, 1825–29, 1831–33. *Biographical Directory of the American Congress, 1774–1949* (Washington, 1950), p. 1574.

126. Joseph Alston (1776–1816), Governor of South Carolina, 1812–14, married Theodosia, daughter of Aaron Burr. His political career was clouded by suspicion that he was involved in Burr's schemes; and his private life was blighted by the early death of his only son and his wife. *DAB*, I, 229.

127. Richard Rush (1780–1859), son of Benjamin Rush, was Secretary of the Treasury during the administration of John Quincy Adams (1825–29). *DAB*, XVI, 231.

128. James Barbour (1775–1842), Governor of Virginia, 1812; United States Senator, 1815; Secretary of War, 1824. *DAB*, I, 590.

129. Abram Myers to James Barbour, Georgetown, March 7, 1828; MS., RG 94, Records of the War Department, Office of the Adjutant General, U.S. Military Academy, Application Papers of Cadets, National Archives.

130. William Drayton (1776–1846), Colonel of Infantry, July 6, 1812; Secretary of War, 1816; member of the House of Representatives, 1825–33. *DAB*, V, 448; see also J. B. O'Neall, *Biographical Sketches of Bench and Bar of South Carolina*, I, 305–23.

131. Judge William Smith (c. 1762–1840), senator from South Carolina, 1816–23, 1826–30; Judge of the Constitutional court of appeals, 1808–16; leader of the states rights movement. *DAB*, XVII, 359.

132. Robert Y. Hayne (1791–1839), senator from South Carolina, 1822–32; leader of the low tariff forces in the Senate; known for his debates with Daniel Webster on the nature of the powers of the Federal government. *DAB*, VIII, 456.

133. See *Dictionary of American History*, IV, 251, where this act is referred to as the "first service pension law." See also W. H. Glasson, *Federal Military Pensions in the United States* (New York, 1918).

134. MS., RG 15, Records of the Veterans' Administration, Revolutionary War Pension File of Isaac Franks S 41549, National Archives. The file contains the certificate of award as of Apr. 8, 1818, issued Dec. 14, 1819, with provision for payment of arrears; and Franks's discharge papers, dated March 12, 1782.

135. Joseph Borden McKean (1764–1826). Attorney General of Pennsylvania, 1800–8; appointed associate judge of the district court for the city and county of Philadelphia, 1817; named president judge, Oct. 1, 1818. *DAB*, XII, 77.

136. Isaac Franks (1759–1822). See Morris Jastrow, "Documents Relating to the Career of Colonel Isaac Franks," *PAJHS*, V (1896), 7–34.

137. "Reduced circumstances" were nothing new in the life of Isaac Franks. Writing to Dr. Benjamin Rush from Ephrata, Lancaster County, Pa., under a partly illegible date, June 25, 1810, Franks informed his correspondent that he was bankrupt: "I must therefore inform you, that some time since in consequence of the unceasing pressures of two of my exorbitant and vindictive creditors, whom you well know, and rather then put my Person in their power, I have been compel'd to take the benefit of the Insolvent Acts. . . . By consent I gave private notice, and as none of them appeared, the President Judge indulged me with a private hearing, and I received honorable attention. So that very few know the circumstances. No, not my dear Children. Therefore Sir, this communication is confidential, for which reason have the goodness to burn this letter; for I do not wish the circumstance made public, and please God, if my health continues, I hope again to be prosperous. . . . The Object Sir of this Letter is, to know if you could Obtain for me a Clerkship, or other suitable station in the mint, Or in some Other Department of the U.S. perhaps some suitable appointment in the Custom House Department under Genl Steel, who knows me as a revolutionary Officer. . . ." Isaac Franks to Benjamin Rush, Ephrata, June 25, 1810; MS., Rush Papers, Library Company of Philadelphia; see W. & W., pp. 197, 439.

138. MS., RG 15, Records of the Veterans' Administration, Revolutionary War Pension File of Elias Pollock S 40279, National Archives.

139. See *Baltimore Directory*, 1819, unpaged. "Polock, Elias, pedlar, 72 Front o t."

140. There is no indication why Elias Pollock (1755–1832) enlisted under the assumed name of Joseph Smith. One possibility is that since he was engaging in a revolutionary activity, he was trying to protect

himself against later prosecution. Another possibility is that as he was unable, in 1778, as in 1818, to write his own name in English letters, he may have been unable to communicate it in any way to the recruiting officer.

141. See *Baltimore Directory*, 1819, unpaged. "Bailey, Thomas, justice of the peace and conveyancer, office 6 Harrison; dwel. Pitt extended o t."

142. See *Baltimore Directory for 1845*, p. 20. "Brice, Hon. Nicholas, chief judge Balto. city court, h. 132 N. Charles st." Brice was not listed in directories for earlier years.

143. A letter from A. D. Hiller, Executive Assistant to the Administrator, Veterans' Administration, Washington, to Mr. Louis M. Levy of Philadelphia, dated Feb. 3, 1937 (attached to Elias Pollock documents) in response to an inquiry, notes that Pollock was "allowed pension on his application. . . . His pension certificate was No. 7373. In September 1823, his name was transferred from Maryland Pension Agency to Philadelphia, Pennsylvania Pension Agency. The place of his residence in Pennsylvania is not shown. . . . Elias Pollock died May 10, 1832, place not stated." Pollock died in Philadelphia and was buried in the Spruce St. Cemetery.

144. The story and text of these documents in Elzas, *JSC*, pp. 154–55, n.

145. Israel B. Kursheedt (1766–1852); see the full note in Schappes, p. 596, n. 5 to document 59.

146. Lucius Levy Solomons (1803–30), see N. Taylor Phillips, "The Levy and Seixas Families . . . ," *PAJHS*, IV (1895), 208.

147. Selina Seixas Solomons (1806–83), see Phillips, *ibid.*, 208; for G. M. Seixas, see below, this Part, note 161.

148. Sullivan appears in the *New York Business Directory 1841*, p. 125, as a member of the law firm of Sullivan and Bowdoins, of 4 New St.

149. I. B. Kursheedt to George Sullivan, New York, Aug. 23, 1831; MS., Lucius L. Solomons Collection; copy from the A.J.A.

150. Both the original (1824) Hebrew *Ketubah* and Kursheedt's (1831) English translation are in the Lucius L. Solomons Collection, together with the attestation as given here and a formal notarization signed by Kursheedt and by Samson M. Isaacks, Notary Public City & County of New York, dated July 11, 1831; copies used from the A.J.A.

151. Probably Samuel Hays (1764–1839), husband of Richea Gratz; see Part Three, note 8. In 1825, this merchant had his shop on "Chesnut above 12th"; Morais, *Jews of Philadelphia*, p. 446.

152. Probably Hayman Marks (1772–1825), an exchange broker, who was connected by marriage with the Seixas family and was active in the work of Congregation Mikveh Israel, having been Parnass, 1815–18. His residence in 1825 was at 68 South Front Street. See Morais, *Jews of Philadelphia*, pp. 45, 292, 446; W. & W., *passim*.

153. Levi Phillips (1754–1832), who had been Parnass of Congregation Mikveh Israel, 1818–20, and, after an interlude of six months, again 1820–21, was a merchant, having his shop at 22 North 4th Street in 1825. See Morais, *Jews of Philadelphia,* pp. 45, 447; W. & W., *passim.* He was not related to Zalegman Phillips; see Stern, pp. 174, 176.

154. Moses Mendelssohn (1729–86), a leader in the German enlightenment and a major precursor of Reform Judaism.

155. See the conclusion of Mendelssohn's *Jerusalem: oder über religiöse Macht und Judentum* (Berlin, 1783), part II, p. 140, n.

156. See this Part, note 83.

157. From Hirsch of Uehlfeld, *Dibre Negidim* (Amsterdam, 1799), pp. 18, 26, as translated by M. Silber, *America in Hebrew Literature* (New Orleans, 1928), pp. 46–49 of English section. Hirsch's Hebrew text is reproduced by Silber, pp. 22–23 of Hebrew section.

158. Jacob George Hieronymus Hahn (1761–1822); see P. C. Malhuysen, *Nieuw Nederlandsch Biografisch Woordenboek,* VIII, 666.

159. Properly, Joannes Lublink de Jonge (1736–1816). A literary figure of the era, he translated into Dutch such English works as Edward Young's *Night Thoughts* and James Thomson's *The Seasons.* Lublink de Jonge was a member of the Dutch national assembly from 1795. See Malhuysen, *Nieuw Nederlandsch Biografisch Woordenboek,* V, 326.

160. Gershom Mendes Seixas (1746–1816) was the most distinguished religious leader among the American Jews of this time. As "minister" of Congregation Shearith Israel in New York, he introduced the practice of delivering sermons in English on days of national thanksgiving or humiliation. He is recorded in *Census,* 1790, New York, p. 117: "New York City and County. . . . Seixas, Gershom. Free white males of 16 years and upward . . . 1; free white males under 16 years . . . 2; free white females . . . 6." See also *DAB,* XVI, 564.

In later times, it was not unusual for Jews to gather in their synagogues, even as Christians gathered in their churches, to beseech the favor of the Lord on their country or to give thanks for His providence. A characteristic expression during the War of 1812 was noted in *Niles Weekly Register,* Saturday, Nov. 13, 1813, pp. 184–85: "The vestry of the Hebrew Synagogue, at Charleston, S.C., feeling grateful towards the Almighty disposer of Events, for having pleased to crown with success the arms of the United States, both by land and sea, appointed Sunday, the 31st ult. as a day of thanksgiving and prayer."

161. Mordecai M. Noah, see Part Four and Part Nine.

162. Isaac Harby (1788–1828); see *DAB,* VIII, 239; and Part Four and Part Five.

163. *Discourse delivered in the Synagogue in New York on the Ninth of May, 1798, observed as a day of Humiliation conformably to a Recommendation of the President of the United States of America* (New York, 1798), pp. 23–25.

164. *Discourse delivered at the Consecration of the Synagogue K. K. Shearith Israel in the city of New York on Friday, the 10th of Nisan, 5578, corresponding with the 17th of April, 1818* (New York, 1818), pp. 18–21, 22–25, 28–31. It was this *Discourse* that Noah distributed so widely, eliciting the response in this Part, Document 7, from John Adams.

165. This memorandum was prepared by Harby for Samuel Gilman, who included the full text in his review of Harby's *Discourse . . . before the Reformed Society of Israelites. . . .* (Charleston, 1825). The Gilman review was published in *The North American Review*, XXIII (July, 1826), 67–79; the excerpt from Harby's memorandum presented here from pp. 72–73. Gilman was pastor of the Unitarian Church in Charleston.

166. David Ramsay (1749–1815) was a physician who also played a leading part in politics and wrote several histories, the earliest of which, *History of the Revolution of South Carolina* (1785), led to charges of plagiarism. *DAB*, XV, 338.

167. John Melish (1771–1822), geographer and merchant, settled in Philadelphia in 1811 and thereafter published a series of volumes on travel, geography, statistics, and political economy. His first publication, 1812, consisted of notes called *Travels in the United States of America, in the Years 1806 & 1807, and 1809, 1810 & 1811*. This work had a reputation for accuracy. *DAB*, XII, 513.

168. Jedidiah Morse (1761–1826), known as "the father of American Geography" because of a series of works, beginning with *Geography Made Easy* (1784), a little text that went through twenty-five editions in its author's lifetime. This was followed by *The American Geography* (1789), later editions of which bore the title *The American Universal Geography* (1795); *The American Gazetteer* (1797); and *A New Gazetteer of the Eastern Continent* (1802). He also wrote histories of New England and of the American Revolution. *DAB*, XIII, 245.

169. Probably Joseph Bellamy (1719–90), distinguished theologian and disciple of Jonathan Edwards, author of many works on religious subjects.

170. Hannah Adams (1755–1831). See *DAB*, I, 60.

171. *A Memoir of Miss Hannah Adams*, written by herself (Boston, 1832), pp. 10–11.

172. In the edition published in Boston, 1817, the article runs for 8½ columns, from p. 128, col. 2, to p. 132, col. 2.

173. Adams, *Dictionary*, where the number given is attributed in a footnote to "a pamphlet, styled, 'The Correspondent,' consisting of letters between eminent persons of France and England. London, 1817," although in the text itself reference is made to "a pamphlet recently published, entitled, 'Of the Jews in the nineteenth century.'" It is interesting to note that Mordecai M. Noah, a year later, accepted the same figure

for the Jewish population of the United States, although in almost every other estimate Noah increased the population figure as given by Miss Adams, so that her total for the Jewish population of the world is 6,598,000, while Noah's total is 7,688,000. Noah, *Discourse delivered at the Consecration of Shearith Israel,* p. 45.

174. Adams, *Dictionary,* p. 132, col. 1.

175. See this Part, note 169.

176. *The History of the Jews from the Destruction of Jerusalem to the Nineteenth Century* (2 vols., Boston, 1812).

177. "I next chose a subject in which I thought it probable that I should not meet with any interference. I formed the design of writing the History of the Jews, though I was sensible that it would require much reading, and that I must wander through a dreary wilderness, unenlivened by one spot of verdure. My curiosity was strongly excited, and I determined to persevere in my attempt to investigate the fate of this wonderful people. . . . I had at this time the privilege of corresponding with the celebrated Gregoire, who had attained great celebrity for the conspicuous part he acted during the French Revolution, and exerted all his energy in the first constitutional assembly to procure the rights of citizens for the Jews. He had the goodness to send me writings in their favor, which increased the interest I felt in this oppressed people." "Mr. Buckminster was so kind as to give me the use of his large and valuable library, which was of great advantage to me in compiling my History of the Jews. In my efforts to complete the work, I was encouraged and animated by his participating in the interest I felt in this extraordinary people. Though entering into the details of the sufferings of the persecuted Jewish Nation, yet the enthusiasm Mr. Buckminster inspired, and the pleasure of conversing with him upon a subject with which he was intimately acquainted, rendered the time I was writing my History one of the happiest periods of my life." *A Memoir of Miss Hannah Adams,* pp. 32–33, 39.

178. Abbé Henri Gregoire (1750–1831), French ecclesiastic and writer, supported the French Revolution. He was named Bishop of Blois in 1792. Among his many books is *Histoire des sectes religieuses* (2 vols., 1810, 1814). See *Dictionnaire de Theologie Catholique,* VI, 1854–63 (including a complete bibliography), and *Lippincott's Pronouncing Biographical Dictionary* (5th ed.), p. 1167.

179. Joseph S. Buckminster (1784–1812), a brilliant Unitarian clergyman who died young, is credited in large measure with the introduction of critical biblical scholarship to America. His library of British and continental scholarly works, numbering about three thousand volumes, was remarkable for the New England of his time. *DAB,* III, 233.

180. Adams, *History of the Jews* (Boston, 1812), II, 204–21.

181. E.g., in *Sulamith,* Vol. VI (1822?), no. 2, pp. 8–18; David

Ottensooser, *Geschichte der Jehudim* (Fuerth, 1821), pp. 123 ff., on which, see also M. Silber, *America in Hebrew Literature*, pp. 52–62.

182. See this Part, Document 54 and note 156.

183. *History of the Jews* (Boston, 1812), I, iii–iv, vi.

184. *History of the Jews* (Boston, 1812), II, 210–21.

185. Judah Monis (1683–1764). See *DAB*, XIII, 86.

186. See *PAJHS*, III (1894), 113.

187. Ezra Stiles (1727–95). See *DAB*, XVIII, 18, and this Part, note 19.

188. Rabbi Chajim Moses ben Abraham Karigal (1733–77). See Grinstein, p. 440; *Universal Jewish Encyclopedia*, VI, 320–21.

189. Dr. Abiel Holmes (1763–1837), father of Oliver Wendell Holmes and grandfather of Justice Oliver Wendell Holmes, Jr., was an early biographer of Ezra Stiles, his father-in-law. Miss Adams's quotations in this section are from Holmes's biography of Stiles (Boston, 1798). See Catherine Drinker Bowen, *Yankee from Olympus* (Boston, 1944), Part I.

190. Gershom M. Seixas, "the presiding rabbi" (Miss Adams's note).

191. The account is an abridgement of a letter "written January, 1811, by Mr. Philip Cohen, a respectable Jewish merchant in Charleston."

192. Emanuel Nunez Carvalho (1771–1817) served as Hazzan in Charleston and Philadelphia. See Elzas, *JSC*, p. 145 and *passim*; Grinstein, pp. 246, 252, 577, and W. & W.

Part Two. Economic Life

1. Robert G. Albion, *The Rise of New York Port, 1815–1860* (New York and London, 1939), pp. 6–8.

2. A less "dreary" interpretation of the economic life of this decade is to be found in Merrill Jensen, *The New Nation; a History of the United States during the Confederation, 1781–89* (New York, 1950); Jensen believes this decade to have been one of booming trade activity.

3. The Neutrality Act of June 5, 1794, reinforcing George Washington's Neutrality Proclamation of April 22, 1793, specifically forbade the outfitting of vessels of foreign belligerent nations in U.S. ports. Carl Russell Fish, *The Foundations of American Neutrality* (Madison, Wis., 1922), contains the texts of the documents of 1793 and 1794. See also Charles M. Thomas, *American Neutrality in 1793; a Study in Cabinet Government* (New York, 1931).

4. Moses Myers (1752/3–1835) settled in Norfolk, Va., in 1786. He established a highly-regarded and successful mercantile house, later taking his sons into partnership. The home of Moses Myers is still regarded as one of the outstandingly beautiful residential buildings of Norfolk. In addition to his regular trading activities, Moses Myers was at various times a consular agent for the Netherlands, Collector of the Port of

Norfolk, and prize-master on behalf of the American Navy, as well as agent of the French Republic. It was his appointment as Collector of the Port of Norfolk that led to the correspondence between Henry Clay and Solomon Etting reprinted above, Part One, Documents 39–40.

5. Stephen Girard (1750–1831). See *DAB*, VII, 319. For some references to Philadelphia Jews who were in business relations with Girard, see W. & W., pp. 342–43.

6. James Swan to Moses Myers, Philadelphia, July 31, 1795; MS., Myers Family Papers; copy in A.J.A. Moses Myers apparently acted in the capacity of unofficial agent prior to his formal appointment in 1795. There is a reference to such activities on behalf of a protest by a French Naval Commander against a breach of the neutrality laws by American officials, March 23, 1794; see *Calendar of Virginia State Papers*, VII, 77. He was certainly involved in French commercial enterprises as early as 1791; see J. B. McMaster, *Stephen Girard* (Philadelphia, 1918), I, 142.

7. Cf., for example, Samuel Mordecai to Samuel Myers, Jr., Richmond, Sept. 20, 1807; MS., Myers Family Papers. For a similar problem in dealing with perishable goods in a glutted market, see the letter of Andrew Tucker to Samuel Myers, Norfolk, March 15, 1807 (MS., Myers Family Papers).

8. See Reznikoff, pp. 66–68, 71–73. For a European account of the Jews of Charleston, by a companion of the Marquis de Lafayette on his American tour in 1825, see Auguste Levasseur, *Lafayette in America in 1824 and 1825* (New York, 1829), II, 62.

9. From 1806 to 1810, the United States Congress attempted, by various legislative measures, to bring commercial pressure to bear on both France and England in order to prevent the encroachments of these belligerent powers on American shipping. First was the Partial Non-Intercourse Act of April, 1806; this was followed by the very unpopular Embargo Act of Dec. 22, 1807, and its supplements; then came the Total Non-Intercourse Act of March 1, 1809; and finally the bill that was nicknamed "Macon's Bill No. 2," which was passed at the last session of Congress in 1810, within a few hours of adjournment. This bill is referred to by Henry Adams as "the measure which produced a war with England," the War of 1812. It abandoned the pretense of direct resistance to France and England, repealed the Non-Intercourse Act of March 1, 1809, thus leaving commercial relations with all the world free of governmental control, but it also authorized the President to proclaim a non-intercourse prohibition against either France or England if these nations did not, within a specified time, revoke their edicts, "that they shall cease to violate the neutral commerce of the United States." For full discussion of the Embargo Act of 1807, see Henry Adams, *History of the United States of America during the Second Administration of Thomas Jefferson* (New York, 1921), II, 152–453. A briefer account, based on Adams's, is to be found in Edward Channing, *The Jeffersonian*

System, 1801–1811 (New York and London, 1906), especially pp. 209–23. The history of Non-Intercourse measures is fully reported in Adams, *op. cit.*, vols. I and II, *passim*, and in Adams, *History of the United States of America during the First Administration of James Madison* (New York, 1921), I, *passim*. W. W. Jennings, *The American Embargo, 1807–1809* (Iowa City, 1921) [University of Iowa Studies in the Social Sciences, vol. VIII, no. 1], studies especially the effects of the Embargo on American commerce; the figures cited by Jennings in his Chapter IX show the tragic decline of American import and export trade during the period when the Embargo Act was in force.

10. A letter from Samuel Mordecai to Samuel Myers, dated at Richmond, May 30, 1808, reveals some of the grounds for tension in the United States (MS., Myers Family Papers).

11. Southern commerce was, in general, hit worst by the Embargo and Non-Intercourse Acts, yet support for the Embargo was strong in the South. "The section which possibly suffered the most, but which certainly complained the least," was the South. For a comprehensive view of the attitude of Southerners to the Embargo, see L. M. Sears, *Jefferson and the Embargo* (Durham, N.C., 1927), pp. 227–52.

12. A printed announcement of this, with signatures, is in the Myers Family Papers.

13. For the preparation of John Myers's trip to Europe, see letter of introduction, May 7, 1810, in French, from Lozee, a merchant in Philadelphia, to Arnould Barthelemy Beerenbrock, "Ex legislateur," of 333 Rue St. Honore in Paris (MS., Myers Family Papers). In this letter, Lozee describes himself as a close friend of both Moses and John Myers and refers to his participation with Moses Myers in the business of outfitting ships. Lozee gives his address as % Vanuxen and Clark, Philadelphia business firm. Another letter of introduction, from J. Moses and Sons in New York to Messrs. Batard, Sampson & Sharpe of London (MS., Myers Family Papers), also speaks of Moses Myers as a close friend and merchant of high reputation. As early as March 4, 1810, John Myers had written to the family friend Joseph Marx of Richmond offering to do any services—presumably of business agency—for Marx while in Europe. Marx's reply, dated at Richmond, March 7, 1810 (MS., Myers Family Papers), expresses regret that John Myers proposes a European trip. In order that John Myers might be able to negotiate agreements with European business concerns, on Nov. 12, 1810 Moses Myers executed a power-of-attorney in the name of John Myers, who was already over in Europe. This instrument signed by Moses Myers was attested, on Nov. 14, 1810, by Robert B. Taylor, notary public. MS., Myers Family Papers.

14. Moses Myers & Son to Messrs. Gibson & Co., Norfolk, July 27, 1810; MS., Myers Family Papers. This letter is the duplicate; the original was sent to the Gibson office in Rotterdam.

15. For an example of the importance of spermacetti candles in trade, see K. W. Porter, *The Jacksons and the Lees; Two Generations of Massachusetts Merchants, 1765–1844* (Cambridge, Mass., 1937), I, 271. See also *Commerce of Rhode Island 1726–1800* (Boston, 1914), 2 vols., *passim* (Collections of the Massachusetts Historical Society, seventh series, nos. IX and X).

16. Moses Michael Hays (1739–1805), first of the Newport community and then of Boston, was an insurance broker, commission salesman, dabbler in real estate and dealer in bills of exchange on London. He was also prominent as an underwriter and was one of the petitioners for a charter for a mutual fire insurance company in Boston in 1798. See N. S. B. Gras, *The Massachusetts First National Bank of Boston 1784–1934* (Cambridge, Mass., 1937), p. 57; J. S. Davis, *Essays in the Earlier History of American Corporations* (Cambridge, Mass., 1917), II, 237.

17. Christopher Champlin (1731–1805), merchant of Newport, owner of the Champlin Mason House from 1791; at his death he was president of the Bank of Rhode Island, and he had also been the first grandmaster of the Masonic order in Rhode Island, *National Cyclopedia of American Biography*, VII, 559; *WPA Guide to Rhode Island*, p. 223. See *Commerce of Rhode Island* (as in note 15 above) for documentary records of the Champlin family commercial affairs and some of the Jews with whom the Champlins did business.

18. Moses Michael Hays to Christopher Champlin, Boston, Nov. 12, 1791; MS., Rhode Island Historical Society, copy from A.J.A.

19. Solomon Lyon (or Lyons) was a prosperous merchant in Philadelphia. W. & W., pp. 408–9, for his taxes in various years; pp. 343, 349, for some of his investments; and *passim*, for his relations in the Jewish community.

20. Lyon's Will, May 26, 1802, indicates his possession of two other properties in the center of Philadelphia, as well as other properties in the Northern Liberties.

21. W. & W., p. 183, call attention to the fact that "The social gradations of the day described Aaron Levy and Solomon Lyons as 'gentlemen,' the Pragers, Michael Gratz and Samuel Hays as 'merchants,' and Abraham Phillips, Moses Nathan and Levy Phillips as 'shopkeepers,'" basing their statement on Edmund Hagan, *The Prospect of Philadelphia* (Philadelphia, 1795), *passim*.

22. G. G. Evans, *Illustrated History of the United States Mint. . . .* (Philadelphia, 1885); David K. Watson, *History of American Coinage* (New York, 1899).

23. Solomon Lyon, Philadelphia, to Mary Habacker, Philadelphia, Indenture, April 28, 1794; MS., A.J.H.S.

24. This property was bequeathed by Solomon Lyon, in his Will, May 26, 1802 (copy in A.J.H.S.), to his daughter, Rachel. By this

time, Mary Habacker was no longer its occupant; the name of the 1802 occupant was Leonard Keehmle.

25. Hilary H. Baker, politically a liberal Jeffersonian, alderman of Philadelphia, was a friend of Benjamin Nones; in 1788, when Congregation Mikveh Israel was in financial straits, Baker made a contribution of one pound, two shillings and six pence. See W. & W., pp. 144, 190; Morais, *Jews of Philadelphia*, p. 20.

26. See the references cited in this Part, note 22.

27. The Schuyler Copper Mine, located in Hanover, Hudson County, New Jersey, was one of the most productive of the early mines in the U.S. It was discovered prior to 1719 by a Negro slave on the Schuyler estate. Before the Revolution, a shaft of close to 200 feet had been sunk. Mining operations were often brought to a halt by the presence of water in the shaft. To cope with this problem, a steam engine was imported, in parts, and erected by Josiah Hornblower about 1755. This engine, an early model, preceding the improved Watt engine, operated on the atmospheric principle of Newcomen's engine. It remained in service for more than 40 years. See J. L. Bishop, *A History of American Manufactures from 1688–1860* (Philadelphia, 1864), I, 546–47; *WPA Guide, New Jersey*, p. 542.

28. Uriah Tracy (1755–1807), Senator from Connecticut, 1796–1807. Previously member of the Connecticut House of Representatives, 1788–93 (Speaker, 1793), States attorney for Litchfield County, 1794–99; member of U.S. House of Representatives, 1793–96. *Biographical Directory of the American Congress, 1774–1949*, p. 1929.

29. For a picture of Jewish participation in the copper trade in post-colonial America, see Mark Bortman, "Paul Revere and Son and Their Jewish Correspondents," *PAJHS*, XLIII (1954), 199–229.

30. Jacob Marks Company to Alexander Hamilton, without place or date, marked "file Dec. 10. 1794," MS., Record Group No. 59, General Records of the Department of State, Miscellaneous Letters, Oct.–Dec., 1794, National Archives.

31. Alexander Hamilton (1755–1804), was Secretary of the Treasury in the cabinet of President Washington. *DAB*, VIII, 171; date of birth as given in *DAB* (1757) has been corrected to accord with recent evidence. See Broadus Mitchell, *Alexander Hamilton: Youth to Maturity, 1755–1788* (New York, 1957).

32. Jacob Marks Co. evidently was an early participant in various facets of the metal trades, particularly copper. Their relation to the Schuyler Copper Mine, suggested in this letter, is further emphasized in an advertisement in the New York *Spectator*, Oct. 4, 1797: "Ore of every kind assayed and purchased. Also leases of mining ground taken. Apply to Frederick Rhode, assayer at Schuylers Copper Mine N.J. or J. Mark & Co. New York." Another advertisement, New York

Daily Advertiser, June 21, 1798, stresses that orders are taken for bolts, sheathing nails and brass castings for machinery, and that old copper, brass, copper ore and pig iron were purchased. Both advertisements appear in R. S. Gottesman, *The Arts and Crafts in New York, 1777–1799* (New York, 1954), pp. 249–50, 261. Later, Jacob Marks and Co. entered the Indian trade and supplied the government with goods and materials designed especially for this trade. See Document 65.

33. Jacob Jacobs (1764–97) is recorded as a householder in the *Census*, 1790, South Carolina, p. 41. See also Reznikoff, *passim;* and Elzas, *JSC, passim.*

34. Recorded in Charleston *Will Book*, XXVI (1793–1800), 640–44.

35. Congregation Beth Elohim. Jacobs's legacy of 10 pounds was a modest one compared with the 200 pounds left by Philip Hart (1727–96). For this and other early bequests, see Reznikoff, p. 245.

36. Rachael Jacobs was the youngest sister of Jacob Jacobs, a daughter of David Jacobs and his wife Richa.

37. Samuel Jacobs (1767–1810) was an officer of a Masonic lodge in Charleston, *PAJHS*, XIX (1910), 86; and at one time a contributor to Congregation Beth Elohim, Elzas, *JSC*, p. 135.

38. Phila (Hays) Nunez (1738–1808) was the sister of Jacobs's wife and the widow of Daniel Nunez (1705–89).

39. Gershon Cohen (1748–1802), a prominent merchant, resided in Charleston during the British occupation of that city in 1780. His patriotism was, however, never called in question. Reznikoff, pp. 47–50. He was a member of the committee of three to raise the money for building the $20,000 "new synagogue" for Beth Elohim in 1792. See Elzas, *JSC, passim.* He had a large household, according to *Census*, 1790, South Carolina, p. 39: "Free white males of 16 years and up- ward . . . 3; free white males under 16 . . . 3; free white females . . . 7; slaves . . . 6."

40. Katey (Caty) Jacobs, a sister of Moses Michael Hays, married Abraham Sarzedas in 1753; after his death, which occurred before 1779, she became Mrs. Jacob Jacobs.

41. Jacob Jacobs apparently was less concerned about slavery than some other Jews of his time. Philip Hart manumitted his slaves by will; see Charleston *Will Book*, XXVI (1793–1800), 397–98. When slaves were not emancipated by will, they might be emancipated by deed. In the *Deed Book*, vol. 2, p. 520, of the Petersburg, Va., Hustings Court, under the date of Oct. 2, 1797, there is a deed of emancipation signed by Samuel Myers on April 20, 1796, which has special interest, since the slave concerned had been purchased only three months before the date of the deed: "I, Samuel Myers, of the Town of Petersburg, in the State of Virginia, do declare, that I did purchase of David Maitland, Trustee on the estate of Simon Fraser deceased (according to his bill of Sale granted to me, dated the fourth day of January 1796) a Mulatto Woman

named Alice, about the age of forty two years. Now therefore I do, for myself, my heirs, executors and administrators, hereby release unto her the said Alice all my right, claim, interest or pretensions of claims whatsoever, as to her person or any estate she may hereafter acquire, without any interruption, from me, or any other person whatsoever claiming by, from, or under me. . . ." The witnesses to this deed of emancipation were M. M. Myers and S. M. Myers. Is it conceivable that in a quarter of a year, Samuel Myers had developed conscientious scruples? See also Part Three, Document 109 and notes thereto. The manumission of slaves by will was forbidden in South Carolina after 1841. See Rosser H. Taylor, *Ante-Bellum South Carolina* (Chapel Hill, N.C., 1942), p. 186.

42. Rebecca (Sarzedas) Cohen (1761–1841) was a daughter of Caty Jacobs by her first husband. Her name appears in *A Census of Pensioners for Revolutionary or Military Service* (Washington, 1841). See Elzas, *JSC*, p. 92.

43. Phillip Cohen (1781–1866) was probably the same "respectable merchant" who supplied Hannah Adams with her information about the Jews of Charleston. See Part One, Document 58, and Stern, p. 31.

44. Jacob J. Cohen (1784–1849). Stern, p. 31.

45. Thomas Osborn (or Osborne) was a delegate from St. Bartholomew's parish in Charleston to the South Carolina Colony Congress in 1775. Later, he was sheriff for many years; see *South Carolina Historical and Genealogical Magazine,* VII (1906), 105.

46. Edward Lowndes, merchant and property owner in Charleston, died in 1801; see *South Carolina Historical and Genealogical Magazine,* VI (1905), 26.

47. Abraham Serzedas Cohen, brother of Philip and Jacob J. Cohen. There is no entry other than his name in Stern, p. 31.

48. Hyam Cohen (1789–1850) served as assistant paymaster in Seminole War, 1836; city assessor of Charleston, 1838–50. See Elzas, *JSC*, pp. 133, 204, 207; Reznikoff, pp. 104–5, 283. Obituary notice in Charleston *Mercury,* Aug. 26, 1850.

49. *Census,* 1790, South Carolina, Charleston district, p. 32, lists Joshua Ward as head of a household consisting of 62 slaves.

50. *Census,* 1790, South Carolina, Charleston, p. 38, lists: "Somersell, William, free white males 16 years and upward . . . 3; free white females . . . 5; slaves . . . 12."

51. *Census,* 1790, South Carolina, Charleston, p. 42, lists: "Taylor, Bennet, free white males 16 years and upward . . . 2; slaves . . . 7."

52. *Charleston Directory for 1829,* p. 90, lists a Thomas L. Jones as an attorney-at-law with offices at 10 St. Michael's Alley. It is questionable whether this is the same person, since *Census,* 1790, South Carolina, lists no fewer than 16 men named Thomas Jones.

53. There has already been much information gleaned from wills by all historians of local Jewish communities. Much, however, still remains

to be done with these documents which reveal family information as well as economic matters, attitudes toward slavery, and devotion to Jewish organizations and to synagogues. Particularly touching passages can be found in some of these wills, e.g., that of David Brandon, probated April 24, 1838: "I do by this present give and do give with my free Will and accord and without any other reason that my wife ['s] Daughter Rachel Depas, Widow of fisher Moses with whom She had two childrens Mariamne and fisher that I love as if they was my own childrens, and having married again with William C. Lambert and having also two other childrens that I love as if they was my own childrens, named Elizabeth Lambert and Samuel Lambert, I leave to my beloved Rachel Lambert whatever I will have at my Demise. . . .

"I recommend my faithful Servant and friend Juellit or Julien free negro, to my Dear Rachel and W. C. Lambert my friend & request them to take him under their protection to treat him well as they would do me and to give him Such portion of my Cloths as they will think useful to him and never to forsake him being the best friend I ever had." Recorded in Charleston *Will Book* H, 1834–39, p. 356.

54. Simon Philipson was in partnership with his brother, Jacob, at 18 Chestnut Street in Philadelphia; see *Philadelphia Directory for 1804*, p. 182. They maintained an Indian trading post in the new territory of St. Louis, Missouri, as well as headquarters in Philadelphia. They were early members of Congregation Rodeph Shalom, the first Ashkenazic synagogue in the United States. A considerable part of their business was in furs and skins: "Missouri Beaver, Dressed Buffalo Hides, Racoon, Muskrat, Bear and other Skins, shaved, in the hair and Indian Dressed Deerskins" read one of their advertisements, in *Poulson's American Daily Advertiser*, July 18, 1812. John Jacob Astor was one of their sources of supply. Later, Simon Philipson and his family moved to St. Louis while his brother Jacob remained in Philadelphia to manage the eastern end of the business. W. & W., pp. 356, 495.

55. The system of discrimination to build up the national trade and commerce of the U.S., began very early with the Act of July 20, 1789, which placed higher tonnage duties on foreign vessels and "granted a rebate of 10% on duties payable on imports when goods were brought to the country in American ships." E. R. Johnson and others, *History of Domestic and Foreign Commerce in the United States* (Washington, 1915), II, 1–30.

56. *Report of the Committee of Commerce and Manufactures, to whom was referred on the Eighteenth of December Last, the Petition of Simon Philipson, of the City of Philadelphia. 20th February, 1805. Read and ordered to be referred to a committee of the whole House, to-morrow* [Washington, 1805].

57. *Philadelphia Directory, 1804*, p. 35 records only one Breithaupt,

but his initial was F., not T. as in the report. He was a merchant, and may have been a friend of Philipson.

58. Thomas Usher Pulaski Charlton (1779–1835), a lawyer in Savannah, who had served as elected representative to the Georgia State Legislature, and, in 1807, as judge of the Eastern circuit in that state, is chiefly remembered as the compiler of the first volume of Georgia court decisions, *Reports of Cases Argued and Determined in the Superior Courts of the Eastern District of the State of Georgia* (1824). *DAB*, IV, 24.

59. Mordecai M. Sheftall (1789–1856) was the fifth son of Levi Sheftall (1739–1809) and his wife Sarah de la Motta (1753–1811). Levi Sheftall was a half-brother of the first Mordecai Sheftall (1736?–97), father of Dr. Moses Sheftall. Thus, Dr. Moses Sheftall, who signed this form, was the cousin of young Mordecai. No correction was made in the printed form, where the consent of the apprentice's father is spoken of. See Stern, p. 193; Edmund H. Abrahams, "Some Notes on the Early History of the Sheftalls of Georgia," *PAJHS*, XVII (1909), 167–86; and Leo Shpall, "The Sheftalls of Georgia," *Georgia Historical Quarterly*, XXVII (1943), pp. 339–49; see also, Malcolm H. Stern, "New Light on the Jewish Settlement of Savannah," *American Jewish Historical Quarterly*, LII (1962–63), 169–99.

60. For comparison with an earlier printed apprenticeship form, see Richard B. Morris, *Government and Labor in Early America* (New York, 1946), pp. 366–67.

61. Photographic copy of the original document from A.J.A.

62. There is comparatively little information about Sabbath and Holy Day observance in our period outside of synagogue records, which are generally pessimistic since they report actions taken to encourage increased observance. See Part Six. Certainly maintenance of Jewish traditions was of great concern to the Sheftall family; see Part Three, Document 93. Another case in point reveals at least Holy Day observance by a Jewish business firm in Richmond, Va. See Ezekiel and Lichtenstein, pp. 128–29, 298. See also this Part, note 94, for another instance of a Sabbath-observing business firm in Wilmington, Del.

63. Levi Sheftall DeLyon, who witnessed this indenture, was yet another cousin of Mordecai Sheftall. DeLyon's mother, Sarah (Sheftall) DeLyon, was a sister of Levi Sheftall. She married Abraham DeLyon, a surgeon in the Revolutionary War, who died in 1835. Levi S. DeLyon later became a judge. See Stern, pp. 41, 193.

64. See this Part, Document 61.

65. For General John Mason, see George Dewey Harmon, *Sixty Years of Indian Affairs* (Chapel Hill, N.C., 1941), *passim.* Originally, the headquarters of the Office of Indian Affairs were at Philadelphia but were later removed to Georgetown. Harmon, *op. cit.*, p. 106, n. 44.

66. Levi Sheftall (1739–1809), see E. H. Abrahams, in *PAJHS*, XVII (1909), Shpall, in *Georgia Historical Quarterly*, XVII (1943).

67. Benjamin Sheftall, see Stern, p. 193.

68. Mordecai Sheftall, see this Part, note 59.

69. John Mason to Jacob Mark, Georgetown, April 10, 1811; MS., RG 75, Records of the Bureau of Indian Affairs, Office of Indian Trade, Letters sent, volume B, National Archives.

70. See also John Mason to Jacob Mark, Georgetown, May 24, 1811; MS., RG 75, Records of the Bureau of Indian Affairs, Office of Indian Trade, Letters sent, volume B, National Archives.

71. John Mason to William Simmons, Georgetown, Feb. 2, 1813; MS., RG 75, Records of the Bureau of Indian Affairs, Office of Indian Trade, National Archives.

72. Mason did write this letter; see J.M. to Ben Sheftall, Georgetown, Feb. 2, 1813; MS., RG 75, Records of the Bureau of Indian Affairs, Office of Indian Trade, National Archives. One of the items in dispute was a charge of $50 "for extra services and store rent." With respect to this, Mason wrote "I must repeat as I said in my letter of 31 May 1809 I cannot in justice to the public find it consistent with my duty to allow it. Mr. Sheftall was in receipt of a fixed salary from this office which was deemed by him equal to his services for it."

73. At this time the Office of Indian Trade was separate from the Indian Department; the latter was an agency of the War Department.

74. John Mason to Ben Sheftall, Georgetown, March 2, 1813; MS., RG 75, Records of the Bureau of Indian Affairs, Office of Indian Trade, National Archives.

75. The expression is quoted from Mason's letter to Sheftall referred to in note 72 above.

76. See this Part, note 9.

77. Richard Leake was an attorney, who in 1820 had his office at 16 South Seventh Street in Philadelphia; McElroy's *Philadelphia Directory for 1820.*

78. For Moses Sheftall, see Part Three, Document 93, and Part Five, Document 178.

79. Richard Leake to Dr. Moses Sheftall, Philadelphia, July 29, 1812; MS., B. H. Levy Collection; copy from A.J.A.

80. The original "Essex Junto" was made up of men of the upper classes of Essex County, Mass., who came together at Ipswich in April, 1778, to consider a new constitution for Massachusetts. The name was later applied to a group of anti-French Federalist extremists, led by Senator Timothy Pickering of Massachusetts, who vigorously opposed the War of 1812.

81. For Philadelphia "society" at this time, see the letters of Rebecca Gratz, in Part Three.

82. President Madison's War Message of June 1, 1812, listed four reasons for going to war; one was the refusal of the British to revoke the Orders in Council (see this Part, note 9, on Macon's Bill No. 2). On June 17, 1812, the Orders in Council were revoked, but this news did not reach the United States in time to prevent the Congressional vote in favor of war, June 18, 1812.

83. The coincidence of names suggests that "Mr. P" is Zalegman Phillips (1779–1839), whose wife Arabella's (1786–1826) maiden name was Solomons; see Stern, pp. 174, 22.

84. Mordecai M. Sheftall, see this Part, note 59.

85. Richard Leake wrote to Moses Sheftall on business and social matters quite often. In a letter dated August 8, 1813, he voiced the opinion "that the British will in the Winter go along our Southern Coast. . . . They can land about 4000 men including sailors & marines. I think they will not trust them far inland for fear of *desertion*. . . . Your forts with *red hot shot* could sink their barges, but you could not prevent in your present state of preparation their landing below fort Jackson." As an amateur strategist he went on to suggest "Lines of Circumval-lation" to prevent such a landing. Later, in the same letter, Leake wrote: "Perhaps the most important subject of our deliberations now is the prospect of *Peace*, it is a fact that cotton has fallen in England, the London paragraphists talk very unfavorably of a peace & of the Russian mediation in a rage. . . . here you may know a mans sentiments by the state of his stock on hand. if he has much goods he wishes war, if he has none on hand, he wants *a speedy peace*, as to the terms he cares not a fig. his pocket & his purse is his political thermometer, which is hot or cool as the tide of goods ebbs or flows" (MS., B. H. Levy Collection, copy from A.J.A.).

86. Robert Fulton (1765–1815), artist, civil engineer, and inventor; his design for a steam-powered war vessel, the *Fulton the First,* was authorized for construction by Congress in 1814. This was to have been a huge paddle-wheel-driven warship; it was constructed but never tested in battle. Fulton's correspondence with Solomon Etting refers to an offer made by a Baltimore syndicate to undertake the construction of this experimental vessel.

87. For Solomon Etting, see Part One, note 59.

88. Robert Fulton to Solomon Etting, New York, Nov. 26, 1814; MS., Fulton Papers, Library of Congress; copy from typescript in the Mendes Cohen Collection, Maryland Historical Society.

89. Another member of the far-flung Myers family who had diffi-culties as a result of the wartime conditions that prevailed was David Myers, commander of a merchant vessel for which he could not get clearance papers.

90. Indeed, they were of much earlier date; by 1699 lotteries were

already prevalent in New England and denounced by an ecclesiastical assembly there as "a cheat" and lottery agents described as "pillagers of the people." See *Dictionary of American History,* III, 303.

91. See below, Part Six, Document 192.

92. See Edwin Wolf, 2d, "Unrecorded American Judaica Printed before 1851," in Handlin, *et al., Essays in American Jewish History* (The American Jewish Archives, Cincinnati, Ohio, 1958), p. 204, number 55.

93. Advertisement, *Delaware Gazette and Peninsula Advertiser,* June 20, 1815. Copy from A.J.A.

94. Jacob da Silva Solis (1780–1829) and his brother Daniel (1784–1869) were in business partnership in Wilmington, Del. In a later issue (Dec. 1815) of the *Delaware Gazette and Peninsula Advertiser* in which this lottery is advertised, the partners also advertised their new venture into wholesale trade in dry goods: "To Country Storekeepers. J. S. & D. Solis, Respectfully inform them and others, that they have opened a wholesale Dry Goods Store, At No. 22, Third street, between King and French streets, where they keep a constant supply of fresh goods suitable to the season, which they will sell at the Philadelphia prices. It is hardly necessary to say how much time and expense may be saved by giving the preference to this new establishment, instead of travelling to and from Philadelphia; particularly when the subscribers will take Delaware and Southern bank notes at par for all new purchasers. Wilmington, Dec. 14, 3 m. N.B. No business transacted on seventh day."

See Part Three, Document 111, and notes for further information on the Solis family.

95. *Report of the Trial of Charles N. Baldwin for Libel, in Publishing, in the Republican Chronicle, Certain Charges of Fraud and Swindling in the Management of Lotteries in the State of New York* (New York, 1818), pp. 8–10, 66–67.

96. Eleazer S. Lazarus (1788–1844) was, by trade, a distiller, very active in congregational affairs in Shearith Israel. See also Part Five, Document 188.

97. Naphtali Judah (1773–1855), see Schappes, pp. 590–91. Schappes states that Judah became a lottery broker some time after the War of 1812; the document above states that Judah had been in this business as early as 1809. See also Edwin Wolf, 2d, "Unrecorded American Judaica . . . ," p. 199, number 35, referring to 1811.

98. Mordecai Myers (1776–1871) was born in Newport. He was brought to New York by his widowed mother when he was four years old. During a brief stay in business in Richmond, he was active in the affairs of Congregation Beth Shalome. When he returned to New York, he became a devoted adherent of the Masonic order and was a member of Congregation Shearith Israel. He was a member of the Tammany Society and an elected representative to the State Assembly in 1828, and again from 1830 to 1834; as a member of a select committee on

legislative chaplaincies, he signed an important report recommending the abolition of fees for chaplains. Later, he removed to Schenectady, N.Y., where he served as mayor in 1853 and 1854. He participated in the War of 1812 as a Captain in the U.S. Infantry. See his *Reminiscences 1780 to 1814 Including Incidents in the War of 1812–1814, Letters Pertaining to his Early Life Written by Major Myers, 13th Infantry, U.S. Army to his Son* (Washington, 1900), and selections from these memoirs in Schappes, pp. 96–99, 127–33; see also Schappes's full notes to these documents, esp. 591–92, and 598–99. For the report on legislative chaplaincies, see Joseph L. Blau, ed., *Cornerstones of Religious Freedom in America* (Boston, 1949), pp. 136–56. See also Pool, *Old Faith*, p. 321 and *passim;* Marcus, *Memoirs of American Jews, 1775–1865* (Philadelphia, 1955), I, 50–75.

99. Solomon Seixas (1787–1840), a son of Benjamin M. Seixas, served as Major in the War of 1812.

100. Not only was a verdict of "not guilty" returned by the jury, but 11 of its members commended Baldwin to the consideration of the state for his public service; the other juror dissented, so this matter was dropped. Two of the jurors in this case may have been Jewish: Isaac Collins and Harmon Shatzel.

101. Asher Marx was, like his brother Joseph, one of the early members of Congregation Beth Shalome of Richmond. See *PAJHS*, IV (1896), 21; XX (1911), 104. Later, he removed to Baltimore; Stern, p. 132.

102. See above, Part One, note 32.

103. Asher Marx to Moses Myers & Sons, New York, June 11, 1819; MS., Myers Family Papers. Three days later, on June 14, 1819, Asher Marx again wrote from New York to Moses Myers, raising the question of a settlement of accounts with Moses Myers & Sons in a rather acrimonious fashion. When several months had passed, the acrimony became so great that Asher's brother Joseph Marx made an effort to settle the matter (Joseph Marx to Moses Myers, Richmond, Nov. 6, 1819; MS., Myers Family Papers). The matter was not settled by this interposition, however, nor could it have been, because of the assignment of all Myers's assets to Lamb & Drummond as trustees. On Feb. 23, 1825, Asher Marx again wrote to Moses Myers & Sons for a settlement; the amount involved was $17,911.36 (Asher Marx to Moses Myers & Sons, New York, Feb. 23, 1824; MS., Myers Family Papers). See also, Joseph Marx to Moses Myers, Richmond, Oct. 30, 1819; MS., Myers Family Papers. In still another letter of advice, dated at Richmond, Oct. 7, 1820, Joseph Marx suggested to Moses Myers that he should take advantage of the state bankruptcy act (Joseph Marx to Moses Myers, Richmond, Oct. 7, 1820; MS., Myers Family Papers).

104. MS., Connecticut State Archives.

105. Moses Judah was a New York merchant of genealogy not known,

although his association with a Connecticut petition suggests the possibility that he is the Moses Judah (died 1851) mentioned in Stern, p. 102. He should not be confused with an older Moses Judah (1735–1822), lawyer and Revolutionary patriot. The younger Moses Judah was active in the New York Manumission Society. See documents in Schappes, pp. 118–21, and notes, p. 597.

106. In 1814, the Saugatuck Manufacturing Company was incorporated for the purpose of manufacturing cotton and woolen cloth in Norwalk, Conn. After a brief period of success, the company fell into difficulties in 1818. A reorganization took place under the auspices of the Saugatuck Manufacturing Association, composed essentially of the original group of managing directors. It was this Association that, in 1819, petitioned for a new act of incorporation under the name of the Richmondville Manufacturing Company. The reorganized company had considerable success. In 1828, one of the original stockholders of the Saugatuck Manufacturing Company, who had been squeezed out by the reorganization, brought suit in chancery for the recovery of his investment of $2,000. "The plaintiff removed to *Louisville*, in *Kentucky*, a thousand miles distant; and since 1816, has had little communication with the company, or its concerns. On his return to this state, in the summer of 1828, he found his right to any portion of his investment, either capital or product, utterly denied, although the concern had been very successful, having sustained no losses, and having, for many years past, made annual dividend of seven *per cent.* upon the whole capital; and measures had been adopted, by which his name had no longer a place among the stockholders, and his whole investment, as well as all the profit arising on it, had been appropriated to other members of the concern." No decision on the legality of the device used to eliminate this stockholder was rendered; his suit was dismissed under the statute of limitations. See Banks vs. Judah, et al. (Conn., 1830), 8 *Reports*, 145 ff.

107. John Hays (1770–1836) was a grandson of Solomon Hays and son of Baruch Hays, both of New York. He was himself born in New York City. See *Universal Jewish Encyclopedia*, V, 256, for a slightly inaccurate biographical sketch. See also John Reynolds, *The Pioneer History of Illinois* [1673–1818] . . . (2d ed., Chicago, 1887), pp. 223–25 and *passim;* Reynolds's sketch is marred by the same inaccuracies as those in the *Universal Jewish Encyclopedia*, but contains many warm and human sidelights revealing the high esteem in which Hays was held by his fellow Illinoisans.

108. This date is wrongly given as 1822 by both sources referred to above. For the correction, see *Journal of the Executive Proceedings of the Senate of the United States of America* (Washington, 1828), III, 234–35, 255. Under date of Monday, Jan. 15, 1821, the Senate heard

a letter, dated Jan. 12, 1821, enclosing a letter to the President (James Monroe) from the Secretary of War (John C. Calhoun) dated Jan. 10, 1821, nominating, *inter alios*, "John Hays, of Illinois to be Agent at Fort Wayne, vice William Turner, displaced." This nomination was tabled without discussion at this time; it was not taken up by the Senate until Saturday, March 3, 1821, at which time it was passed without debate.

109. This appointment is completely overlooked in both biographical sketches referred to above. See *Journal of the Executive Proceedings. . . .*, III, 375–76, for the original appointment by President Monroe, May 10, 1824, and confirmation by the Senate, May 12, 1824; also see *ibid.*, III, 586, for renomination by President John Quincy Adams, Dec. 27, 1827, and p. 594 for confirmation of the reappointment by the Senate, Jan. 21, 1828.

110. [Lewis Cass (?)] to John Hays, Detroit, Oct. 11, 1820; MS., National Archives.

111. At this time, there was an awkward distribution of the conduct of Indian affairs: An independent agency, the Office of Indian Trade, headed by a superintendent, was in charge of all matters relating to trade with the Indians. We have seen (this Part, Documents 65 through 67) some aspects of the work of this office. The political relations between the U.S. government and the Indians were carried on through the War Department, whose Secretary at this time was John C. Calhoun. As an Indian Agent, Hays's immediate supervisor would be the Governor of the State or Territory, acting *ex officio* as Commissioner of Indian Affairs and reporting to the Secretary of War. At this time, Lewis Cass was Civil Governor of the Michigan Territory, having been appointed to that position by President James Madison in 1813. Cass's attitude toward the Indians was sympathetic but firm, and during his territorial administration, Indian affairs were well-handled. For discussion of the general problem, see George Dewey Harmon, *Sixty Years of Indian Affairs, 1789–1850* (Chapel Hill, N.C., 1941) and Laurence F. Schmeckebier, *The Office of Indian Affairs* (Baltimore, 1927). A more personal account, by the man who was, in 1820, superintendent of Indian Trade and one of the early advocates of more humane solutions of Indian problems is to be found in Thomas L. M'Kenney, *Memoirs, Official and Personal. . . .* (New York, 1846), vol. I. Cass's activities as *ex officio* Commissioner of Indian Affairs for Michigan Territory are discussed in Andrew C. McLaughlin, *Lewis Cass* (Boston and New York, 1899), and, more vividly, in Frank B. Woodford, *Lewis Cass, the Last Jeffersonian* (New Brunswick, N.J., 1950).

112. On the matter of factories for the production of goods for Indian trade, see Ora B. Peake, *A History of the United States Indian Factory System, 1795–1822* (Denver, 1954).

113. These "annuities," disbursed by the Indian agents on the author-

ity of the War Department, were payments fixed by the treaties between the United States and various Indian tribes, often as compensation for Indian lands turned over to the United States.

114. The letter book in the National Archives contains copies only of letters sent; there is no indication who signed the letter. In this case, it was either Lewis Cass himself or a deputy.

115. Moses Lopez (1739/44–1830), descendant of early Jewish settlers of Newport, was the last Jew of the original community to leave Newport, in 1822, shortly after the death of his brother, Jacob (1750–1822). He is recorded in *Census, 1790, Rhode Island,* p. 21, Newport "Lopez, Moses, Free white males 16 and upward . . . 3; free white females . . . 1." See Morris A. Gutstein, *The Story of the Jews of Newport, Two and a Half Centuries of Judaism, 1658–1908* (New York, 1936), and the more popular account, by the same author, *To Bigotry No Sanction: A Jewish Shrine in America, 1658–1958* (New York, 1958).

116. Stephen Gould was a Quaker and non-resister. At one time, he earned his living as a watchmaker. See George C. Channing, *Early Recollections of Newport, R.I. from [1793–1811]* . . . (Newport, 1868), p. 230. An earlier letter from Joseph Lopez, a New York relative of Moses Lopez, reveals at least one basis for the keen sense of friendship that Moses Lopez had for Stephen Gould. From this it appears that Gould had helped to care for Moses's brother, Jacob Lopez, during his last illness: "Its contents conveys by request of my Kinsman Moses Lopez the melancholly tidings of the Exit of his much lamented Brother Jacob. this sudden & unexpected event, proves truly very grievous to me & all his connections here. . . . It affords much consolation to observe that during his illness he has experienced the benevolent attentions of his surrounding friends. this severe visitation to my worthy Kinsman Moses under his inferior state of health, is no doubt very agonizing to his feelings. . . . I am under great obligations for your friendly attentions towards him in his forlorn state & for the circumstantial detail you have related of the distressing scene that has recently taken place. from that circumstance I am further induced to trespass on your goodness to crave you will use your best exertions to prevail on Cousin Moses to embark for this place by the first Packet after the receipt of this, leaving the adjustment of his concerns to be completed at a proper Season. in the interim by a change of objects & an excursion by Water, may in some measure contribute to alleviate the distress of his mind, & to restore him the enjoyment of better health" (Joseph Lopez to Stephen Gould, New York, March 21, 1822; MS., Collection of David Jacobson, copy from A.J.A.).

117. A short time before this, Abraham Touro, formerly of Newport but then of Boston, had paid for the construction of a brick wall around the Jewish cemetery at Newport to replace the old wooden fence which

was in bad condition. The new wall cost Touro about $1,000. Pool, *Portraits Etched in Stone*, p. 26.

118. Moses Lopez to Stephen Gould, New York, Dec. 5, 1825; MS., Collection of David Jacobson, copy from A.J.A.

119. Aaron Lopez Gomez (died, 1860), a storekeeper in New York; see Moses Lopez to Stephen Gould, New York, Feb. 6, 1826; MS., Collection of David Jacobson, copy from A.J.A. Cf. Grinstein, p. 222.

120. The Newport Bank stood at 3 Washington Square; it was incorporated in 1803 with capitalization of $120,000.

121. Many other letters from Lopez to Gould are in the Jacobson collection. All deal with similar business matters and make clear the difficulties involved, even as late as 1828, in carrying on business activities where there was no currency standard or uniform banking regulation. A passing comment in a letter of August 3, 1828 indicates that Moses Lopez was Sabbath-observing: "Your sa[i]d letter Coming to hand just at the beginning of our Sabath when you will know we do not attend to any business will I am sorry to say be the means of your keeping in suspence two days longer as I could not before avail myself of the Mail" (Moses Lopez to Stephen Gould, New York, Aug. 3, 1828; MS., Collection of David Jacobson, copy from A.J.A.).

122. David Nathans (1793–1878) and his father Isaiah Nathans (1766–1843) are recorded in the *Philadelphia Directory for 1830*, p. 140, as merchants, at 252 N. Second street. In McElroy's *Philadelphia Directory for 1837*, p. 162, however, Isaiah Nathans is listed as "gent.," and his address given as 31 Margaretta, suggesting that he had by then retired. See also W. & W., *passim*, and Stern, p. 164.

123. Other letters from David Nathans to his father are printed below, Part Seven, Documents 238–41.

124. David Nathans to Isaiah Nathans, Pittsburgh, July 7, 1826; MS., Nathans Family Papers in the collection of Mrs. Melvin M. Franklin, copy from A.J.A.

125. Business affairs were an important incidental on David Nathans's western trips which were undertaken as an agent of the Masonic order.

126. Charles Shaler (1788–1869) was a lawyer and politician first in Ohio, and then in Pittsburgh, Pa., after 1813. See Leland D. Baldwin, *Pittsburgh: The Story of a City* (Pittsburgh, 1937), pp. 240, 280, 289; and the fuller biographical sketch in John N. Boucher and others, *A Century and a Half of Pittsburgh and Her People* (New York, 1908), I, 467 and *passim*.

127. Ephraim Pentland had a stormy journalistic career in Pittsburgh from the year 1805; he had already (though only 20) served an apprenticeship on the Philadelphia *Aurora*. See Leland D. Baldwin, *Pittsburgh: The Story of a City* (Pittsburgh, 1937), pp. 180, 182, 285, 289, 353.

128. A later letter of this 1826 series testifies that not all of David

Nathans's time was spent on business or Masonic affairs. Writing from Batavia, New York, Aug. 17, 1826, David assured his father that the long detour into New York State had been undertaken because thus he could make better speed to his next stop in Pennsylvania, the direct roads being so poor. However, "I have visited a number of places much to my Satisfaction Several Indian villages, Falls of Niagara, Lockport &c . . . I have Several Indian presents and Specimens, for my dear Father & Mother Brothers and Sister" (MS., Nathans Family Papers, copy from A.J.A.).

129. Some further indication that all was not well in the economy may be gleaned from a letter of Rebecca Gratz to Benjamin Gratz, March 12, 1827, referring to the bankruptcy of her brothers in 1825: "Two or three months ago our Nieces commenced employing themselves in manufacturing little ingenious articles by which they hoped to obtain the means of lightening the difficulties that were gathering around them. I suggested to them the probability of their being able to dispose of some of them in Kentucky and offered to apply to you on the subject. accordingly a small box has been forwarded to your address, which we beg you will have the goodness to place in some store, or dispose of in any way you think proper. they enclosed a paper with the *highest prices* at which the articles could be sold here, but without by any means limiting them, and will be very grateful to you for having them sold to the best advantage your fashionable market may afford. Our sister & the girls make every exertion to bear as they ought the reverses of fortune, and as time soothes their regret for more irretrievable losses, are recovering their cheerfulness. Mr. Hays has taken a counting-house and with his son Henry's assistance is endeavoring to make a living. they will all unite their efforts & I hope with success" (R.G. to Benjamin Gratz [Philadelphia], Mar. 12, 1827; MS., A.J.H.S.). Such a reversal of fortune for the Hays family of Philadelphia is certainly indicative of a worse downturn than the price index would suggest.

130. Samuel Hays Myers (1799–1840) was the son of Samuel Myers (1755–1836), who settled in Richmond about 1798, and Judith Hays (1767–1844) of Boston, his wife. He was the oldest of six children of this couple. He married Eliza K. Mordecai (1809–61), daughter of Jacob Mordecai of Richmond. Myers was active in the affairs of Congregation Beth Shalome.

131. This was probably Judah Hays (1770–1832) originally of Boston, son of Moses Michael Hays (1739–1805), and inheritor of his fortune who was for a time in partnership with Abraham Touro (1777/78–1822), his cousin. He was one of the founders of the Boston Athenaeum. See *Universal Jewish Encyclopedia*, V, 257.

132. Israel I. Cohen (1750–1803) and his wife Judith Solomon (1766–1837) lived in Richmond where they had nine sons, seven of whom lived beyond infancy, and one daughter. The oldest of these

children, Jacob I. Cohen, Jr., was born in 1789 and died in 1869. After Israel Cohen's death, his widow took her young family to live in Baltimore, where they achieved an outstanding business success. See Ezekiel and Lichtenstein, pp. 29–31, for the Cohen family; see also Part One and this Part, Document 85, for further materials on the Cohens.

133. Samuel H. Myers to Judah Hays, Richmond, Aug. 11. 1826; MS., Virginia Historical Society.

134. Undoubtedly Jacob Mordecai (1762–1838), his future father-in-law. See Ezekiel and Lichtenstein, pp. 23–25, for a brief sketch of Jacob Mordecai, who was twice married, first to Judith Myers (1762–96) and then to Rebecca Myers (1776–1863), further evidence of the interconnection of the two families.

135. Samuel H. Myers never did truly "settle down in business," but instead practiced law.

136. The reference is clearly to his forthcoming marriage, which had probably already been arranged.

137. The elder Samuel Myers; see this Part, note 130.

138. A little later, in Aug., 1828, business conditions were still poor in Philadelphia, though better in the western part of the state. David Nathans, writing to his father, Isaiah Nathans, from Pittsburgh, Aug. 28, 1828, said: "Business is lively here yet as I have been informed not so much so at the present as it has been. . . . I have been looking out for a Good place for Business but as yet have discovered no place in which a fortune is to be made. . . . I hope that Business has revived in Philad. and that you may not have any reason to Complain . . . and I hope that after my return we shall be enabled to do a better business than we have of late" (David Nathans to Isaiah Nathans, Pittsburgh, Aug. 28, 1828; MS., Nathans Family Papers, copy from A.J.A.).

139. For a history and details of the Tariff Acts of 1816, 1819, 1824, 1828, and 1833, see Frank William Taussig, *The Tariff History of the United States* (8th ed., New York, 1931), still the most useful general history.

140. Joseph Gratz (1785–1858); see Part Three, note 72.

141. Richard Rush (1780–1859), lawyer, diplomat, and statesman. He was the son of Dr. Benjamin Rush. *DAB*, XVI, 231.

142. Benjamin Gratz (1792–1884), see Part Three, note 68.

143. Samuel D. Ingham (1779–1860), Secretary of the Treasury, 1829–31, when he resigned, ostensibly because he refused to recognize the wife of his colleague, John H. Eaton, socially. *DAB*, IX, 473.

144. George David Rosengarten (1801–90), born in Hesse-Cassel, in Germany, migrated to the United States before 1827. He married Elizabeth Bennett, by whom he had five sons and two daughters, 3 of whom Joseph George (born 1835), Adolph George (born 1838), Samuel George (born 1827), are identified by Morais, *Jews of Philadelphia,*

passim. McElroy's *Philadelphia Directory for 1837,* p. 190, lists "G. T. Rosengarten, chemical lab., c. Sth. 7th and Vine, h 24 Palmyra Row," probably the same person. According to a communication from Edwin Wolf, 2d, the firm Rosengarten founded is still doing business as Merck & Co.

145. Joseph Gratz to Richard Rush, Philadelphia, March 7, 1828; MS., RG 56, Records of Department of Treasury, National Archives.

146. See this Part, Document 63.

147. Benjamin Gratz to Samuel D. Ingham, Philadelphia, April 1, 1831; MS., RG 56, Records of Department of Treasury, National Archives.

148. Joseph Anderson (1757–1837), appointed by President Madison to the post of Comptroller of the Treasury, held office until July 1, 1836. *DAB,* I, 267.

149. James Nelson Barker (1784–1858), appointed by President Van Buren to the post of First Comptroller of the Treasury, Mar. 1, 1838; he lost this office on April 19, 1841, but was later named acting comptroller, Sept. 14, 1841. *DAB,* I, 603.

150. George D. Rosengarten to James N. Barker, Philadelphia, May 29, 1839; MS., RG 56, Records of Department of Treasury, National Archives.

151. Thomas Stewart, who was born in Ireland, was serving at this time as Appraiser for the Customs office at Philadelphia. He was appointed prior to 1829 and is still listed in the same position in 1843. See *Official Register of the United States,* various years.

152. George B. Wood and Franklin Bache, *The Dispensatory of the United States of America* (3d ed., Philadelphia, 1836) would have been the official pharmaceutical authority at the time of this letter; other revised editions have kept the work up-to-date, the latest being the 25th ed. revised in 1955.

153. Algernon S. Roberts, a druggist, was senior member of the firm of A. S. & E. Roberts, doing business at 76 S. Second Street, Philadelphia, at this time. See McElroy's *Philadelphia Directory for 1837,* p. 187.

154. Elias M. Durand (1794–1873), pharmacist and botanist, after immigrating to the United States from his native France in 1816, spent seven years in Baltimore before opening a drugstore at the corner of 6th and Chestnut sts. in Philadelphia in 1825. This store became an informal clubhouse for the physicians of Philadelphia. *DAB,* V, 538.

155. As far back as March 19, 1823, we find Abraham L. Hart of Philadelphia in correspondence with J. Anderson, Comptroller of the Treasury, over an action of the Customs officials at the Port of New York. See Abraham L. Hart to Jo Anderson, Philadelphia, March 19, 1823; MS., RG 56, Records of Department of Treasury, National Archives. This was Abraham Luria Hart (1789–1872) who seems to have run a music shop in Philadelphia; W. & W., *passim,* and Stern, p. 74A.

The actual importer was not Hart, but Joseph Dreyfous, an Alsatian-Jewish immigrant of 1816, in the jewelry business in Philadelphia; Hart's part was that he had signed the bond for Dreyfous who shared a store at 30 South Fourth St. with Hart in 1825. On Dreyfous, see W. & W., p. 493; Morais, *op. cit.*, p. 445. A similar situation, more tactfully handled by the Collector of the Customs in Savannah, is revealed in a scrawled memorandum: "On the 15. July 1819, the Collector at Savannah, on the application of Mr. Minis, surety to the duty bonds of Mr. Isaac Cohen, was authorized to grant indulgence on them, of 6. 9. and 12. months."

Isaac Cohen had gone into bankruptcy; Minis had written on June 26, "His insolvency authorises me to believe that I shall have to meet their payments in addition to my own."

Instructions from the Comptroller of the Treasury advising the Collector at Savannah to grant Minis's request, dated July 15, 1819, were not transmitted to Minis for 3 months. MS., undated memorandum, RG 56, Records of the Department of Treasury, National Archives.

Still another query, this time regarding a "Small Claim for return Duties on the Seven Cases Choppers," was raised by the Philadelphia publishing firm of E. L. Carey and Abraham Hart. When this partnership was formed in 1829, young Hart (1810–85) was only 19 years old; this helps in understanding the very personal tone of their letter to the Comptroller of the Treasury: "We can assure you although the amount is Small, it would be hard for us to loose [sic] it, as we are young men in Business . . ." Carey & Hart to J. Anderson, Philadelphia, May 11, 1833; MS., RG 56, Records of the Department of Treasury, National Archives; see also W. & W., p. 353 and *passim*.

156. Some small part of Moses Myers's financial anxiety during this period must have been alleviated by the news that he was to receive a legacy of $5,000 under the will of his friend and distant family connection, Abraham Touro (1777/78–1822) of Boston. A letter from Touro to Myers, dated at Boston, Aug. 26, 1822 (MS., Myers Family Papers), condoles with Myers on his losses, but also speaks of the losses that Touro had sustained; the cases were hardly comparable. When Abraham Touro died, soon after the writing of this letter, he bequeathed $100,000 to his younger brother, Judah Touro (1775–1854) and $50,000 to various institutions as well as making smaller bequests to Moses Myers and others. See Schappes, p. 660, n. 54. The letter of Aug. 26, 1822, also refers to some services of Moses Myers in connection with Touro's financial affairs in Norfolk.

When news of the Touro bequest reached Myers, he executed a deed transferring $3,500 of the total amount to his son, Myer, and the balance to his son Frederick. (Moses Myers of Norfolk, deed Nov. 11, 1822, disposing of the bequest to him from Abraham Touro; MS., Myers Family Papers).

157. Frederick Myers to Moses Myers, Norfolk, May 1, 1827, with petition enclosed; MS., Myers Family Papers, copy in A.J.A. John Myers was also active on his father's behalf. On May 2, 1827, he wrote to ex-President James Madison: "Dear Sir: I believe you know both personally, & by reputation, my father, Moses Myers esq of Norfolk, who is put in nomination by his friends for the office of Collector of that port, now vacant. He has never asked his government for an office, during a long life of activity, & many public services & acts of patriotism. Now retired from business, & not in easy circumstances, this trust is asked. It is one of very moderate emolument indeed, but it is respectable, & suited to his moral habits, & mercantile experience. It is a maxim with me not to ask, what cannot with perfect propriety be granted. May I solicit from you a few lines in his behalf to the Secretary of the Treasury, or President?

"The only excuse I can offer for this freedom, is the little acquaintance you have of me while Aid-de-Camp to General Taylor during the last War. Upon that remembrance likewise I beg to be most respectfully presented to Mrs. M." (John Myers to James Madison, Washington, D.C., May 2, 1827; MS., Madison Papers, Library of Congress).

158. Moses Myers's nomination for the position of Collector of the Customs for the district of Norfolk and Portsmouth, Va., was proposed by President John Quincy Adams in a communication to the United States Senate, Dec. 19, 1827; this communication was placed before the Senate on Monday, Dec. 24, 1827. Approval of the appointment of Myers came on Tuesday, January 15, 1828, by a comparatively close recorded vote of 24 to 16. See *Journal of the Executive Proceedings of the Senate of the United States of America,* III, 579–80. It was this appointment that supplied the occasion for the exchange of letters between Solomon Etting and Henry Clay (see Part One, Documents 39, 40).

159. Petition, Norfolk and Portsmouth merchants and citizens to the President of the United States, undated (copy) of original; MS., Myers Family Papers.

160. Philip I. Cohen, who died in 1852, was the second son of Israel I. and Judith (Solomon) Cohen. Since he was only a boy of ten at the time of his father's death in 1803, he must have moved from Richmond to Baltimore with his mother; indeed, he is listed in the *Baltimore Directory for 1835,* p. 32, as dwelling on "Charles St. near Franklin." The wide business interests of the Cohen family (see this Part, Document 87) must have found him in Virginia for much of the time; he appears as one of two witnesses to the deed (this Part, note 156) in which Moses Myers disposed of his legacy from Abraham Touro.

161. Thomas Gatewood of Virginia, Naval officer of the port of Norfolk, was nominated to office by James Monroe, May 24, 1824 and confirmed by the Senate, May 26, 1824; John Q. Adams renominated him

on Dec. 28, 1827 and he was confirmed again by the Senate, Jan. 9, 1828. See *Executive Journal of the Senate*, vol. III, *passim*.

162. This controversy bred considerable correspondence which may be found in RG 56, Records of the Department of Treasury, National Archives.

163. Moses Myers to Joseph Anderson, Norfolk, Jan. 15, 1828; MS., RG 56, Records of the Department of Treasury, National Archives.

164. Acts of the Seventeenth Congress of the U.S. . . . 3 Dec. 1821 . . . 8 May 1822, Statute I, Chap. CVII, "An Act further to establish the compensation of officers of the customs and to alter certain collection districts, and for other purposes," 3 U.S. Statutes at Large, 693. Sec. 7 sets the commissions of the collector at Norfolk at 13¼% of all monies received; sec. 10 places a limitation of $3,000 on the total emoluments after deduction of expenses for any collector (except some specifically dealt with in secs. 8 and 9).

165. See this Part, note 4.

166. Benjamin Etting (1798–1875). See Part Three, note 101.

167. Samuel Etting (1796–1862) of Philadelphia, for example, Benjamin's cousin, had business relations with Robert Garrett & Co. in Baltimore. On Jan. 22, 1833, he wrote to the Baltimore house, offering various trade goods, some from China, at lower prices, after March 4 of that year: "The reduction of duties that takes place in March next, in many articles in which you are interested." The list includes Cassia at 17 and 17½ cents and Young Hyson Tea at 55 to 68 cents (Samuel Etting to Messrs. Robert Garrett & Co., Philadelphia, Jan. 22, 1833; MS., Garrett Family Papers, Library of Congress). Again, on August 6 of the same year, he wrote: "We have the Globe in today from Canton; at foot I annex (as near as I can come at it) a list of her Teas; she brings much fewer than was expected. I am told that many of her Invoices will be brought to auction at once. I should be pleased to execute your orders for such as you may want." The list includes Young Hyson, Imperial, Gun Powder, Hyson, Souchong, Powchong, H Skin, and Pecca. (Samuel Etting to Messrs. R. Garrett & Co., Philadelphia, Aug. 6, 1833; MS., Garrett Family Papers, Library of Congress; copy from A.J.A.).

168. See Part Three, Document 107.

169. Joshua Moses (1780–1837) was a member of Congregation Shearith Israel, a freemason, and merchant. He was among a group who petitioned the Trustees of Congregation Shearith Israel, in 1829, for the right to purchase family plots in the cemetery. See Pool, *Portraits Etched in Stone*, p. 86.

170. The invoice is dated at Canton, Dec. 9, 1831; it bears an endorsement by Joshua Moses dated March 26, 1832. Allowing for the fact that 1832 was a leap year, the elapsed time *from the dating of the invoice* was only 109 days; a week or more must have slipped by

between the date of the invoice and the clearing of the Canton River, for the time recorded for this voyage of the ship Atlantic was but 98 days! See Carl C. Cutler, *Greyhounds of the Sea: The Story of the American Clipper Ship* (New York, 1930), pp. 80–82, for a full discussion of record runs from 1810 to the 1830s. Cutler says, "It was not until the 26th of March, 1832, that the marks of the *Russell* [96 days in 1815] and *Chasseur* [96 days in 1816] were again approached. On that date the Philadelphia built ship *Atlantic* passed Cape Henlopen 98 days from Macao, under command of Captain McCall."

171. Invoice of Merchandise shipped by Benjamin Etting . . . 1831; MS., copy from A.J.A.

172. Egon C. Corti, *The Rise of the House of Rothschild* (New York, 1928) tells the story of this European financial structure to 1830; the same author's *The Reign of the House of Rothschild* (New York, 1928) carries the Rothschild saga to 1871. Both volumes are based on papers in the firm's archives and on official documents. It is interesting that Corti, with all his thoroughness, has nothing whatever to say about the relations of the House of Rothschild with the American government.

173. Robert Phillips (1789–1833) and his brother Isaac (1791–1851) were immigrants from England to Philadelphia, shortly before 1813. The fact that they were English-speaking apparently speeded their integration; they applied for membership in Congregation Mikve Israel in 1813 and were fairly active. Their first partnership, as "merchants" was already established in 1820; according to the Philadelphia *Gazette*, Dec. 7, 1824, this partnership was dissolved on Jan. 1, 1825. If so, it was reestablished as a banking firm some years later. See W. & W., *passim;* Morais, *Jews of Philadelphia*, p. 285; Schappes, p. 229. It may be that their relationship to the House of Rothschild was forwarded by the fact that Isaac Phillips had married, in 1822, Sarah, the daughter of John Moss (1771–1847), "the most successful Jewish importer in the city." W. & W., pp. 347, 461–62.

174. See Part One, note 62, and Part Two, note 132.

175. For an interesting brief study of the French Spoliation Claims, see Richard A. McLemore, *The French Spoliation Claims, 1816–1836; a Study in Jacksonian Diplomacy* (Nashville, Tenn., 1933). The part played by the House of Rothschild in negotiating these claims is not mentioned by McLemore. It is conceivable that the Rothschilds offered to handle the European fiscal end of this matter in order further to embarrass the French regime after 1830.

176. Roger Brook Taney (1777–1864) had been appointed by President Andrew Jackson to the cabinet post of Secretary of the Treasury on Sept. 23, 1833; he held the office for less than a year, until June 24, 1834. Later he was appointed Chief Justice of the United States Supreme Court, *DAB*, XVIII, 289.

177. R. & I. Phillips to Roger B. Taney, Philadelphia, April 19, 1834;

MS., RG 56, Records of Department of Treasury, National Archives. Robert Phillips was no longer alive at the time of this correspondence, but the firm continued under its old name.

178. Nathan Mayer de Rothschild (1777–1836), third son of Mayer Amschel Rothschild, the founder of the dynasty, was the head of the London branch; because of his talents, he was the leading figure in the dynasty after his father's death in 1812. He and his four brothers were ennobled by the Emperor of Austria.

179. The Paris branch of the House of Rothschild was headed, at this time by James Mayer de Rothschild (1792–1868), youngest of the five sons of Mayer Amschel Rothschild.

180. The original headquarters of the firm at Frankfort retained the name of the founder, Mayer Amschel Rothschild (1743–1812), although at this time the oldest son, Amschel Mayer de Rothschild (1773–1855), was its head.

181. Originally known as Karl Mayer Rothschild (1788–1855), later ennobled as Baron Charles de Rothschild, he was the fourth son of Mayer Amschel Rothschild and head of the Italian branch of the firm at Naples.

182. The fifth branch, in Vienna, headed by Baron Solomon Mayer Rothschild (1774–1855), second son of Mayer Amschel Rothschild, is inexplicably missing from this list.

183. De Rothschild Freres to R. & I. Phillips, Paris, May 17, 1834; MS., RG 56, Records of Department of Treasury, National Archives. This is, of course, not the original MS. letter, but a copy.

184. R. & I. Phillips to Roger B. Taney, Philadelphia, June 20, 1834; MS., RG 56, Records of Department of Treasury, National Archives.

185. See this Part, Document 80.

186. See this Part, Document 81.

187. It is noteworthy that this name, phonetically spelled here, is correctly spelled "Taney" on the outside mailing address for this letter.

188. John Forsyth (1780–1841) was appointed Secretary of State by President Andrew Jackson in 1834; he remained in that office through the remainder of Jackson's term of office and also was retained in the same post through the entire administration of President Martin van Buren. *DAB*, VI, 533.

189. Levi Woodbury (1789–1851) was appointed Secretary of the Treasury by Andrew Jackson, June 27, 1834, to succeed Roger B. Taney. Woodbury remained in this office until 1841, when he retired with the Van Buren administration; he later served in the United States Senate. *DAB*, XX, 488.

190. John Forsyth to Levi Woodbury, Washington, Aug. 6, 1834; MS., RG 56, Records of Department of Treasury, National Archives.

191. Barings of London, see Ralph Willard Hidy, *The House of Baring in American Trade and Finance; English Merchant Bankers at Work, 1763–1861* (Cambridge, Mass., 1949).

192. William Willink, Jr., of Amsterdam. No further information.

193. N. M. Rothschild to John Forsyth, London, Sept. 29, 1834; MS., RG, 59, General Records of the Department of State, National Archives. Some question must have arisen at this time about the use of titles of nobility in addressing the Rothschilds for we find that, on Oct. 30, 1834, R. & I. Phillips communicated to John Forsyth a copy of a letter they had received under the date of Sept. 22, 1834: "With reference to the correspondence between you and the Honble John Forsyth of the Department of State at Washington you have made some little error which the following will elucidate.

" 'The Title of Baron has been conferred to my Four Brothers & Myself by the Emperor of Austria.' " (R. & I. Phillips to John Forsyth, Philadelphia, Oct. 30, 1834; MS., copy, RG 56, Records of Department of Treasury, National Archives).

194. The fifth auditor of the Treasury at this time was Stephen Pleasanton of Delaware, who was appointed to this position prior to 1829 and retained it until 1853.

195. J. I. Cohen, Jr. & Brothers, to Levi Woodbury, Baltimore, May 27, 1835; MS., RG 56, Records of the Department of Treasury, National Archives.

196. On Jan. 15, 1835, a bill was presented to the French chamber of deputies to authorize payment to the United States of the sum fixed in the treaty of July 4, 1831 (see William M. Malloy, *Treaties, Conventions, International Acts, Protocols, and Agreements between the United States of America and other Powers, 1776–1909* [Washington, 1910], pp. 523–26). Meantime, President Jackson's annual message of 1834 (Jackson to Congress, Dec. 1, 1834, in James D. Richardson, *A Compilation of the Messages and Papers of the Presidents, 1789–1902* [Washington, 1902], III, 100–7) had been very vigorous in the language it used in speaking of the failure of the French to honor the terms of the treaty of 1831. The President's message became known in Paris on Jan. 8, 1835 and caused a great sensation. So the bill of Jan. 15, 1835, though supported by the commercial and manufacturing classes, was opposed by the anti-regime Frenchmen, and could not be passed save by the addition of a crippling amendment, offered by Deputy Valaze, requiring that the United States offer "satisfactory explanations" to the French government before any payments were made. With the amendment, the bill passed the deputies late in April, 1835. See McLemore, *The French Spoliation Claims . . .* , pp. 10–13.

197. David I. Cohen (1800–47), fifth of the brothers.

198. James Howard was the president of the Franklin Bank of Baltimore at this time. He resided on Frederick Street, between Baltimore and Second sts. See *Baltimore Directory for 1835*, p. 127.

199. James Howard to Levi Woodbury, Baltimore, May 28, 1835; MS., RG 56, Records of Department of Treasury, National Archives.

200. William F. Frick was an attorney in Baltimore. See *Baltimore Directory for 1845*, p. 45.

201. William Frick to Levi Woodbury, Baltimore, May 29, 1835; MS., RG 56, Records of Department of Treasury, National Archives.

202. Benjamin I. Cohen (1797–1845) was the fourth of the Cohen brothers.

203. See this Part, note 132.

204. See "Proceedings of the Convention to promote the Trade and Commercial Interests of the City of Baltimore, Dec. 22, 1834," clipping, unidentified, in Mendes Cohen Collection, Maryland Historical Society.

205. James W. Zacharie was a well-established merchant and, in 1822, a partner in the mercantile house of Zacharie and Turner, "9 St. Louis, n. Chartres," in New Orleans. See *New Orleans Directory for 1822*, unpaged.

206. See this Part, note 189.

207. A similar concern, though not in the context of "booster" organizations, was manifested by Harmon Hendricks (1771–1838), in a letter to Churchill Caldom Cambreleng (1786–1862), who was in 1830 chairman of the House Committee on commerce and navigation, foreign affairs, ways and means. Cambreleng served in Congress as representative from N.Y. in nine consecutive congresses, 1821–39. In this letter, dated at New York, May 21, 1830 (MS., National Archives), Hendricks expresses his hopes that the United States will recognize the newly-won independence of Haiti, because until this recognition shall be granted, discriminatory duties will be charged against American merchants trading in the Haitian market. Hendricks apparently did not wish the subject to be raised publicly unless he was sure of affirmative action: "A direct application to Your Government, if rejected, might be attended with results which I do not desire, and I wish you would favor me with your opinion on the subject. If you could oblige me by naming the circumstance in its proper quarter, it would be adding very much to the favor I ask."

208. J. W. Zacharie to Levi Woodbury, New Orleans, Sept. 10, 1837; MS., RG 56, Records of the Department of Treasury, National Archives.

209. Such an enumeration, based on *The Philadelphia Directory for 1825*, may be found in Morais, *Jews of Philadelphia*, pp. 445–48. A vast amount of information may be gleaned from the pages and especially the notes of W. & W. Unfortunately this type of research is too infrequently pursued; most of the older community histories preferred to list only the more successful Jews of their towns.

210. Some exceptions will be seen in Part Eight. It is noteworthy that in 1838 a group of Jews proposed, in a letter to the Trustees of Congregation Anshe Chesed of New York, the establishment of an agricultural colony, to be named Sholem, in Ulster County, N.Y. See Grinstein, pp. 119–22, for discussion and the text of the letter to Anshe Chesed.

211. Many Jewish business men in Philadelphia and New York acted as land brokers and tax agents. See W. & W., *passim*. See also the advertisement of M. Myers & Co., 107 Water Street, New York City, in the New York *Enquirer*, July 7, 1826, p. 2. Myers maintained a "military and General Agency office" remitting taxes to Missouri, Illinois, and Ohio for lands held there, and offered to purchase land in the Arkansas Territory for his customers.

212. Moses Elias Levy (c. 1782–1854) was a "pioneer" settler in Florida, whose second son, David, who called himself David Levy Yulee (1810–86), became, in 1845, Florida's first United States Senator. There is much information on Moses Levy in Samuel Proctor, "Pioneer Jewish Settlement in Florida, 1764–1900," *Proceedings of the Conference on the Writing of Regional History in the South* . . . (Miami Beach, 1956), especially pp. 85–95. See also Leon Huhner, "Moses Elias Levy, Florida Pioneer," *The Florida Historical Quarterly*, XIX (1941), 319–45. Proctor notes that one of Levy's plans was to establish a Jewish settlement on the land in Florida, a hope for which financial support never developed. See, on this, Elfrida D. Cowan, "Moses Elias Levy's Agricultural Colony in Florida," *PAJHS*, XXV (1917), 132–34.

213. Moses E. Levy to James Whitcomb, Washington, June 19, 1840; MS., RG 49, Records of the General Land Office, Docket 250, National Archives. The original folder also contained confirmation of this claim and a survey of the tract of land lying on Black Creek, East Florida. Docket 249 also contains materials relating to Moses E. Levy's land claims ranging in date from 1817 to 1888.

214. The problems that arose in connection with the title to land in Florida were the result of the transfer of sovereignty from Spain to the United States. The validity of the older Spanish titles and the verification of title transfers that took place shortly before the territory was acquired by the United States were always difficult procedures. See, for example, H. Rattenburg to John Quincy Adams, Secretary of State, Jan. 16, 1823; MS., RG 59, General Records of the Department of State, National Archives.

215. James Whitcomb (1795–1852) was appointed commissioner of the General Land office by President Jackson in 1836, served in that position until the end of Van Buren's administration, 1841. Then he moved to Indiana where he established a large and lucrative law practice, and was twice elected Governor of the State and then United States Senator. *DAB*, XX, 82.

216. Mordecai and Osborne to Comptroller of the Treasury and enclosed affidavits, Petersburg, Va., Oct. 8, 1838; MS., RG 56, Records of Department of Treasury, National Archives.

217. John W. Campbell, a native of Virginia, was Collector of Customs at Petersburg in 1838. *Official Register*, 1837, 1839.

218. The Collector of Customs in Petersburg, Va., previous to Campbell was Charles D. McIndoe, a Virginian. *Official Register*, 1835.

219. In 1837, George Wolf of Pennsylvania was First Comptroller of the Treasury Department; he resigned and was appointed Collector of the Customs for the district of Philadelphia, effective March 1, 1838. On that date, James N. Barker, who had held the Philadelphia position, replaced Wolf as First Comptroller of the Treasury. *Executive Journal*, V, 75, 76, 80; *Official Register*, 1837, 1839.

220. C. F. Osborne was president of the Petersburg Railroad, running from Petersburg, Va., westward to the Roanoke River, somewhere north of the proposed terminus of the Raleigh and Gaston Railroad. A short connecting line, the Greensville and Roanoke, was projected. Geo. Washington Mordecai (1801–71) was the son of Jacob Mordecai (1762–1838) and his second wife, Rebecca (Myers); he settled in Raleigh, N.C., and won eminence as a lawyer, president of the Raleigh and Gaston Railroad, and president of the Bank of North Carolina (from 1845).

221. The Raleigh & Gaston Railroad, one of the first of the short but important railways of the South, is discussed in detail in Cecil K. Brown, *A State Movement in Railroad Development* (Chapel Hill, N.C., 1928), chap. IV, pp. 45–62.

222. For the drawback and rebate provisions of the "Railroad Iron Bill" of 1832 in relation to iron imports used in railroad construction, see the excellent discussion of the conflict between the need of the American iron manufacturers for protection and the equal and opposite need of the railways for duty-free importation in Lewis H. Haney, *A Congressional History of Railways in the United States to 1850* (Madison, Wisc., 1908), pp. 298 [132]–326 [160].

Part Three. The Family and Social Life

1. Moses Sheftall (1769–1835). "Member of the Georgia legislature, and also had been a Judge of the County Court," *PAJHS*, XIX (1910), 91; in the B. H. Levy Collection, A.J.A., is a letter dated at Savannah, Jan. 22, 1802, from E. R. Duke, Adjutant of the Chatham County Militia to Moses Sheftall, enclosing Sheftall's "appointment, made some time since as Surgeon To the Same Regiment."

2. Solomon Bush (1753–1795), after distinguished service in the Revolution, rising to the rank of Colonel, was unsuccessful as an applicant for federal office. He may have received some medical training in England, or his title of "Doctor" may have been a courtesy title. See W. & W., pp. 154–58 and *passim*.

3. MS. Letter to Mrs. F. Sheftall, dated at Philadelphia, February 14, 1791, in B. H. Levy Collection, copy in A.J.A.

4. Mordecai Sheftall (1735?–97), the son of Benjamin Sheftall, was one of the first white children born in the Georgia colony. He was a prominent merchant and Revolutionary patriot. See *JE*, XI, 252. Mordecai Sheftall's exciting account of his capture by the British in 1778 is reprinted in Schappes, pp. 55–58. Bancroft's *Census*. . . . *Savannah*

. . . , p. 23, records him as judge of the Court of Common Pleas of the City of Savannah.

5. MS. Letter, Moses Sheftall to Mordecai Sheftall, Nov. 16, 1790, in the B. H. Levy Collection, copy in A.J.A.

6. *Census*, 1790, Pennsylvania, p. 228, records Levy Phillips, shop-keeper, at Race Street South, Philadelphia. A Levy Phillips was Parnass of Mikveh Israel congregation, Philadelphia, 1818–20; a Levi Phillips, Merchant, of 22 North 4th Street is listed in the *Philadelphia Directory for 1825.* These three reports probably refer to the same person. See H. S. Morais, *The Jews of Philadelphia* (Philadelphia, 1894), pp. 45, 447.

7. Thomas Leeming (1748–97), Revolutionary patriot, soldier, lawyer, and merchant, lived in Philadelphia, where he died of yellow fever. *DAB*, XI, 75.

8. Samuel Hays (1764–1839) was the husband of Richea Gratz and a trustee of the first Jewish cemetery in Philadelphia.

9. The religious problem that young Sheftall refers to here is that the Bush family had, by this time, virtually apostasized. Solomon Bush, at his death in 1795, was buried in the Quaker cemetery. The Sheftalls, on the other hand, had retained their close adherence to Judaism. W. & W., pp. 127–28, report "a case of an unusual conditional *halitzah,* or leviration, the release of obligation to marry a brother's widow. On that occasion, the bride-to-be, Mathias Bush's daughter Eleanor (Elka-lah), removed the ceremonial shoe from the foot of Georgia's Sheftall Sheftall, who promised that he would grant her a formal leviration within three months after his brother's death by which she would be freed to marry whom she pleased. . . . The shoe, an essential artifact in the ancient ceremony, is still treasured at Mikveh Israel." W. & W. also cite part of a letter (Moses Sheftall to Mordecai Sheftall, Philadelphia, Dec. 1, 1791, MS., Sheftall Papers, A.J.H.S.) in which Moses Sheftall explains, "in my former letter I mentioned something respecting her Religion which I think proper to Explain, bad Examples are very apt to be Catching and as she frequently comes to town to her Brothers she may possibly come into some of his mode of Living." Plate no. 23, opposite p. 240 in W. & W., reproduces the Hebrew promise of Halitzah given by Sheftall Sheftall in 1791 from the Mikveh Israel Archives.

10. Pierce Butler (1744–1822), *DAB*, III, 364.

11. Benjamin Rush (1745–1813), the distinguished patriot, physician, and philanthropist.

12. There are six householders of the name of Gunn listed in the *Census*, 1790, Pennsylvania.

13. Sauerkraut was a major preoccupation of Moses Sheftall during this visit. See letter, Moses Sheftall to Mordecai Sheftall, Dec. 5, 1790, in MS. in the B. H. Levy Collection, copy in A.J.A.: "not being able to procure any sour Crout you will receive by Capt. Burrows a barrel

of very Excellent Cyder Marked M. S. which I request you will substitute for the Crout." In this letter, Moses Sheftall repeats the account of his courtship. This indicates the uncertainty of mail delivery in this period, and adds to the credibility of Miss Bush's insistence that she had not been truant in replying to the correspondence of her suitor.

14. There are three householders named Burrows listed in *Census, 1790, Pennsylvania.*

15. Rachel (Gratz) Etting (1764–1831), second wife of Solomon Etting (see Part One, note 59), was very newly wed at the time of this letter; her marriage to Solomon Etting took place on October 26, 1791. Etting's first wife, Rachel Simon, had died Jan. 14, 1790. Furthermore, the Solomon Ettings had just taken up residence in Baltimore. For details, see Aaron Baroway, "Solomon Etting, 1764–1847," *Maryland Historical Magazine*, XV (1920), 1–20.

16. Barnard Gratz (1738–1801), trader and merchant, was a partner of his brother Michael and Joseph Simon in Lancaster, Pa. See Frederic Shriver Klein, *A History of the Jews in Lancaster* (Lancaster, Pa., 1955), pp. 16–19.

17. MS. letter in Etting Papers, The Historical Society of Pennsylvania. Copy from A.J.A.

18. *Census, 1790, Maryland*, p. 21, records Benjamin Levy (1726–1802) of Baltimore, head of a family consisting of himself, 2 "free white females," and 1 slave. Rachel Levy was the daughter of Nathan Levy of Philadelphia, her husband's half brother. See Stern, p. 109.

19. Sally Etting (1776–1863), a sister of Reuben Etting. See Philipson, *Letters*, p. 389, and Stern, p. 49.

20. Shinah (Solomon) Etting (1744–1822), widow of Elijah Etting, and mother of Solomon and Reuben Etting, and Rachel (Gratz) Etting's mother-in-law. Mrs. Etting long survived her husband (he died in 1778), and is listed in *Baltimore Directory, 1819*, unpaged: "Etting, Mrs. widow, Fayette near Paca."

21. Mrs. Myer S. Solomon was Catherine Bush before her marriage. See Stern, p. 49.

22. Simon Gratz (1773–1839) was the oldest son of Michael Gratz and the brother of Rebecca Gratz. See Philipson, *Letters*, xv.

23. Richea Gratz (1774–1858) was the second daughter of Michael Gratz and the sister of Rebecca Gratz. See Philipson, *Letters*, x; *JE*, VI, 82.

24. Miriam Gratz (1750–1808), daughter of Joseph Simon. See Klein, *History of the Jews in Lancaster*, p. 17; Osterweis, *passim*.

25. MS. in Mordecai Collection, Duke University Library (?); copy from A.J.A.

26. Samuel Hays (1764–1839) was at this time Richea's betrothed and later her husband. *JE*, VI, 82.

27. Joseph Simon (1712–1804), see Philipson, *Letters*, p. 246.

28. Leah Phillips (1764–1842), daughter of Joseph Simon, sister of Miriam Gratz, and aunt of Rebecca Gratz. Philipson, *Letters*, p. 139.

29. Levi Phillips (see above) was the husband of Leah (Simon) Phillips; his death is reported in a letter of Rebecca Gratz, December 31, 1832: "Levi Phillips death has left his poor blind wife entirely destitute." Philipson, *Letters*, p. 139.

30. Shinah Schuyler (born 1762), daughter of Joseph Simon and aunt to Rebecca Gratz, had married Dr. Nicholas Schuyler of Albany or Troy, N.Y., in 1782, against the wishes of her father. Dr. Schuyler had served as a surgeon in the Revolutionary army. Only when Joseph Simon lay on his deathbed, in 1804, was a reconciliation effected, through the intervention of Rebecca Gratz. See Osterweis, pp. 73–75.

31. MS., Schuyler Papers in Library of Congress; copy from A.J.A.

32. Simon Gratz, see this Part, note 22.

33. Hyman Gratz (1776–1857), fourth child of Michael and Miriam (Simon) Gratz, brother of Rebecca Gratz. Philipson, *Letters*, x.

34. Frances (Fanny) Gratz (1771–1852), oldest child of Michael and Miriam (Simon) Gratz. Philipson, *Letters*, x.

35. Miriam (Simon) Gratz.

36. Reuben Etting (1762–1848), older brother of Solomon Etting, married Frances Gratz in 1794. The couple moved to Baltimore, where Solomon Etting and his second wife, Rachel (Gratz), a cousin of Frances (Gratz), had lived since 1791.

37. The use of personal letters to convey business intelligence as well as family news was usual in this period, when newspapers were less common than today. The Gratzes owned land in upper New York state.

38. Samuel Hays; see this Part, note 25.

39. Rebecca Gratz (1781–1869), fifth child of Michael and Miriam (Simon) Gratz. See Osterweis for the most recent attempt at a biographical sketch of this energetic and dynamic social leader of the Philadelphia Jewish community and active participant in the broader social life of her generation. Her services to the Jewish community were both in benevolent associations and in religious education; for some further account of activities with which she was closely connected, see Part Five.

40. Maria Fenno, a minor literary lady of the age, was the second wife of Judge J. Ogden Hoffman.

41. Josiah Ogden Hoffman (1766–1837) was one of the most gifted lawyers of this period, excelling in commercial and maritime law. He was also a social aristocrat and arbiter, described as "a court of last resort in the quiddities of minuets and precedence at table." In 1798, he became attorney-general of the State of New York, a position in which he served until 1801. Seven years later he was chosen recorder of the city of New York and remained in that office until 1815. *DAB*, IX, 114.

42. Washington Irving (1783–1859), who was to achieve distinction

and international fame as a writer of history and fiction, immortalizing the Dutch ethnic group in his *Knickerbocker History of New York* and other works, studied law in Judge Hoffman's office. Here, he met and became engaged to Matilda Hoffman, his mentor's daughter. Matilda's early death in 1809 (see Philipson, *Letters*, p. 59) prostrated Irving, and it was Rebecca Gratz's kindness that deeply impressed him at this time. See *DAB*, IX, 505; Philipson, *Letters*, xix–xx.

43. Philipson, *Letters*, contains fewer than half of the letters that are known to exist in manuscript. There are substantial collections of Gratz letters in the library of the A.J.H.S. and in A.J.A.

44. Copy from A.J.A.

45. Two reasons may be adduced for the failure to celebrate Washington's Birthday. The first is that during the early years of the United States there was a widespread concern lest the country slide back into monarchial institutions; one way to prevent this, it was thought, was to prevent undue reverence to any individual. The second, and more political reason was that Washington, originally the hero of all Americans, had become the hero of the Federalist Party. The Jeffersonian administration discouraged the celebration of Washington's Birthday because such a celebration might redound to the glory of the opposition party.

46. Thomas Abthorpe Cooper (1776–1849), one of the outstanding tragic actors of his age, made his American debut in Philadelphia on Dec. 9, 1796. Later he played in New York and Charleston as well, remaining in America for 23 years. His characterizations of Hamlet and Macbeth were rated below only those of Kemble and Garrick. See *National Cyclopedia of American Biography*, X, 260; G. C. D. Odell, *Annals of the New York Stage* (New York, 1927), I, 452, II, 125 f. Isaac Harby of Charleston, S.C., mentioned Cooper in his "Defence of the Drama" (Part Five, Document 154) as well as publishing a critical essay on Cooper's Othello. See Henry L. Pinckney and Abraham Moise, *A Selection from the Miscellaneous Writings of the Late Isaac Harby, Esq.* (Charleston, S.C., 1829).

47. Samuel Ewing, it is believed, was the love of Rebecca Gratz's life. Because of religious differences, she would not marry him; because of her love, she would marry no one else. She retained a close friendship with members of his family. He was a lawyer. His father, Dr. John Ewing (1759–1802), was a Presbyterian minister, first provost of the University of Pennsylvania, a Hebraist, and a theologian. See W. B. Sprague, *Annals of the American Pulpit* (New York, 1858), III, 216–19; *DAB*, VI, 236.

48. James K. Paulding (1778–1860), as an author, is best remembered as "the chief Dutch interpreter of the New York Dutch." His career in politics led him to the post of Secretary of the Navy in Martin Van Buren's cabinet, 1837–41; *DAB*, XIV, 321. There is an extended authorized sketch in E. A. and G. L. Duyckinck, *Cyclopedia of American Literature* (New York, 1856), II, 1–6.

49. Rebecca Gratz maintained a very close interest in the social scene: "Our city is not so gay as yours. We have not had one private dance yet—but tea parties without number—we have been at three within the last week, but not such as used to give such a terrible name to Philadelphia tea parties. They are more sociable and of course more pleasant. . . . I do not think I shall go to an Assembly this winter. The cotillion parties are better suited to my taste." R.G. to Maria Fenno Hoffman, January, 1807; MS., A.J.H.S. "Sophia Dallas is going to be married to Richard Bashe very shortly and Patty Jones to a Mr Adams. . . . there are also several other weddings talked of. . . . Andrew is expected home this spring, but not a married man, poor fellow! he has *another* disappointment to bewail, but I guess this loss is greater to his purse, than his heart." R. G. to Maria Fenno Hoffman, March 25, 1805; MS., A.J.H.S.

50. Rebecca Gratz to Mrs. Ogden Hoffman (Maria E. Fenno), March 7, 1809; A.J.H.S.

51. See this Part, note 41.

52. Probably Charles Nicholas, a friend of Rebecca's youth. See Osterweis, p. 218.

53. Rebecca Gratz's strain of romanticism, so characteristic of her era, reveals itself throughout her correspondence. That element in the romantic temper which produced "Gothic" novels and consumptive heroines, as well as Rebecca's very real and deep concern for Matilda Hoffman's health, is visible in this passage. Maria Fenno Hoffman, too, wallowed in a sentimental readiness to expect the worst, and in at least one case Rebecca had to administer a corrective: "Miss Pemberton whose death you lament with so much sensibility is much better she has been extremely ill and I suppose the relapse gave rise to the report of her death. The family are prepared to take her to Charleston and Mr. Goellet has his hopes renewed, but her situation is very precarious, and perhaps they will not be able to accomplish their design. Mr. Goellet is a faithful lover. he has attended her constantly during the whole summer. I hope she may recover and reward his attachment with many years of happiness." R. G. to Maria E. Fenno, Nov. 23, 1802, A.J.H.S. What a plot lay herein for a minor fiction writer.

"My poor friend Peggy Ewing is again reduced to the brink of the grave. . . . She is again attacked with chills & fever, night sweats & raising of blood, and I fear will ere long fall a victim, sweet interesting patient sufferer! her path has been thickly strewn with thorns in this world.

"Disappointment & death have torn from her the friends & relations most dear to her heart. and the chill hand of adversity & dependence rob[b]ed her of those fair prospects which bloomed in her youth." R. G. to Mrs. Ogden Hoffman, February 26, 1809; A.J.H.S.

"She [Peggy Ewing?] gave us a sad account of poor Becky whose long engagement was last week dissolved. . . . I fear [she] will fall victim to disappointed affections. She neither sleeps, nor eats, is at private lodgings in the country . . . alledging that her greatest wish is to be alone. Mr Powel has, I suspect, acted a villains part. . . . of all disappointments, this is the most severe. death of friends is an evil, which Nature inflicts, and Nature sustains us through, but the treachery of a lover, after so long an attachment, is a shock which I think she never can recover from. his death would have been less severe." R. G. to Mrs. Ogden Hoffman, July 24, 1808, A.J.H.S.

54. The three MS. letters dated in June, 1811, from the Myers Family Papers, tell the story of this affair.

55. An extract from the MS. diary of Richard D. Arnold; copy from the typescript in A.J.A., pp. 1–4, 5–6, 8–9. Richard D. Arnold (1808–76) was a physician and politician; born in Savannah, Ga., he began his medical practice there in 1832, the year of the duel he records. In 1833, with William Bulloch, he was owner and co-editor of the Savannah *Georgian.* He was also one of the leaders of the Union Democrats of Lower Georgia (the anti-nullification wing of the Democratic Party). *DAB,* I, 371; A. Wilson, *Historic and Picturesque Savannah* (Boston, 1889), pp. 128, 153.

56. James Jones Stark was elected as a member of the Georgia legislature from Glynn County. A contemporary, Robert Habersham, described him thus in his diary for Aug., 1832: "Stark had been a disipated young man, and had broken the heart of his mother. All his family had dropt off except one sister, Poor girl! She has worn black for a long time, bereft of all that was dear to her, but now the last sad blow has fallen. Her amiable and affectionate heart bled over the remains of her ill fated brother until his body was carried away, and then she fell into a stupor from which she has not yet recovered. He was a brave, honorable young man, very promising in his profession, and with excellent talents. He did not have a moment to defend himself but was shot down before he could utter a word." Copy of relevant sections of Habersham's diary in A.J.A.

57. Philip Minis (born 1805) was the son of Isaac Minis and Divina Cohen. He studied to be a physician and was commissioned Assistant Surgeon in the U.S. Army, April 12, 1826. In 1836, he became a major and resigned from the army in 1837. He served also as Disbursing Agent for the Indian Department and played a significant role during the Cherokee removal. See W. Harden, "The Minis Family," *Georgia Historical Quarterly,* I (1917), 45–49. He married Miss Sarah A. Livingston of New York, by whom he had seven children. W. Harden, *A History of Savannah and South Georgia* (Chicago and New York, 1913), II, 556.

58. Perhaps Daniel Sturges, surveyor general, who had designed the Great Seal of Georgia in 1799. See Knight, *Georgia Landmarks,* II, 95. More probably a younger member of Sturges's family.

59. Thomas S. Wayne, later became City Marshal (see *Savannah*

Directory for 1867, p. 168). He was also one of the founders of Ogle-
thorp Lodge no. 1, Odd Fellows, instituted in 1842. Joseph Bancroft,
Census of the City of Savannah. . . . (Savannah, 1848), p. 45.

60. There were two physicians by the name of Waring in Savannah
in 1867: "J. J. Waring, office. S.W. corner of Bull and Perry Sts.," and
"W. R. Waring of 110 State St.," *Savannah Directory for 1867*, p. 167.

61. Mary Elizabeth Fenno was a sister of Maria (Fenno) Hoffman.
She met her future husband while he was "reading" law in the office
of her brother-in-law.

62. Giulian Crommelin Verplanck (1786–1870), author and politician,
was a principal in the Columbia College commencement riot of 1811.
He was a member of one of the more prominent Dutch families of New
York. *DAB*, XIX, 253.

63. MS. R.G. to Mrs. Gulian [sic] C. Verplanck, August 17, 1812;
A.J.H.S.

64. MS., R.G. to Mrs. Giulian C. Verplanck, June 10, 1812; A.J.H.S.

65. P. Pedersen was the Danish chargé d'affaires and consul general
in Philadelphia. He maintained his office at 212 Mulberry St., *Philadelphia Directory, 1811*, p. 250; same in *Directory, 1814*, unpaged.

66. Anne Philipine de Peters, married Louis Casimir Elisabeth Moreau-
Lislet (1767–1832), Louisiana jurist and politician, *DAB*, XIII, 157.

67. Mordecai Myers may well be a member of the Savannah family
(referred to by Stern as Myers III). If so, he was born in 1794 and died
in 1865; he would have been 18 years old at the time of writing this
letter; see Stern, p. 155.

68. Benjamin Gratz (1792–1884), youngest child of Michael and
Miriam (Simon) Gratz. Ben Gratz settled in Lexington, Ky. There is
a considerable body of correspondence between Rebecca Gratz and her
"baby" brother and his family. See this Part, note 93.

69. From copy in the A.J.A.

70. Rebecca Gratz, in a letter to Mrs. Verplanck, Aug. 17, 1812
(A.J.H.S.), supplies travel notes of a trip to Harpers Ferry in the western
part of Virginia (later West Virginia). She has nothing to say about the
young ladies of the area, but she draws a sharp contrast between the
natural beauty of the scenery and the poor conditions of the roads. "The
road is so intolerable that having walked and rode alternately, we gladly
retired as soon as the ceremony of a meal including dinner and supper
could be administered."

71. Sarah Gratz (1779–1817) was the fifth child of Michael and
Miriam (Simon) Gratz.

72. Joseph Gratz (1785–1858) was the seventh child of Michael and
Miriam (Simon) Gratz. "Barnard Gratz in 1798 mentioned in a letter
to his nephew Simon that he was 'sincerely sorry for been Dissoppointed
by Injoyment of Jose bar mitzwa hope he performit well in Reading his
parsha.'" W. & W., p. 255 (citing Barnard Gratz to Simon Gratz, Balti-

more, March 7, 1798, MS., in the possession of Edwin Wolf, 2d). This provides one of the few early references to religious practices that we have.

73. "A soldier called this morning to inform us you were well. Thank Heaven, your excellent constitution enables you to bear the privations of a camp life, but we should like to hear *how* you bear them. It is reported here you are too strict a disciplinarian. I hope the tale is exaggerated. the severity of a camp must be hard enough to all, but an officer may support his own dignity and yet soften the toil of his soldiers by suavity of manners and gentle deportment." (Rebecca Gratz to Benjamin Gratz, Sept. 12, 1814, MS., A.J.H.S.)

74. Such references are occasionally to be found in the letters of Rebecca Gratz, e.g.: "the 10th of April is Passover. Would I might expect you to keep it with us, when you went away I did certainly hope to see you at that time. You must at least let me know where you will be at that period. On Thursday next is Purim no longer a mirthful festival with us, it passes away without celebration; but more solemn feasts are more permanently observed." Rebecca Gratz to Benjamin Gratz, March 7, 1819, MS., A.J.H.S.; Philipson, *Letters,* p. 17; W. & W., p. 256.

75. Rebecca, Sarah, and Joseph Gratz to Benjamin Gratz, Philadelphia, Sept. 28, 1814. MS., A.J.H.S.

76. Edward Ingersoll, "attorney at law, 156 Walnut," *Philadelphia Directory, 1820,* unpaged.

77. Philip Syng Physick (1768–1837), friend of Benjamin Rush, was one of the outstanding surgeons of his time. *DAB,* XIV, 554. McElroy's *Philadelphia Directory for 1837,* p. 174, lists his office at 123 S. 4th St.

78. Dr. P. is, of course, Dr. Physick; Dr. K. is probably Dr. Adam Kuhn.

79. Daughter of William Rawle (1759–1836), Philadelphia lawyer and philanthropist. *DAB,* XV, 400.

80. Mention of members of the Ogden family occurs from time to time in the Gratz letters; see Philipson, *Letters,* p. 60. McElroy's *Philadelphia Directory for 1837,* p. 190, lists Catherine Ogden, a widow. This is probably the "cate" of the letter.

81. Judith and Lewis J. (Levi or Levy) Cohen (1800–68) were children of Joseph Cohen (1745/46–1822) by his second marriage to Hannah Moses (died 1800). Joseph Cohen had an older son, Solomon (1782–1854), by his first wife, Rose Barnet; see Stern, p. 27.

82. MS., Charles Cohen Papers, Philadelphia, Pa.; typescript copy from A.J.A.

83. Solomon Jacobs (1775–1827), served the city of Richmond as Recorder, equivalent to president of the Board of Aldermen, and acting Mayor. This is the highest municipal office to have been held by a Richmond Jew in the period of our concern. Three times he was elected Grand Master of the Masonic order in the State, the only Jew to have

held this position in Virginia. He was Parnass (president) of Congregation Beth Shalome. He represented the French government in the tobacco market and also acted as an agent of the Rothschilds. His epitaph
is reported to be the only one in the Hebrew Cemetery in Richmond
to refer to slavery. See Ezekiel and Lichtenstein, pp. 41–43. The epitaph
reads "In memory of/ SOLOMON JACOBS,/ who died on the 12th day of
Hesvan, 5588/ aged 52 years./ During a hopeless and painful illness,
which he/ bore with great patience and unshaken fortitude,/ he manifested in no ordinary degree his perfect/ reliance on the mercy of God,
and his entire/ conviction of the truth of the Mosaic Dispen-/ sation.
He passed a life of activity and use-/ fulness with unblemished integrity:
called to/ offices of distinction in the municipality of/ the city and other
corporate institutions, he/ discharged his duty with firmness and ability./
Fond as a Husband./ Indulgent as a Father./ Kind as a Master./ Hospitable and benevolent as a Man./ Steady, useful, and disinterested as a
Friend/."

84. Esther (Hetty) Jacobs (born 1790) was the daughter of Benjamin
Nones (1757–1826) of Philadelphia.

85. Solomon Jacobs to Hetty Jacobs, Richmond, Sept. 7, 1817, MS.,
The Valentine Museum, Richmond, Va. In a postscript addressed to his
father-in-law, Jacobs was a bit more specific in describing business conditions: "Times here entirely *idle*. U.S. B[ank] Stock keeps pace here
with yr *market*, which rules the roost *in this article* every where. I heard
yesterday that last accounts from philada [show] it at a pause. It has
ascended with the rapidity of an air Balloon and may descend like lightening. It must burst over some poor heads. No prospect of divident can
justify the rapid rise."

86. Solomon Jacobs to Hetty Jacobs, Richmond, Aug. 11, 1816, MS.,
The Valentine Museum, Richmond, Va.

87. Except for Mr. Wilkinson, who may have been a white overseer,
the individuals named in this paragraph were apparently Negro slaves
belonging to the Jacobs household.

88. Thomas Pym Cope (1768–1854), merchant and philanthropist,
came to Philadelphia in 1786. His firm, Cope and Thomas, laid the
foundation for a line of packets to Europe. He served in the state Legislature in 1807, and was president of Mercantile Library Company. *DAB*,
IV, 421. The "draft" referred to in the text was actually written on part
of this letter, and there is now a gap in the MS. where it was removed
for cashing.

89. One of the prominent Jewish families of Philadelphia. See W. &
W., *passim*.

90. Emanuel Nunez Carvalho had been teacher in Congregation
Nidche Israel of Barbados, 1799–1808; Polonies Talmud Torah, New
York, 1808–11; hazzan of Congregation Beth Elohim of Charleston, 1811–
15. In 1815, he became temporary minister of Congregation Mikveh

Israel in Philadelphia; in 1817 he died. The sermon to which Jacobs refers in this letter is probably Carvalho's *Sermon preached on Sunday . . . July 7, 1816, on Occasion of the Death of the Rev. Mr. Gershom Mendes Seixas* (Philadelphia, 1816). "It should also be noted that Carvalho's sermon . . . in 1816 was the first one known to have been delivered in a Philadelphia synagogue, and definitely the first to have been printed." W. & W., pp. 249–50; 454.

91. Solomon Jacobs to Hetty Jacobs, Richmond, July 15, 1817, MS., The Valentine Museum, Richmond.

92. Possibly Mordecai Lyons (1792–1845); see Stern, p. 129.

93. Benjamin, youngest of the Gratz boys, married Maria Gist, daughter of Colonel Nathaniel Gist of the Revolutionary Army, in 1819, after he had moved to Lexington, Ky., to care for the western affairs of the family. A portrait of Ben and Maria Gratz by Sully is now in the possession of the Clay family in Lexington, Ky. Although Rebecca was profoundly disturbed by her brother's marriage out of the Jewish faith, she found in Maria a person so sympathetic that she was able to correspond with Maria for many years as a confidante and intimate. The marital affairs of her brothers could scarcely have made Rebecca Gratz very happy. Simon had seven or more children; "but whether he was married to their mother is unknown"; at all events, their mother (identified as Mary Smith) was not Jewish, and the children were brought up as Christians. Jacob Gratz also had a son; however there is no record of his having married. Hyman and Joseph Gratz remained unmarried, and apparently also childless. Both Benjamin Gratz's first wife, Maria Cecil Gist, and his second, Anna Maria (Boswell) Shelby, were non-Jews; and Benjamin's children were brought up as Christians. See W. & W., p. 240; Philipson, *Letters*, xx. See this Part, note 68.

94. Rebecca Gratz to Maria (Gist) Gratz, Philadelphia, Oct. 3, 1820, MS., A.J.H.S.

95. Mrs. Boswell was the mother of Anna Maria (Boswell) Shelby, later to be Benjamin Gratz's second wife.

96. Rachel Gratz (1783–1823) married Solomon Moses (1774–1857) in 1806; Horace, the eighth of their nine children, was born Aug. 10, 1820, a little less than two months before the date of this letter.

97. Mrs. Biddle, might be the wife of either James Biddle (1783–1848), naval officer assigned in 1817 to take possession of the Oregon territory (*DAB*, II, 240), or of Nicholas Biddle (1786–1844), litterateur, scholar, statesman, and financier (*DAB*, II, 243).

98. Ellen Hays (1800–55) was the daughter of Samuel and Richea (Gratz) Hays.

99. Col. Morrison of Kentucky.

100. The only person by the name of Sally Etting listed by Stern (p. 49) was born in 1776 and died in 1863. She was an aunt of Benjamin Etting; but, on Stern's information, she was unmarried. None of the

Etting men of the generation before Benjamin was married to a woman of the name of Sarah or Sally.

101. Benjamin Etting (1798–1875), son of Reuben and Frances (Gratz) Etting.

102. See Part Two, Document 81.

103. Sally Etting to Benjamin Etting, Baltimore, May 19, 1825, MS., Etting Papers, The Historical Society of Pennsylvania.

104. While most such casually mentioned names are unidentifiable, here it is possible that this is Mrs. Mary Caton, wife of Richard Caton, of 14E Lombard Street in Baltimore. See *Baltimore Directory for 1845*, p. 26, and Matchett's *Baltimore Directory for 1847–8*, p. 62.

105. Poor Sally Etting apparently received recent personal attention from her nephew. Her many requests were taken care of: "I recd the Crapes yesterday and was a little surprised at no letter but this day the letter was sent me by I don't know who nor do I know who brought the Bundles" (Sally Etting to Benjamin Etting, Baltimore, June 29, 1825, MS., Etting Papers, The Historical Society of Pennsylvania). But young Benjamin did not write and although a visit to Baltimore seemed to have been rumored in the summer of 1825, he did not visit. Perhaps he was kept so busy running errands that he had no time for correspondence: "I am always troubling you Henry and Richea Etting tells me your Aunt Becky [Rebecca Gratz, whose older sister Frances was Benjamin Etting's mother] has the best receipt for Preserving Pine Apples that can be. I have a large quantity to do & if her receipt is better than I shall be glad to have it. . . . I wish it by return of Mail as they are going to England Monday or Thursday. Send it in her hand as yours is not always plain enough to read" (Sally Etting to Benjamin Etting, Baltimore, July 7, 1825, MS., Etting Papers, The Historical Society of Pennsylvania). Possibly, the constant whining and complaining made any answer difficult: "If I did not judge you by myself my dear Child I should think you had forgot you ever had an Old Aunt who loves you sincerely. Tis two months since I have had a line from you indeed I believe tis three do you think that right when you knew I have been unwell all summer" (Sally Etting to Benjamin Etting, Baltimore, Sept. 8, 1825, MS., Etting Papers, The Historical Society of Pennsylvania).

106. Gratz Etting (1795–1849) was the son of Reuben and Frances (Gratz) Etting. He had a distinguished academic record at his graduation from the University of Pennsylvania. During the War of 1812, he served in the U.S. Navy. When he returned, he practiced law and took an active part in the political strife of his period on the democratic side.

107. As a partisan Democrat, Gratz Etting would, of course, be particularly interested in publicizing Jackson, the party's outstanding candidate for the presidency.

108. Gratz Etting to Benjamin Etting, Bellefonte, Jan. 15, 1826, MS., Etting Papers, The Historical Society of Pennsylvania.

109. There are many firm names in *Philadelphia Directory, 1820*, that include the name "Smith" but none styled "Smith & Co."

110. John Rianhard is listed in *Philadelphia Directory, 1820*, unpaged, at 179 High st; P. L. Senat is listed as a commission merchant in the McElroy's *Philadelphia Directory for 1837*.

111. Probably Benjamin J. Phillips (1776–1830), son of Jonas Phillips.

112. Henry Etting (1799–1876), son of Reuben and Frances (Gratz) Etting, served in the United States Navy.

113. Isabella Etting (1801–55), younger sister of the writer.

114. The distaste of Southern liberals for the institution of slavery persisted until 1831. Slavery was regarded as an economic necessity and a moral evil, even by such advocates as John Taylor of Caroline. During the legislative sessions of 1830–31 there was actually a discussion of ending slavery in Virginia. At the very time when these discussions were going on, however, Virginia suffered a slave uprising, and almost simultaneously, Thomas R. Dew, in his *Review of the Discussions* in the Legislature offered the first positive argument for slavery. Dew was made President of William and Mary College; Virginia realigned herself with the states of the Deep South in the proslavery camp. See C. H. Ambler, *Sectionalism in Virginia* (Chicago, 1910), pp. 185–200; E. L. Fox, *The American Colonization Society, 1817–1840* (Baltimore, 1919). Of all the states south of the Mason-Dixon line, Virginia had both the largest number of free Negroes and the largest number of slaves. In 1830, there were 47,548 free Negroes and 469,757 slaves in that state. See U.S. Bureau of the Census, *Negro Population 1790–1915* (Washington, 1918), p. 57. After 1830, there was a marked percentage decrease in manumissions in all the states as the liberal influence of the Revolutionary period sank beneath the weight of economic pressures. C. G. Woodson, *Free Negro Heads of Families in the United States in 1830* (Washington, 1925), p. xviii. See Luther P. Jackson, *Free Negro Labor and Property Holding in Virginia, 1830–1860* (New York, 1942). Among other Richmond Jews who manumitted their slaves by testament or otherwise are Isaiah Isaacs and Jacob I. Cohen. See Ezekiel and Lichtenstein, pp. 15, 20, 327–29, and 330–35.

115. Isaac H. Judah (1761–1827), son of Hillel and Abigail (Seixas) Judah, of New York. He settled in Richmond in 1784, becoming a prominent merchant; he lived on the north side of L st., "near Bacon's branch" *Richmond Directory 1819*, p. 53. He served, it is said, as the first reader of Congregation Beth Shalome. See Ezekiel and Lichtenstein, *passim.*

116. Will of Isaac H. Judah.

117. Perhaps a nephew of Isaac H. Judah, although no one of this name appears in Stern's listing. See Ezekiel and Lichtenstein, *passim.* *PAJHS*, XI (1902), 92, reports a David Judah as enlisting in the Revolutionary forces; this cannot be the same person, but may be an otherwise unrecorded member of the Judah family.

118. The expression suggests that these mulatto boys were the illegitimate children of Isaac H. Judah, who was never married.

119. Sarah Judah (1760–1842) married Ralph de Paz in 1798; see Stern, p. 102.

120. Rebecca Judah (1782–1867) married Isaac B. Seixas in 1809; see Stern, p. 102.

121. Manuel Judah (1769–1834), "merchant, corner of E and 6th sts." *Richmond Directory,* 1819, p. 53. See Ezekiel and Lichtenstein, *passim;* Stern, p. 102.

122. Baruch H. Judah (1763–1830) was keeper of the Virginia Museum in 1821; see Ezekiel and Lichtenstein, pp. 134–35; Stern, p. 102.

123. Gershom Seixas Judah (born 1767), see Ezekiel and Lichtenstein, *passim.*

124. Rachel Judah (1772–1863) married Zalma Rehine (1757–1843) in 1800. Rehine, a native of Westphalia, was a shopkeeper in Richmond until he moved to Baltimore in 1828 or 1829. In Baltimore he was active in the organization of a synagogue; indeed, he lent his home for religious services during the organization period. By his marriage Rehine was connected with the Seixas, Marks, and Kursheedt families. See Richmond Husting Court, Deed Book 49, pp. 393–96. Rehine was, also, uncle of Isaac Leeser who became spiritual head of Congregation Mikveh Israel of Philadelphia in 1829 and the outstanding spokesman of American Jewry in the 1840s. See Ezekiel and Lichtenstein, pp. 37–40.

125. Frances (Gratz) Etting (1771–1852).

126. Benjamin Etting (1798–1875).

127. To Harriet Marx (1802–80) of Baltimore.

128. Henry Etting (1799–1876); see this Part, note 112.

129. Frances Etting to Benjamin Etting, Philadelphia, March 26, 1828; MS., Etting Papers, The Historical Society of Pennsylvania.

130. Gratz Etting (1795–1849).

131. Moses Nathans (1811–49) was the son of Isaiah Nathans, merchant, of 252 North Second Street, Philadelphia; he married Benveneda V. Solis (1815–93) on November 30, 1831.

132. Daniel Solis (1784–1867), at this time was in business in Wilmington, Del. His brother, Jacob da Silva Solis (1780–1829), had been his business partner and had been active in soliciting funds for Congregation Shenarai Chasset, New Orleans, as well as for Congregation Bene Israel, Cincinnati. Daniel Solis soon afterwards moved to Philadelphia where he served the Jewish community as *shohet* (ritual slaughterer). See Schappes, p. 609; W. & W., *passim,* and especially pp. 252–53 and 456.

133. Daniel Solis to Moses Nathans, Wilmington, Del., Nov. 17, 1830; MS., Nathans Family Papers, copy from A.J.A.: "Dr. Sir[,] I this day I had. Your honorable Letter put In my hand by Mrs Solis and I am Extremley oblige to You for Your honorable Intension to my Daughter but beg to be Excused to answer it at preasent as I have wrote to Your

farther on the Subject and as Soon as I recd the answer I will write to You in the Interim Do Not Let it Debar ous of the pleasure of Your honorable Company[.] I subscribe My self You obt St Daniel Solis" Daniel Solis to Isaiah Nathans, Wilmington, Del., Nov. 17, 1830; MS., Nathans Family Papers, copy from A.J.A.:

"Dear Sir[,] I this Day Recd a Letter from Your Son Moses wherein he has made me honourable proposals of Marriage for My Daughter I have wrote to him beging to be Excused answering it Untill I hear from You

"Sir as I have no wish that any part of my family Should Intrude into the bosom of anothers, without there will and approbation I therefore take the Liberty to inform You of it, Wishing You to Let Me know Your pleasure on the Subject. I subscribe my self You Obt Daniel Solis

"PS. pleas to give Myne and Mrs Solis and Famley respects to Mrs Nathans and famley"

In the same collection are to be found a number of letters from Miss Solis to Moses Nathans and to his sister, Isabelle, "her chosen friend," all, where dated, being from the end of the year 1830.

134. Moses Nathans to Daniel Solis, Philadelphia, Nov. 14, 1830; MS., Nathans Family Papers; copy from A.J.A.

135. Cohen was admitted to the bar in 1829. He was a leader in the States Rights Party and served as Secretary of the States Rights and Free Trade Convention, Charleston, Feb. 22 and 25, 1832. See Schappes, p. 613.

136. Other Charleston Jews who enlisted in the Washington Volunteers were J[acob] Cohen, Jr., and Columbus Moise (1810–71), son of Dr. Aaron Moise. See Reznikoff, pp. 105, 282. Leon Dyer of Baltimore also served in the Florida campaign. See Henry Cohen, "Settlement of the Jews in Texas," *PAJHS*, II (1894), 148, and Samuel Proctor, "Pioneer Jewish Settlement in Florida," *Proceedings* of the Conference on the Writing of Regional History in the South, Miami Beach, Feb. 15, 1956 (Miami Beach, 1956), p. 94.

137. The Jackson Administration, carrying out the policy set by John C. Calhoun in the Cabinet of James Monroe, sought to remove all Eastern Indians to reservations west of the Mississippi. A treaty of removal negotiated with some of the chiefs of the Seminoles in Florida was repudiated by the tribe led by Osceola. The war in the Florida Everglades which ensued lasted until 1842 despite Osceola's capture by treachery. Although in this prolonged war the Seminoles were gradually forced from their original habitat, the white forces were in constant state of fear and anxiety because of their proximity to the swamps and to the non-white population of the Everglade region. The campaign of 1836 was a major effort in the struggle to dislodge the obstinate Indians. See Grant Foreman, *Indian Removal* (New York, 1932); Katherine T. Abbey, *Florida, Land of Change* (Chapel Hill, N.C., 1941).

138. Myer M. Cohen, *Notices of Florida and the Campaigns* (New York, 1836), pp. 143–53.

139. Colonel Abbott Hall Brisbane (died 1861) of South Carolina was a military engineer. A graduate of West Point, he was commissioned in 1825 and served on topographical duty; in 1828 he resigned. He served in The Seminole War, 1835–36, as colonel of South Carolina volunteers. After the war, he was mustered out and became interested in the development of railroads. Appleton's *Cyclopedia of American Biography*, I, 378.

140. In M. M. Cohen, *Notices of Florida*, pp. 159–61, there is a listing, "as accurate as I am able to render it," of the officers of the left wing of the army in Florida. In the list of Captains of Brisbane's Regiment appear the names of J. Jones, George Henry, P. Quattelbaum, T. S. Hibbler and P. M. Doucin.

141. B. B. Strobel, surgeon of Brisbane's Regiment. "The ever diligent Dr. Strobel is wiping alternately the lancet and double barrelled gun, wherewith he is so well qualified to draw blood." Cohen, *Notices of Florida*, p. 138.

142. Adjutant A. G. Magrath, Brisbane's Regiment.

143. Major N. G. Walker, Brisbane's Regiment.

144. Major Edmund Kirby. See Heitman, *Historical Register . . . U.S. Army*, I, 603.

145. On George McDuffie (1790–1851), a prominent political leader in South Carolina; see Part Four, note 162.

146. Presumably Captain George Henry, Brisbane's Regiment.

147. Abraham Eustis, Brigadier General, commanded the left wing of Gen. Winfield Scott's army in this Florida campaign. See Jacob R. Mott, *Journey into Wilderness*, ed. by Jacob F. Sunderman (Gainesville, Fla., 1953); and Heitman, *Historical Register . . . U.S. Army*, I, 408.

148. First Lieutenant J. F. Kennedy, First Regiment Artillery.

149. Rebecca Gratz to Maria Gist Gratz, Philadelphia, January 14, 1838; MS., A.J.H.S.

150. Joseph Gratz.

151. Benjamin Gratz, husband of the recipient of this letter.

152. Richea (Gratz) Hays.

153. Samuel Etting (1796–1862), husband of Ellen Hays; son of Solomon and Rachel (Gratz) Etting.

154. Harriet Marx, daughter of Joseph Marx of Richmond, married Benjamin Etting (1798–1875), on whom see this Part, note 101.

155. Joseph Marx (1772–1840), merchant of Richmond, Va., married Richea Myers of New York, a cousin of Rebecca Gratz. See Ezekiel and Lichtenstein, pp. 47–50; Philipson, *Letters*, p. 94.

156. Benjamin Etting.

157. Dr. Simon Gratz Moses (1813–97), son of Solomon and Rachel (Gratz) Moses, was graduated from the Medical College of the Univer-

sity of Pennsylvania in 1835; he married Mary P. Ashe, Jan. 24, 1838, at Wilmington, N.C. See Philipson, *Letters,* xvi–xvii, 249; *Catalogue of the Medical Graduates of the University of Pennsylvania* (Philadelphia, 1839).

158. Francis Preston Blair (1791–1876), Democratic politician, was one of the chief organizers of the Republican party in the 1850s; he rejoined the Democratic party after the Civil War. His sons Montgomery (1813–83) and Francis Preston, Jr. (1821–75) also had active political careers.

159. Miriam Gratz Etting (1807–78) daughter of Reuben and Frances (Gratz) Etting, niece of Rebecca Gratz. Philipson, *Letters,* pp. xiii, 398.

160. Henry Etting (1799–1876), youngest son of Reuben and Frances (Gratz) Etting, became a midshipman in the United States Navy, Jan. 1, 1818. Commissioned as Captain in 1861, he served in the Navy until his death; his latest commission was dated March 3, 1876. See Philipson, *Letters,* xiii–xiv.

161. Rebecca Gratz had purchased not a dress, but yard goods for the making of a dress; her question is whether her sister-in-law was in deep mourning, in which case the purchased material would not have been "of present use."

162. Miriam Moses (born 1808) was one of the children of Solomon and Rachel (Gratz) Moses, whose upbringing was taken over by Rebecca Gratz when their mother died in 1823. Miriam married Solomon Cohen of Georgetown, S.C., Nov. 30, 1836. Philipson, *Letters,* 227. Later the Cohens returned to Savannah, Ga., where Solomon Cohen had practiced law before his marriage and had served as attorney for Dr. Philip Minis in his 1833 trial, following his duel with Starke. See this Part, Document 99, and Thomas Gamble, *Savannah Duels and Duellists, 1733–1877* (Savannah, 1923), p. 195.

163. Rebecca Gratz to Miriam Cohen, Philadelphia, Dec. 4, 1838; MS., Library of the University of North Carolina. Octavus Cohen (1814–76) was Miriam Cohen's brother-in-law.

164. Rebecca Gratz to Miriam Cohen, Philadelphia, Feb. 10, 1839; MS., Library of the University of North Carolina.

165. James Kirke Paulding (1778–1860), *DAB,* XIV, 321.

166. Julian Meyers, probably the son of Mordecai Myers (1794–1865) and Sarah Henrietta (Cohen) Myers (1799–1886), Miriam Cohen's sister-in-law, was named midshipman, March 2, 1839; passed midshipman, July 2, 1845; commissioned Master, Feb. 21, 1854; dismissed Dec. 6, 1861. *List* . . . . *Navy* (New York, 1901), p. 400.

167. The pseudo-scientific cult of phrenology, or the reading of character traits from the outward conformations of the skull, enjoyed a great vogue in the United States beginning in the 1820s. The work of pioneer European phrenologists, Gall and Spurzheim, was introduced by American disciples like Dr. Charles Caldwell of the medical faculty of Transyl-

vania University. Spurzheim visited the United States in 1832; his personal charm and sympathetic insight into human nature and his demonstration of the surgical technique of brain dissection won him many friends and admirers. Certain aspects of phrenology had been discussed earlier, in the medical writings of Dr. Benjamin Rush. Myer M. Cohen included some interesting remarks on phrenological characteristics of Indians in his *Notices of Florida and the Campaigns* (New York, 1836), pp. 170–71. See Merle Curti, *The Growth of American Thought* (New York, 1943), pp. 341 ff. Rebecca Gratz discussed her interest in phrenology in a letter to her sister-in-law, Mrs. Benjamin Gratz two days before the date of this letter.

Rebecca Gratz to Maria (Gist) Gratz, Philadelphia, Feb. 8, 1839; MS., A.J.H.S. "You ask me my dear Sister, what books we are reading besides the bible? Why we have accompanied you thro' palestine with John Stevens, and had all our veneration excited in the wonderful views of the excavated city, and our patriotism warmed amidst the desolation of Jerusalem!! and are now deeply interested with George Combe & Spurtzeim on the science of phrenology. Combe has just finished a course of the most interesting lectures I ever listened to, and many a time have I wished for you, to exercise your mind in this study of nature through a medium, which if not true (which I believe it is) is so ingenious and plausible, in the lessons of Combe, that it opens a channel of thought leading to high and holy contemplations. If you have not read a small work of his on the Constitution of Man I can recommend it, as highly interesting & useful. What you would particularly like in his lectures, is his application of phrenology to the improvement of education, and he addresses it to women—mothers particularly with good effect, and gives examples from numerous anecdotes that has fallen under his own observation, in the experience of 20 years devoted to practical science, he is quite different in practice & precept to Dr. Caldwell, for he applies it to daily use."

168. Dr. George Combe (1797–1847), Scottish physician who visited America and preached the phrenological gospel. See Curti, *Growth of American Thought*, p. 341.

169. Of the University of Pennsylvania.

170. Lucretia Coffin Mott (1793–1880), reformer and Quaker preacher; she was especially active as an advocate of temperance, peace, women's rights, and abolition. She organized the American Anti-Slavery Society in 1833. *DAB*, XIII, 288. See L. C. M. Hare, *The Greatest American Woman, Lucretia Mott* (New York, 1937).

171. Probably the wife of F. Eckard, M.D., who is one of 4 persons of the name of Eckard listed in McElroy's *Philadelphia Directory for 1837*.

172. Benjamin Gratz.

173. Maria (Gist) Gratz, wife of Benjamin Gratz.

174. Simon Gratz (1773–1839) was at this time at odds with his brother Hyman over the distribution of property held by them in the years of their partnership (1797–1827).

175. Louisa Gratz (1801–88) was the daughter of Simon Gratz; her mother was Mary Smith. All seven children of Simon Gratz seem to have been brought up as Christians. Louisa became a convert to Judaism in 1851. See W. & W., p. 240.

176. Reuben Etting.

177. Richea (Gratz) Hays.

178. J. L. Stephens, *Incidents of Travel in Egypt, Arabia Petraea, and the Holy Land.* 2 vols. (New York, 1837).

179. William Hickling Prescott (1796–1859), *History of the Reign of Ferdinand and Isabella* (Boston, 1837).

180. This may be Frank M. Etting (1833–90), who was chosen official historian of the Centennial Celebration in 1876. See W. & W., p. 388, n. 21.

181. Maria Minis (1829–53), daughter of Abraham and Mabel (Henry) Minis, was a half sister of Dr. Philip Minis. See W. Harden, "The Minis Family," *Georgia Historical Quarterly*, I (1917), 49. See also Philipson, *Letters*, p. 203.

182. Rebecca Gratz to Maria Gratz, [Philadelphia], Jan. 9, 1839; MS., A.J.H.S.

183. Reuben Etting.

184. Louisa Gratz, daughter of Simon Gratz; see this Part, note 22.

185. At a minimum, this refers to the fact that Simon Gratz's children were reared as Christians. It may mean more; as W. & W. point out (p. 240), Simon "had seven children, but whether he was married to their mother is not known." Stern, p. 64, accepts but does not date a marriage.

186. The roots go back to the dissolution of partnership of S. and H. Gratz, and led to litigation; see Gratz against Gratz (Pa., 1834); 4 Rawle 410. As in so many other instances, business difficulties were followed by personal rancor.

187. Simon died in the year of this letter.

188. Rachel Cohen (1825–1913).

189. Benjamin I. Cohen (1797–1843) of Baltimore, son of Israel I. Cohen (1750–1803) and Judith (Solomon) Cohen of Richmond. See Ezekiel and Lichtenstein, pp. 29–31. After Israel Cohen's death, his widow moved her young family (the oldest, Jacob I. Cohen, Jr., was then only 13), to Baltimore. See I. Blum, *The Jews of Baltimore* (Baltimore, 1910), p. 5.

190. Benjamin I. Cohen to Rachel Cohen, MS., in Mendes Cohen Collection, Maryland Historical Society.